STUDIES IN EVANGELICALISM
edited by
Kenneth E. Rowe &
Donald W. Dayton

1. Melvin E. Dieter. *The Holiness Revival of the Nine-teenth Century.* 1980.

2. Lawrence T. Lesick. *The Lane Rebels: Evangelicalism and Antislavery in Antebellum America.* 1980.

3. Edward H. Madden and James E. Hamilton. *Freedom and Grace: The Life of Asa Mahan.* 1982.

4. Roger H. Martin. *Evangelicals United: Ecumenical Stirrings in Pre-Victorian Britain, 1795-1830.* 1983.

5. Donald W. Dayton. *Theological Roots of Pentecostalism.* 1987.

6. David L. Weddle. *The Law as Gospel: Revival and Reform in the Theology of Charles G. Finney.* 1985.

7. Darius L. Salter. *Spirit and Intellect: Thomas Upham's Holiness Theology.* 1986.

8. Wayne E. Warner. *The Woman Evangelist: The Life and Times of Charismatic Evangelist Maria B. Woodworth-Etter.* 1986.

EDITOR'S NOTE

The current resurgence of Evangelical religion has highlighted the important role of this force in the formation of American and British culture. This series will explore its roots in the Evangelical Revival and Awakening of the eighteenth century, its nineteenth-century blossoming in revivalism and social reform, and its twentieth-century developments in both sectarian and "mainline" churches. Diversity within Evangelicalism will be highlighted--the search for holiness, the Millennial traditions, Fundamentalism, and Pentecostalism. I am pleased to publish Donald Dayton's study of the theological roots of Pentecostalism as number five in the series.

Donald W. Dayton is Professor of Theology and Ethics at Northern Baptist Theological Seminary in Lombard, Illinois, a Chicago suburb. A lay member of the Wesleyan Church of America, Dr. Dayton graduated with honors from Houghton College, studied church history and theology at Yale Divinity School and library science at the University of Kentucky, and took the doctorate in contemporary theology and ethics at the University of Chicago. He has published an impressive list of articles, contributed essays to many collections, and edited several more, including a forty-eight-volume reprint series "The Higher Christian Life: Sources for the Study of the Holiness, Pentecostal and Keswick Movements 1830-1920." His *Discovering an Evangelical Heritage* has become a standard introduction to the movement and is now in its second edition.

Kenneth E. Rowe
Drew University
Madison, New Jersey

164 Old-time Power

C. D. T.

CHARLIE D. TILLMAN

1. They were in an up-per cham-ber, They were all with one ac-cord,
2. Yes, this pow'r from heav'n de-scend-ed With the sound of rush-ing wind;
3. Yes, this "old-time" pow'r was giv-en To our fa-thers who were true;

When the Ho-ly Ghost de-scend-ed, As was prom-ised by our Lord.
Tongues of fire came down up-on them, As the Lord said He would send.
This is prom-ised to be-liev-ers, And we all may have it, too.

CHORUS

O Lord, send the pow'r just now. O Lord, send the pow'r just now.

O Lord, send the pow'r just now, And bap-tize ev-'ry one.

THEOLOGICAL ROOTS OF PENTECOSTALISM

by
Donald W. Dayton

Foreword by Martin E. Marty

Studies in Evangelicalism, No. 5

The Scarecrow Press, Inc.
Metuchen, N.J., & London
1987

This edition is published simultaneously with Francis Asbury Press, an imprint of Zondervan Publishing House, 1415 Lake Drive S.E., Grand Rapids, Michigan 49506

/

Library of Congress Cataloging-in-Publication Data

Dayton, Donald W.
  Theological Roots of Pentecostalism.

  (Studies in evangelicalism ; no. 5)
  Bibliography: p.
  Includes indexes.
  1. Pentecostalism--History of doctrines. I. Title. II. Series.
BR1644.D39 1987 b   273'.9   87-10522
ISBN 0-8108-2037-4

To Jeff

CONTENTS

FOREWORD

Students who have difficulty with dates of historical events sometimes welcome hearing about American Pentecostalism. One way to read the story is to see this movement "erupting" in a healing service in Topeka, Kansas, where a Miss Agnes Ozman was heard "speaking in other tongues," as the disciples of Jesus did on the first day of Pentecost in the Christian calendar. The modern event occurred on New Year's Eve, 1900. The group which encouraged and heard Miss Ozman regathered the next morning, the first morning of the new twentieth century. In such terms, then, it is easy to see Pentecostalism precisely as a twentieth-century phenomenon.

In such terms, also, this book is about the nineteenth century, for it is a prehistory of the now-familiar Pentecostal movement which sweeps the Christian world and attracts so much attention. Naturally, it is author Donald W. Dayton's task to show that the modern movement was more complicated than if it were only a wondrous tempest in a Topeka teacup from which other wonders flowed. Dayton is interested in the growing of the leaves—if we may risk developing the tea metaphor—and that means reaching behind the trees to the roots themselves. He shows that there are many kinds of groves and trees and leaves and cups, without for a moment taking away from the turn-of-the-century events.

To claim that no one has noticed the prehistory and history is no longer appropriate or fair. Charles Edwin Jones in 1974 published a 7,338-entry *Guide to the Study of the Holiness Movement*, and Jones dropped the other shoe in 1983, *A Guide to the Study of Pentecostalism*. Though it adds 9,883 more items, Dayton has to say that "these bibliographies are, of course, not complete. . . ." They do suggest that the movement is one of the better noticed, recorded, and preserved among modern Christian phenomena.

Why has it gone overlooked? One can hazard a safe guess that most humans, most Americans, most historians, and even many historians of American religion have never read one of these thousands of items. Until recently, say a generation ago, Pentecostalism was seen as a movement of illiterates, "hillbillies," "rednecks," "snakehandlers," or "holy rollers," who were at the margins of culture but who would remain there, without needing or leaving literature of much notice.

That has changed. Pentecostalism is widespread as an agent in the growth of Christianity in sub-Saharan Africa, which may become the numerical center of at least Protestant Christianity in this generation. It is strong wherever Christianity is growing. In America it has "seeped northward" from its early mid-South and southeastern strongholds. The great-grandchildren of the founders now run multimillion-dollar television and publishing empires and are familiar figures to the thirteen or more million regular dial-turners who watch the "electronic church." They have, since the mid-sixties, not just sleeked up their image so that "deprivation theories" no longer work to explain them, as Dayton so nicely suggests. Now the undeprived upper-middle classes in Catholicism and some of mainstream Protestantism also have substantial Pentecostal movements.

As the movement and its tentacles and connections grew and its phenomena became more visible, so did curiosity grow. On that scene came Donald W. Dayton, whose own library of four thousand items on the subject gave him a head start and whose earlier bibliographical work gave him momentum. The University of Chicago Divinity School was quite eager to have someone of his background, knowledge, and ability to help expound a movement of such importance. Here is a result of one of his efforts, the tracing of a prehistory. It will serve to demythologize and perhaps to remythologize the world view of most non-Pentecostals who read it.

Pentecostal Christians will also find reasons to consult the work. Some of them, Dayton notes, do not really want a history. One of the claims of some Spirit-filled Christians is that the Spirit simply descended on their antecedents after nineteen relatively quiet centuries, but almost exactly as this Spirit came on the original Pentecost. If so, to study anything that happened before this new descent, or (as will be clear on later pages) before this experience of a "latter rain," would be beside the point and would detract from the miraculous character of the outpouring. They have no choice, it is clear from this book, but to see that there were ignitings before the flame reached them, that there were roots to the growth they reaped. Because Dayton is so informed and respectful, they could not have chosen a more empathic if still critical historian to do this accounting.

The history-less Pentecostal will soon see herself as others see her. That is, her roots will be part of the Wesleyan tradition, for it draws chiefly on John Wesley's doctrine of salvation and other aspects of his reform movement on Anglo-soil. Yet not just any and all Wesleyans matter. Those that do, have their time and place. The ones that Dayton demonstrates to be determinative have a "Made in America" patent and stamp on them. Also pending is his patented development of the theme that a certain kind of "perfectionism" comes into play.

In no time at all, one is drawn to see that Pentecostalism is much more than and indeed something other than "speaking in other tongues." Dayton shows how at least four elements— salvation, healing, baptism of the Holy Spirit, and a second coming of Christ outlook—were fused by the pioneers. He is successful at demonstrating that these four elements together made up a single whole, which had its own inner logic. To pull at any one of the four has an effect on the other three and on the whole, and Dayton intricately works with and weaves them all. The logic holds. These people were not inconsistent, ecstatic ignoramuses. They checked out their experiences, and though they could not agree—the Jones books list many, many scores of denominations which grew out of the beginnings— they could disagree with those who stood outside the logic entirely.

Members of movements who hear about scholarly efforts resent "reductionism," one form of reduction theory or method which tells them and the world that they are "nothing but" something else. Pentecostals do not want to be "nothing but" deprived people who seek advancement in God's favor by claiming the Spirit. They are not and do not want to be "nothing but" marginal people who need a new wedge in the culture. They are not "nothing but" people with psychosexual hangups or theological confusions. One may still make judgments of social and psychological character, and these can inform the study of Pentecostalism just as it would illumine inquiry into High Church Upper-Class Anglicanism or any other movement. Yet Pentecostalism is also "something more," and that something more includes theology of the sort expounded here.

One might say of Dayton, as he says of Jones, that his book is "not complete" nor does it "complete" the Jones books. Yet it is a very important statement, one without which subsequent commentators on Pentecostalism are not likely to give intelligent accountings. Here a new contribution to Christian theology and popular movements comes under a scholar's eye. Pentecostals chose well in attracting the notice of Dayton. They would and will, if they are attentive and fair-minded, call this a "blessing" of these latter days.

Martin E. Marty
The University of Chicago

THEOLOGICAL ROOTS
OF PENTECOSTALISM

34 PREACH THE FOURSQUARE GOSPEL

A. S. M.

AIMEE SEMPLE McPHERSON.

1. Foursquare we stand for the liv - ing Word, For the Word of God,...... Tell-ing
2. Un - furl your ban-ners and for-ward go, Oh, ye ran-somed host...... Trusting
3. Catch up your shield oh, ye liv - ing Church! Christ of Gal - i - lee, ... Bore all
4. Lift up your eyes, then un - to the hills, Lift your voice and sing ...... The clouds

to all the sto - ry of Je - sus, Stem of Jes-se's rod..... Man of Sor-rows
in Je - sus, might-y Bap - tiz - er, With the Ho - ly Ghost... Lion of Ju - dah,
our sickness, car-ried our sor-rows, Set the pris-'ner free .... Lift the fall - en,
of Heav-en, a - flame with glo - ry, Greet the com-ing King ... Swift as wings of

and of grief, Dy - ing on the tree;...... Might-y Re-deem - er, glo - ri - ous
King of Kings, Lord of Lords is He;...... Cloth-ing His Church with pow-er to
help the faint, Dry the weep-ing eye; ...... Come, bring your sickness to thy Phy-
ea-gle's flight, Shall He come a - gain;...... Clad in His glo - ry, and robed in

CHORUS.

Sav-iour, Je - sus of Cal - va - ry......
wit - ness, Lead-ing to vic - to - ry..... Preach the Foursquare Gospel, The Foursquare
si - cian, For He is pass-ing by;.....
hon - or, And with His saints shall reign....

Gos - pel, Clear let the Foursquare message ring, (let it ring) Je - sus on - ly Sav-

iour, Bap-tiz - er and Heal-er; Je - sus the com - ing King. (the com-ing King.)

CHAPTER I

TOWARD A THEOLOGICAL ANALYSIS OF PENTECOSTALISM

The Pentecostal movement has—naturally enough, it must be admitted—generally been interpreted primarily in terms of its most characteristic feature, glossolalia, or "speaking in tongues." This has been true both within and without the movement. Carl Brumbeck's classic apologia for Pentecostalism, *What Meaneth This?* is basically a defense of the practice of glossolalia.[1] Similarly, the critical literature has tended to denounce Pentecostalism with the epithet, "the modern tongues movement."[2] The apparently broader study of recent developments by Roman Catholic Kilian McDonnell, *Charismatic Renewal and the Churches,* is essentially a survey of psychological and sociological research on glossolalia.[3]

   Though of course not without its value, such an approach to Pentecostalism has several limitations. In the first place, glossolalia fails to define the movement adequately in such a way as to distinguish it fully from other religious movements. Until the recent appearance of the "Charismatic movement" or "neo-Pentecostalism" within the traditional churches, such a definition served reasonably well to distinguish the Pentecostal churches from other Christian churches. "Pentecostal" churches were those whose members "spoke in tongues." But the practice of "glossolalia is actually a common religious phenomenon,"[4] occurring in a great variety of contexts. In America, for example, glossolalia has appeared in such groups as the Shakers and Mormons of the nineteenth century.[5] In spite of some common features, such movements are only very indirectly related to Pentecostalism. Glossolalia, therefore, by itself cannot serve to define Pentecostalism or to distinguish it fully from other Christian and religious movements.

Second, such a concentration on glossolalia among interpreters of Pentecostalism precludes an adequate understanding of the movement by encouraging the ahistorical claims of its advocates that Pentecostalism emerged *de novo* either about 1900 in a small Bible college near Topeka, Kansas, under the leadership of "Holiness" evangelist Charles F. Parham, or half a dozen years later in a black mission on Azusa Street, Los Angeles, depending on the set of claims to which one gives the most credence.[6] Both critics and, to a lesser extent, apologists have been inclined to center their attacks or defenses in attempts to discount or establish a historical line of those advocating and practicing this "gift of the Spirit" within the Christian tradition. Such an orientation to glossolalia has discouraged careful theological and historical analysis of developments in the late nineteenth century and has encouraged an immediate jump to such earlier antecedent movements as the "Irvingites" of the 1830s, among whom in Britain many Pentecostal-like practices and theological claims emerged.[7]

Third, the attention given to the practice of glossolalia has diverted interpreters from theological categories of analysis. Sociological and psychological categories have been more regularly employed.[8] Until the recent appearance of glossolalia in the cultural and ecclesiastical mainstream, the phenomenon has largely been understood as an abnormal response to some form of "deprivation," whether sociological or psychological.

Even when theological analysis has been attempted, the concentration on glossolalia has foreshortened the theological analysis by restricting the type of questions considered. The result has been that typical theological analysis of Pentecostalism has centered almost exclusively on questions of pneumatology, especially the doctrine of the baptism in the Holy Spirit and the gifts of the Spirit.[9] Although such an understanding is a decided advance over those interpretations of Pentecostalism which see only glossolalia, it still fails, as we shall see, to grasp the logic of the more complicated *gestalt* of the theological themes that constituted at least original Pentecostalism. Such reductionism in the treatment of Pentecostal theology not only prevents the fullest understanding of the movement, but also precludes critical evaluation of its most distinctive claims.

SEEKING A COMMON PATTERN

These limitations of efforts to interpret Pentecostalism primarily in terms of glossolalia raise the question of whether it might not be possible to offer an alternative analysis that penetrates beneath the practice of speaking in tongues to a fuller understanding of the theological claims supporting that practice—and to do this in such a way as to enable the interpreter to understand the precise historical and theological relationship of Pentecostalism to antecedent and related theological and ecclesiastical traditions.

At first blush, any effort to reduce the bewildering variety of Pentecostal traditions to a common theological pattern seems doomed to failure. Fortunately, however, much of the variety within Pentecostalism is derived from cultural factors, such as divisions along racial lines or by allegiance to a founder whose charismatic leadership has produced a given faction perpetuating his or her own idiosyncratic practices and convictions.[10] For our theological purposes, these factors may largely be ignored.

But even the formalized statements of belief and doctrine within Pentecostalism reflect an amazing variety, containing not only the classical and common doctrines of the Christian church usually amplified by various additions on Pentecostal distinctives—tongues, baptism in the Spirit, and so forth), but also often "articles of faith" on such topics as foot washing, church property, the usefulness of camp meetings, and membership in secret societies or labor unions.[11] Such statements are also not always to be trusted in the search for a characteristic theological understanding of Pentecostalism. Often they are appropriated from other ecclesiastical and theological traditions and then expanded in Pentecostal directions, often in an apparent effort to assert "orthodoxy" and historical continuity with more classical Christian traditions. The 1948 "Statement of Truth" of the Pentecostal Fellowship of North America, for

example, was taken verbatim from the "Statement of Faith"
promulgated five years earlier by the National Association of
Evangelicals—with the exception of article 5:

> We believe that the full gospel includes holiness of heart
> and life, healing for the body and baptism in the Holy
> Spirit with the initial evidence of speaking in other
> tongues as the Spirit gives utterance.[12]

This statement does provide some clues in the search for
a *gestalt* of characteristically Pentecostal claims, especially
when amplified by further clues provided by an emerging
consensus in the effort to develop a typology of Pentecostal
groups. David W. Faupel, elaborating the work of such
predecessors as Klaude Kendrick and Everett Moore, divides
Pentecostal churches and movements into three groups according to their distinctive theological themes:

1. Those teaching a doctrine of sanctification in the Wesleyan
   Holiness tradition (the "three works of grace"—Pentecostals who maintain that Christian experience normally finds
   expression in a pattern of conversion, "entire sanctification" as a distinct subsequent experience, and a
   further baptism in the Holy Spirit empowering the believer
   for witness and service, evidenced by speaking in tongues);
2. Those reducing this pattern to "two works of grace" by
   collapsing the first two into one "finished work" supplemented by a process of gradual sanctification (thus advocating a pattern focusing on conversion and a subsequent
   baptism in the Holy Spirit as just defined); and
3. Those holding a "Oneness" or "Jesus Only" view of the
   Godhead (thus proclaiming an "Evangelical unitarianism"
   of the Second Person of the Trinity).[13]

While the third of these types is in many ways the most
novel and deserves sympathetic analysis in its own right,[14] it
is also clear, at least for our purposes, that it is primarily a
subgroup of the second type evoked by a subsidiary problem.
The Oneness movement is a variation within Pentecostalism
produced by a literalistic effort to harmonize the trinitarian
baptismal formula in Matthew 28:19 with the pattern more
common in Acts (especially Acts 2:38) of baptism in the name

of the "Lord Jesus" or "Jesus Christ." This branch of Pentecostalism resolves this difficulty by affirming the pattern in Acts 2:38 and related passages and arguing from Colossians 2:9 that Jesus is the full manifestation of the Godhead in this dispensation. Though touching on broader issues, such as a dispensational understanding of the trinitarian involvement of God in human history and the larger Pentecostal problem of relating the work of the Spirit to the work of Christ, this cluster of ideas expresses nothing universally characteristic of Pentecostalism. The Jesus Only movement derives, both theologically and historically, from the second, or "two works of grace," branch of Pentecostalism.

TWO CONFLICTING PATTERNS

Our problem, then, is to develop a theological analysis of Pentecostalism that is characteristic of both major types of the movement and that, if possible, helps explain why Pentecostalism separated into these two strands. But to focus too quickly on the tension between the "two works of grace" and the "three works of grace" would produce a soteriological reductionism not unlike that produced by too early a concentration on glossolalia. The article above from the "Statement of Truth" of the Pentecostal Fellowship of North America (PFNA) uses the expression "full gospel" and draws attention to "healing for the body" as well as "holiness" and the baptism in the Holy Spirit.

The term "full gospel" is characteristically used within Pentecostalism and describes a constellation of themes partially submerged in the larger PFNA doctrinal statement. These themes of the "full" or "whole gospel" are spelled out as follows in an early statement:

> During the Reformation God used Martin Luther and others to restore to the world the doctrine of justification by faith. Rom. 5:1. Later on the Lord used the Wesleys and others in the great holiness movement to restore the gospel of sanctification by faith. Acts 26:18. Later still he used various ones to restore the gospel of Divine healing by faith (Jas. 5:14, 15), and the gospel of Jesus's second coming. Acts 1:11. Now the Lord is using many witnesses

> in the great Pentecostal movement to restore the gospel of
> the baptism with the Holy Ghost and fire (Luke 3:16; Acts
> 1:5) with signs following. Mark 16:17, 18; Acts 2:4; 10:44–
> 46; 19:6; 1:1–28:31. Thank God, we now have preachers
> of the whole gospel.[15]

This passage suggests the five themes included in the "whole
gospel—the three works of grace" strand of Pentecostalism
plus two more, "Divine healing by faith" and "Jesus's second
coming." These two extra themes may be added to the
teachings of either branch of Pentecostalism and regularly
occur in passages listing the distinctive themes of Pentecostalism. This constellation of motifs recurs throughout the whole
Pentecostal tradition.

The pattern appears, for example, at the very beginning
when the students at Bethel Bible College were straining
toward the final link in the chain of Pentecostal teachings. As
their teacher, Charles F. Parham, reported:

> In December of 1900 we had our examination upon the
> subject of repentance, conversion, consecration, sanctific-
> ation, healing, and the soon coming of the Lord. We had
> reached in our studies a problem. What about the second
> chapter of Acts? . . . I set the students at work studying out
> diligently what was the Bible evidence of the baptism of
> the Holy Ghost.[16]

This assignment raised the question that resulted a few days
later in the emergence of Pentecostal theology when student
Agnes N. Ozman would "receive the Holy Spirit" and purportedly speak in the Chinese language.[17]

A similar pattern appears in the black denomination
called the First Baptized Holiness Church of God of the
Americas, formed by merger in 1926, but tracing its roots back
to 1898. The basis of union contained the following doctrinal
themes among the denominational commitments: repentance,
regeneration, justification, sanctification, Pentecostal baptism,
speaking with other tongues as the Spirit gives utterance,
divine healing of the body and the premillennial second
coming of Christ.[18] Likewise, the pattern may be found in the
Apostolic Faith Mission, one of the oldest Pentecostal bodies,
tracing its origin directly to the Azusa Street Revival that
launched Pentecostalism into worldwide notice and notoriety:

> This church . . . places special emphasis on the need of
> having three definite, separate, spiritual experiences
> wrought out in the heart and life: JUSTIFICATION,
> SANCTIFICATION, THE BAPTISM OF THE HOLY
> GHOST. . . . These doctrines concerning spiritual experi-
> ence, together with the teachings on Divine Healing, the
> Imminent Second Coming of Jesus—premillennial . . .
> provide the solid, scriptural foundation on which the
> church stands.[19]

This pattern is, if anything, clearer in the other main
branch of Pentecostalism, where the second theme of sanctification drops out to leave an emphasis on the "full gospel"
as a "four-fold gospel." Modern Assemblies of God theologian
Stanley Horton organizes his *Into All Truth*, a denominational
training manual, around "four fundamental teachings—salvation, healing, the baptism in the Holy Spirit, and the second
coming of Christ," because "these four teachings have received
special emphasis and illumination by the Holy Spirit during
the present-day pentecostal revival."[20] This pattern, however,
finds even clearer expression in the work of Aimee Semple
McPherson, controversial founder of the International Church
of the Foursquare Gospel, whose basic message she summarized as follows:

> Jesus saves us according to John 3:16. He baptizes us with
> the Holy Spirit according to Acts 2:4. He heals our bodies
> according to James 5:14−15. And Jesus is coming again to
> receive us unto Himself according to I Thessalonians
> 4:16−17.[21]

THE COMMON FOUR-FOLD PATTERN

We will take this latter four-fold pattern as the basis of
our theological and historical analysis. Though the five-fold
pattern was historically prior and thus has certain claims for
our attention, the four-fold pattern expresses more clearly and
cleanly the logic of Pentecostal theology. It is, moreover,
contained within the more complex pattern and thus has a
certain claim to be at least logically, if not historically, prior to
the five-fold pattern. These four themes are well-nigh universal
within the movement, appearing, as we have been arguing, in

all branches and varieties of Pentecostalism,[22] whereas the theme of entire sanctification is finally characteristic of only the Holiness branch. To opt for the more streamlined four-fold pattern is not to ignore the Holiness branch. The theological and historical reasons for its existence will be clearly revealed as we work with the more universal pattern.

It must be immediately admitted that all the elements of this four-fold pattern occur separately or in various combinations in other Christian traditions. Even the four-fold pattern itself is somewhat anticipated in, for example, the "four-fold gospel" of A. B. Simpson, founder of the late nineteenth-century Christian and Missionary Alliance, who spoke of Christ our "Saviour, Sanctifier, Healer and Coming King."[23] But the emergence of this pattern is in fact the last step in the complex process of development that culminated in Pentecostalism. Its significance will emerge later in our story. It is nonetheless possible to argue that this four-fold pattern provides an analysis of Pentecostalism that is sufficiently characteristic of the movement as a whole to be used as the basis of historical and theological analysis.

Other analyses might well be offered, but the value of this one is demonstrated (1) empirically, as we have been arguing, in that it appears so widely in the literature of Pentecostalism; (2) theologically, as we will indicate momentarily, by the way in which it permits the logic of Pentecostal thought to be explicated; and (3) historically, as the whole of this study will demonstrate, in that tracing the emergence of these four themes reveals, perhaps for the first time with full clarity, the story of the roots of Pentecostal theology.

The fuller meaning of the discrete elements of the four-square gospel will be made clearer as the historical emergence of each is traced. Here we are concerned to demonstrate how these elements are linked together into a distinctive constellation that expresses the inner logic of the movement. Though discretely present elsewhere, these four themes coalesce within Pentecostalism in such a way as to reinforce one another. The characteristic logic of this linkage can be seen most easily by exploring three early names given to the movement: the "Pentecostal Movement," the "Apostolic Faith," and the "Latter Rain Movement." All three of these expressions occur in the title given by Charles F. Parham to his first report of the new phenomenon, "The Latter Rain: The Story of the Origin of the Original Apostolic or Pentecostal Movements."[24]

THE PENTECOSTAL HERMENEUTIC

Exploring the first of these titles, the "Pentecostal Movement," reveals how the first two elements of the four-fold gospel, salvation/justification and baptism in the Holy Spirit, are linked together. This pattern is grounded in a distinct hermeneutic, a distinctively Pentecostal manner of appropriating the Scriptures. In contrast to magisterial Protestantism, which tends to read the New Testament through Pauline eyes, Pentecostalism reads the rest of the New Testament through Lukan eyes, especially with the lenses provided by the Book of Acts. W. J. Hollenweger comments, "The Pentecostals and their predecessors based their views almost exclusively on the Gospel of Luke and the Acts of the Apostles."[25]

But to turn from the Pauline texts to the Lukan ones is to shift from one genre of literature to another, from didactic to narrative material.[26] Narrative texts are notoriously difficult to interpret theologically.[27] Pentecostals read the accounts of Pentecost in Acts and insist that the general pattern of the early church's reception of the Spirit, especially as it is in some sense separated in time from the church's experience of Jesus, must be replicated in the life of each individual believer.

In making this claim, Pentecostalism stands in a long tradition of a "subjectivizing hermeneutic." Claude Welch, for example, indicates that a part of the turn toward subjective experience in Pietism was the insistence that "the drama of the race—of Creation, Fall and Redemption—is to be reenacted in each life." Within Pietism "the true birth of Christ is his birth in our hearts, his true death is in that dying within us, his true resurrection is in the triumph of our faith."[28] The "higher life" antecedents to Pentecostalism in the nineteenth century used a similar approach to Scripture in appropriating elements of the Old Testament *Heilsgeschichte* devotionally. The exodus from Egypt, the wilderness wanderings, and crossing the Jordan River into the Promised Land all became stages in the normative pattern of the spiritual pilgrimage from conversion into the "second blessing" ("Beulah Land").[29]

Thus Assemblies of God historian William Menzies suggests that

> the Pentecostal movement is that group of sects within the Christian Church which is characterized by the belief that the occurrence mentioned in Acts 2 on the Day of Pentecost not only signaled the birth of the church, but described an experience available to believers in all ages. The experience of an enduement with power, called the "baptism in the Holy Spirit," is believed to be evidenced by the accompanying sign of "speaking with other tongues as the spirit gives utterance."[30]

This captures the key claim of Pentecostalism and indicates why it carries the name that it does. The movement's distinctive way of reading the New Testament leads it to the conclusion that, as in the early church, the modern believer becomes a disciple of Jesus Christ and receives the fullness of the Spirit's baptism in separate events or "experiences." In this manner the first two elements of the four-square gospel are tied together by a distinctive hermeneutic.

But to raise the question of the availability of the experience of Pentecost to every generation is to raise implicitly the question of the permanent validity of the phenomena apparently reported in the New Testament—not only the charismata such as glossolalia, but, what is even more difficult, the question of divine healing, also designated in the New Testament as a "gift of the Spirit."

Pentecostalism affirms the integral place in Jesus' ministry of literal miracles of healing and insists that these are to be experienced in our own time because they are part of the post-Pentecost experience of the early church as reported in the Book of Acts. These miracles of healing are not only part of the salvation and relief brought to humanity in the gospel, but are also a sign of reassurance to the believer and witness to the unbeliever. Charles F. Parham wrote in 1902:

> Christ did not leave his believing children without signs of distinction to follow them that the world might know who were Christians and who were not. Neither did he

send forth his servants to preach vague speculative theories of a world to come, but with mighty power for the relief of suffering humanity; feeding the hungry, clothing the naked; healing the sick; casting out devils; speaking with new tongues; confirming the word of inward benefit—wrought in Jesus Christ—by these outward visible signs.[31]

In this quotation a key word is "power." One of the pre-Pentecostal "higher life" teachers, Andrew Murray, stated:

Wherever the Spirit acts with power, there He works divine healings. . . . If divine healing is seen but rarely in our day, we can attribute it to no other cause but that the Spirit does not act with power.[32]

If, then, the Pentecostal "enduement with power" is available to all generations, then the power of the Spirit will manifest itself in our own day in miracles of divine healing, at least in the lives of those who have truly experienced the Pentecostal baptism and know to look for such blessings.

In making this claim, Pentecostals reveal a "restoration-ist" motif that flies directly in the face of the tendency of classical Protestantism to argue that the charismata and "supernatural gifts of the Spirit" ceased with the close of the apostolic era. Illustrative of this way of handling the supernatural element in the New Testament is Benjamin B. Warfield, an advocate of the old Princeton Theology who used the doctrine to refute the pre-Pentecostal healing movements of the late nineteenth century. While granting to the Pentecostals that the "Apostolic Church was characteristically a miracle-working church," Warfield insisted that this state of affairs was

the characterizing peculiarity of specifically the Apostolic Church, and it belonged therefore exclusively to the Apostolic age. . . . these gifts . . . were part of the creden-tials of the apostles as the authoritative agents of God in founding the church. Their function thus confined them distinctively to the Apostolic Church, and they necessar-ily passed away with it.[33]

Pentecostals, however, argue from the unchangeableness of God[34] that the nature of the apostolic church in this respect is normative for all time. In claiming to restore the supernatu-

ral elements of the apostolic era, the movement claimed to be
in effect the "Apostolic Faith"—a name frequently used by
early adherents and applied by them to a large number of early
journalistic efforts and institutions. One advocate put it this
way in a book entitled *The Apostolic Faith Restored:*

> There is, in the religious world of today, a great activity of
> the Lord's Spirit known as the Pentecostal or Apostolic
> Faith Movement. . . . the honest-hearted thinking men and
> women of this great movement have made it their en-
> deavor to return to the faith and practice of our brethren
> who served God prior to the apostasy. They have made the
> New Testament their rule of life. . . . The Pentecostal
> Movement . . . leaps the intervening years crying *"Back to
> Pentecost."* . . . this work of God is immediately con-
> nected with the work of God in New Testament days. Built
> by the same hand, upon the same foundation of the
> apostles and prophets, after the same pattern, according to
> the same covenant . . . they do not recognize a doctrine or
> custom as authoritative unless it can be traced to that
> primal source of church instruction, the Lord and his
> apostles.[35]

This assertion, then, of direct access to the experience of
Pentecost leads quickly to the claim to have restored the
"apostolic faith" and all the supernatural elements reported in
the New Testament. Among these is divine healing, which
becomes not only a gift of God to his people in suffering, but
also a sign of the Spirit's presence to the believer and a form of
witness to the unbeliever in the work of evangelism.

THE "LATTER RAIN" MOVEMENT

But such a claim to have restored the apostolic faith
raises severe apologetic questions for Pentecostals. How can it
be that something apparently so rare in the history of the
church can claim to be an essential manifestation of Christian
faith and practice? Pentecostals had two answers to this
question. Some adherents—usually pressing the evidence
beyond its limits—claimed that it was possible to "establish a
fellowship of faith and practice"[36] by unearthing in most ages
of the church persons and movements that experienced

speaking in tongues and other gifts of the Spirit. But there was also another response to this question, one truer to the logic of at least early Pentecostalism. This answer was bound up in the doctrine of the latter rain, a teaching that illustrates how the expectation of the imminent return of Christ is linked in Pentecostal thought to the other elements of the four-square gospel.

In early years Pentecostalism often took the name "Latter Rain Movement."[37] The classic expression of this doctrine is found in *The Latter Rain Covenant* by D. Wesley Myland.[38] The account of Pentecost in Acts 2 quotes the prophecy from the Book of Joel that in the "latter days" the Spirit will be poured out on all humanity. Pentecostals were, therefore, immediately attracted to the Book of Joel[39] and to hints there, in James 5:7–8, and elsewhere in Scripture of an "early" and a "latter" rain.

Physical rainfall in Palestine comes in two main seasons, in the spring to accompany planting and in the fall to ripen the crops for harvest. This literal rainfall pattern provides the image by which Pentecostals understand their own relationship to the apostolic church and to the imminent end of the age. The original Pentecost of the New Testament was the "early rain," the outpouring of the Spirit that accompanied the "planting" of the church. Modern Pentecostalism is the "latter rain," the special outpouring of the Spirit that restores the gifts in the last days as part of the preparation for the "harvest," the return of Christ in glory. Myland insisted that

> now we are in the Gentile Pentecost, the first Pentecost started the church, the body of Christ, and this, the second Pentecost, *unites* and *perfects* the church into the coming of the Lord.[40]

Myland went so far as to plot the physical rainfall in Palestine as a part of a related argument that an increasing amount of rain in the late nineteenth century paralleled the spiritual emergence of Pentecostalism, confirmed its validity, and indicated that the end was imminent.[41]

Though the specific parallels with Palestinian rainfall lost their value, the broader Latter Rain doctrine provided a key missing premise in the logic of Pentecostalism. It gave the movement a sense of having a key role in the approaching climax of history as the means by which God was preparing the "bride," the church, to meet her Lord. Mrs. Mary B. Woodworth-Etter, a somewhat neglected figure in Pentecostalism, described her "special call for this work" in a vision by these words:

> . . . to give the Household of Faith their Meat in due season; to give the Last Call to the Gentile sinners, the Last Call to the Marriage Supper of the Lamb, for His wife is about to enter the marriage relationship . . . ; and to get those who have been called to be established, to be faithful and true, that they may be anointed with the Holy Ghost and with power, and sealed with proper knowledge of His coming.[42]

But beyond indicating the special task to be performed in the "last days" by the rise of Pentecostalism, the Latter Rain doctrine also explained why the gifts and miracles should reappear after such a long "drought." Mrs. Woodworth-Etter explained: "God says before Jesus comes, these same 'signs and wonders' shall come to pass; the sick shall be healed, devils cast out, people shall speak with tongues—just before he comes."[43] These "signs and wonders" not only tie the eschatological themes into the whole complex of the four-square gospel, but the Latter Rain framework makes the great apologetic problem of Pentecostalism into a major apologetic asset.[44] The long drought from post-apostolic times to the present is seen to be a part of God's dispensational plan for the ages. What seemed to make the movement most illegitimate— its discontinuity with classical forms of Christianity—has become its greatest legitimation.

This, then, is something of the inner logic by which the elements of the four-fold gospel of Pentecostalism cohere. The fact that this logic does exist and can be so explicated confirms to a certain extent the appropriateness of a theological analysis emphasizing this distinctive pattern of four themes, *gestalt*. Tracing the development and interplay of these themes enables the historical and theological genesis of Pentecostalism to be understood, perhaps for the first time, at least in detail. That complicated story will constitute the rest of this study.

NOTES

1. Carl Brumbeck, *What Meaneth This?: A Pentecostal Answer to a Pentecostal Question* (Springfield, Mo.: Gospel Publishing House, 1946).
2. See the survey of this literature in Horace S. Ward, Jr., "The Anti-Pentecostal Argument," in Vinson Synan, ed., *Aspects of Pentecostal-Charismatic Origins* (Plainfield, N.J.: Logos International, 1975), pp. 99–122. The equation of Pentecostalism and glossolalia is seen, for example, in an early Lutheran critique of the movement by H. J. Stolee; originally published as *Pentecostalism* (Minneapolis: Augsburg, 1936), it was reissued in an unaltered edition in 1963 as *Speaking in Tongues*.
3. Kilian McDonnell, *Charismatic Renewal and the Churches* (New York: Seabury, 1976), the best guide now available to the growing social scientific literature on the subject of glossolalia.
4. John T. Bunn, "Glossolalia in Historical Perspective," in Watson E. Mills, ed., *Speaking in Tongues: Let's Talk About It* (Waco, Tex.: Word Books, 1973), p. 46.
5. George H. Williams and Edith Waldvogel, "A History of Speaking in Tongues and Related Gifts," in Michael Hamilton, ed., *The Charismatic Movement* (Grand Rapids: Wm. B. Eerdmans, 1975), especially pp. 81–89.
6. This disputed issue depends in part on whether the white or the black origins of Pentecostalism are stressed and in part on whether the first statement of the full Pentecostal theology or the beginnings of its worldwide impact are sought. Present theological concerns dictate here a focus on the former event. For the issues involved, see Leonard Lovett, "Black Origins of the Pentecostal Movement," in Synan, *Aspects of Pentecostal-Charismatic Origins*, pp. 123–41.
7. See this tendency in ch. 2, "Antecedents of Modern Pentecostalism," in John T. Nichol, *Pentecostalism* (1966; reprint, Plainfield, N.J.: Logos International, 1971, under the title *The Pentecostals*), pp. 18–24, a standard historical treatment of the movement. More recent efforts treat late nineteenth-century developments in more detail. See especially Frederick Dale Bruner, *A Theology of the Holy Spirit* (Grand Rapids: Wm. B. Eerdmans, 1970), pp. 35–55 and related appendixes; Vinson Synan, *The Holiness-Pentecostal Movement in the United States* (Grand Rapids: Wm. B. Eerdmans, 1971); and the 1975 essay cited above by George H. Williams and Edith Waldvogel, "A History of Speaking in Tongues and Related Gifts," already containing intimations of Waldvogel's dissertation, "The 'Overcoming Life': A Study in the Reformed Evangelical Origins of Pentecostalism" (Ph.D. diss., Harvard Divinity School, 1977). Literature emphasizing the Irvingite antecedent includes Andrew Landale Drummond, *Edward Irving and His Circle, Including Some Considerations of the "Tongues Movement" in the Light of Modern Psychology* (London: James Clarke, 1937); Larry Christenson, "Pentecostalism's Forgotten Forerunner," in Synan, *Aspects of Pentecostal-Charismatic Origins*, pp. 15–35, summarizing *A Message to the Charismatic Movement* (East Weymouth, Mass.: Dimension, 1972); and Charles Gordon Strachan, *The Pentecostal Theology of Edward Irving* (London: Darton, Longman and Todd, 1973).

8. The literature is surveyed by McDonnell, *Charismatic Renewal and the Churches,* an effort to refute the "deprivation" theories of the emergence of Pentecostalism.

9. This tendency is evident, for example, in the best theological interpretation of Pentecostalism to date, Bruner's *Theology of the Holy Spirit.* This University of Hamburg dissertation consists almost entirely of an extended exegesis of the relevant texts in Acts and the Corinthian epistles. See also James D. G. Dunn, *Baptism in the Holy Spirit* (London: SCM Press, 1970; also Naperville, Ill.: Allenson, 1970; and Philadelphia: Westminster, 1977).

10. These factors are indicated in the standard surveys of Pentecostalism, perhaps most helpfully in Synan, *The Holiness-Pentecostal Movement in the United States.*

11. The fullest collection of this material is in W. J. Hollenweger, *Handbuch der Pfingstbewegung* (Geneva: privately published, 1965–67). This ten-volume Zürich dissertation has been deposited by the author in major libraries around the world and is available from the Board of Microtext of the American Theological Library Association. Extracts have been published in various languages (English, French, German, and Spanish) with differing contents. The English edition is published as *The Pentecostals* (London: SCM Press; and Minneapolis: Augsburg, 1972).

12. The full statement is in Nichol, *Pentecostalism,* pp. 4–5. Nichol uses this fact to classify Pentecostalism as a subgroup of American Fundamentalism or Evangelicalism.

13. David W. Faupel, *The American Pentecostal Movement: A Bibliographical Essay,* Occasional Bibliographic Papers of the B. L. Fisher Library, no. 2 (Wilmore, Ky.: B. L. Fisher Library, Asbury Theological Seminary, 1972), building on the earlier work of Everett L. Moore, "Handbook of Pentecostal Denominations in the United States" (M.A. thesis, Pasadena College, 1954), and Klaude Kendrick, *The Promise Fulfilled: A History of the Modern Pentecostal Movement* (Springfield, Mo.: Gospel Publishing House, 1961).

14. This analysis is provided by David Reed, "Aspects of the Origins of Oneness Pentecostalism" in Synan, *Aspects of Pentecostal-Charismatic Origins,* an advance report on "Origins and Development of the Theology of Oneness Pentecostalism in the United States" (Ph.D. diss., Boston University, 1978). In addition to standard surveys, two insider accounts are helpful: Fred J. Foster, *Think It Not Strange* (St. Louis: Pentecostal Publishing House, 1965), and Frank J. Ewart, *Phenomenon of Pentecost* (Houston: Herald Publishing House, 1947; rev. ed., Hazelwood, Mo.: World Aflame Press, 1975).

15. H. S. Maltby, *The Reasonableness of Hell* (Santa Cruz, Calif.: n.p., 1913), pp. 82–83.

16. Charles F. Parham, "The Latter Rain," reprinted in Sarah E. Parham, *The Life of Charles F. Parham, Founder of the Apostolic Faith Movement* (Joplin, Mo.: Tri-State Printing, 1930; reprint, Joplin, Mo.: Hunter Printing, 1969), pp. 51–52. See the same pattern in her own preaching in a sermon, "Earnestly Contend for the Faith Once Delivered to the Saints," in Robert L. Parham, comp., *Selected Sermons of the Late Charles F. Parham, Sarah E. Parham, Co-Founders of the Original Apostolic Faith Movement* (n.p., 1941), pp. 9–22.

17. This is reported in Parham's essay, "Latter Rain," and more fully in Agnes N. Ozman LaBerge, *What God Hath Wrought* (Chicago: Herald Publishing, n.d.).

18. This statement is reported in *Religious Bodies: 1936*, vol. 2, pt. 1 (Washington: U.S. Government Printing Office, 1941), p. 696. See the more elaborate statement of faith, similar but lacking a clause on the Second Coming, in the first issue of *Apostolic Faith* (September 1906), the organ of the Azusa Street Mission and its black leader, W. J. Seymour. The early issues of *Apostolic Faith* have been reprinted by Fred T. Corum in *Like As of Fire* (Wilmington, Mass.: n.p., 1981), and the text of the statement is available in an appendix to Hollenweger, *The Pentecostals*, p. 513.

19. *A Historical Account of the Apostolic Faith, Trinitarian-Fundamental Evangelistic Organization* (Portland, Oreg.: Apostolic Faith Mission Headquarters, 1965), pp. 20–21, delineating its "doctrinal foundation." Elsewhere (pp. 31–32) the "doctrines of Christ, as spoken by Him" are listed with proof texts as Justification and Salvation, Sanctification, the Baptism of the Holy Ghost, Divine Healing, the Second Coming.

20. Stanley Horton, *Into All Truth: A Survey of the Course and Content of Divine Revelation* (Springfield, Mo.: Gospel Publishing House, 1955), p. 13.

21. Raymond L. Cox has compiled the writings of Aimee Semple McPherson around this pattern as *The Four-Square Gospel* (Los Angeles: Foursquare Publications, 1969), p. 9. See the similar way of expressing Pentecostal doctrine in Britain in the work of George Jeffreys, the founder of the Elim Foursquare Gospel Alliance, whose teachings are expressed in *The Miraculous Foursquare Gospel—Doctrinal*, vol. 1 (London: Elim Publishing, 1929), especially ch. 1, pp. 1–11. Similarly, D. Wesley Myland reports in *The Latter Rain Covenant and Pentecostal Power with Testimonies of Healings and Baptism* (Chicago: Evangel Publishing House, 1910; reprinted with new pagination by A. N. Trotter of Billings, Missouri [Springfield, Mo.: Temple Press, 1973]), being accosted in camp meeting with the greeting, "What are you doing? Still preaching the four-fold gospel?" (p. 119).

22. This pattern could also be traced outside classical Pentecostalism in the Charismatic movement or "neo-Pentecostalism" and perhaps in Third-World manifestations like certain of the African Independent Churches. The belief in divine healing is pervasive and may well be more characteristic of these movements than glossolalia. Joseph H. Fichter's sociological study of the Catholic Charismatic movement not only indicates the prominence of belief in healing, but also finds among elements of "heterodoxy" in the renewal prayer groups that a majority of participants agree that "accepting Jesus as my personal Savior means that I am already saved" and that "the second coming of Christ is imminent." See his *Catholic Cult of the Paraclete* (New York: Sheed and Ward, 1975), ch. 3, especially p. 44. The doctrine of the baptism of the Holy Spirit has also been carried into traditional churches, but at this point, especially in Catholicism, there has been an effort to critique this doctrine exegetically and substitute such expressions as "release of the Spirit." On this see, for example, Simon Tugwell, O.P., *Did You Receive the Spirit?* (New York: Paulist Press, 1972; also, London: Darton, Longman and Todd, 1972).

23. A. B. Simpson, *The Four-Fold Gospel* (New York: Gospel Alliance Publishing, 1925). A preface traces the theme back forty years earlier. Other late nineteenth-century figures revealing a fascination with variations on these four themes would include R. A. Torrey, Andrew Murray, and A. J. Gordon, though always without glossolalia.

24. The title of ch. 7, by Parham himself, in *The Life of Charles F. Parham*.

25. *The Pentecostals*, p. 336.

26. Critics of Pentecostalism, especially from classical Protestant traditions, have on occasion identified this as the major flaw of Pentecostal exegesis and hermeneutics—that it starts with narrative rather than didactic texts in the Scriptures. See, for example, John R. W. Stott, *Baptism and Fullness: The Work of the Holy Spirit Today* (Downers Grove, Ill.: InterVarsity, 1976), p. 15.

27. One of the few efforts to approach Pentecostal claims in terms of this issue is Gordon D. Fee, "Hermeneutics and Historical Precedent—A Major Problem in Pentecostal Hermeneutics," in Russell P. Spittler, ed., *Perspectives on the New Pentecostalism* (Grand Rapids: Baker, 1976), pp. 118–32.

28. Claude Welch, *Protestant Thought in the Nineteenth Century, vol. I, 1799–1870* (New Haven: Yale University Press, 1972), p. 28.

29. This common pattern is perhaps epitomized in Martin Wells Knapp, *Out of Egypt into Canaan; Or, Lessons in Spiritual Geography* (Boston: McDonald and Gill, 1889; and a series of later editions and reprints).

30. Menzies proposes this definition in *Anointed to Serve* (Springfield, Mo.: Gospel Publishing House, 1971), p. 9, the most recent history of the dominant white American Pentecostal denomination. This definition is also adopted by Faupel, *The American Pentecostal Movement*, p. 9.

31. *A Voice Crying in the Wilderness*, 4th ed. (Joplin, Mo.: Joplin Printing, for Robert L. Parham, 1944), pp. 44–45. This book was first published in 1902.

32. Andrew Murray, *Divine Healing* (New York: Christian Alliance Publishing, 1900), p. 26.

33. *Counterfeit Miracles* (New York: Charles Scribner's Sons, 1918; reprint, London: Banner of Truth, 1972), pp. 5–6. This book has also been issued as *Miracles: Yesterday and Today, True and False* (Grand Rapids: Wm. B. Eerdmans, 1953).

34. This appeal is regularly explicit. See, for example, Maltby, *The Reasonableness of Hell*, p. 84; *Selected Sermons of the Late Charles F. Parham*, Sarah E. Parham, p. 18; B. F. Lawrence, *The Apostolic Faith Restored* (St. Louis: Gospel Publishing House, 1916), pp. 13–14; Mrs. M. B. Woodworth-Etter, *Signs and Wonders* (Indianapolis: privately published, 1916), pp. 192–93.

35. Lawrence, *The Apostolic Faith Restored*, pp. 11–12.

36. Ibid., p. 12. Lawrence was apparently one of the first adherents to develop such a lineage, the validity of such attempts becoming soon the major focus of Pentecostal apologetics and critique.

37. See "The Wonderful History of the Latter Rain" by Miss Lilian Thistlethwaite, an early report of the events that transpired at Charles F.

Parham's Bethel Bible College, ch. 8 of *The Life of Charles F. Parham*, pp. 57–68. The *Latter Rain Evangel* was a journal published from 1908 in T. B. Barratt, *In the Days of the Latter Rain* (London: Simpkin, Marshall, Hamilton, Kent, 1909).

38. D. Wesley Myland, *The Latter Rain Covenant and Pentecostal Power.*

39. See, for example, Aimee Semple McPherson, *Lost and Restored* (Los Angeles: Foursquare Bookshop, n.d.), an elaborate interpretation of church history and of the process by which the "apostolic faith" is "lost and restored" in terms of the prophetic imagery of the Book of Joel, especially the passages surrounding the one quoted in Acts 2.

40. Myland, *The Latter Rain Covenant*, p. 101.

41. Argued by means of the rainfall chart appended to the original edition indicating that "forty three percent more rain fell between the years 1890 and 1900 than fell from 1860 to 1870" (p. 95).

42. Woodworth-Etter, *Signs and Wonders*, pp. 189–90.

43. Ibid., p. 535.

44. Despite this demonstration of the necessity of eschatology and the doctrine of the latter rain to the inherent logic of Pentecostalism, there remain some questions at this point. There is, as mentioned above, no article on eschatology in the first *Apostolic Faith* statement of 1906 (see note 18 above), and the latter rain doctrine did tend to drop out of Pentecostalism (only to reappear, however, in the radical Latter Rain revitalization movement of the 1940s), though broader themes of eschatology remained. Such developments may indicate that the eschatological element is not as integral to Pentecostal logic as the other elements. Nils Bloch-Hoell, for example, says that the theme is vibrant but not crucial, in *The Pentecostal Movement* (Oslo: Universitetsforlaget, 1964), pp. 154–56. More likely is the fact that such apocalyptic orientation is the first element to yield to the forces of institutionalization in such movements. Robert Mapes Anderson argues that eschatology is in fact the central element in the Pentecostal message in *Vision of the Disinherited: The Making of American Pentecostalism* (New York: Oxford University Press, 1979), ch. 5. And David W. Faupel is arguing in a dissertation in progress at the University of Birmingham (England) that the latter rain theme is the key to understanding Pentecostalism. I am arguing here that eschatology is *a* crucial element, but not *the* central theme of Pentecostalism.

31 Love Divine

CHARLES WESLEY

JOHN ZUNDEL

1. Love di - vine, all love ex - cel - ling, Joy of heav'n, to earth come down!
2. Breathe, oh, breathe Thy lov - ing Spir - it In - to ev - 'ry troubled breast!
3. Come, Al - might - y to De - liv - er; Let us all Thy life re - ceive;
4. Fin - ish then Thy new cre - a - tion; Pure and spot - less let us be.

Fix in us Thy hum - ble dwell - ing; All Thy faith - ful mer - cies crown.
Let us all in Thee in - her - it, Let us find that sec - ond rest.
Sud - den - ly re - turn, and nev - er, Nev - er - more Thy tem - ples leave.
Let us see Thy great sal - va - tion, Per - fect - ly re - stored in Thee:

Je - sus, Thou art all com - passion; Pure, un - bound - ed love Thou art.
Take a - way our bent to sin - ning; Al - pha and O - me - ga be;
Thee we would be al - ways bless - ing, Serve Thee as Thy hosts a - bove,
Changed from glo - ry in - to glo - ry, Till in heav'n we take our place,

Vis - it us with Thy sal - va - tion; En - ter ev - 'ry trembling heart.
End of faith, as its be - gin - ning, Set our hearts at lib - er - ty.
Pray, and praise Thee with - out ceas - ing, Glo - ry in Thy per - fect love.
Till we cast our crowns be - fore Thee, Lost in won - der, love, and praise.

CHAPTER II

METHODIST ROOTS
OF PENTECOSTALISM

If we may assume, at least provisionally, the adequacy of our analysis of Pentecostalism into four basic theological themes, we may now use these as clues in seeking the theological roots of Pentecostalism. Such a search, of course, has its dangers and problems. To the committed Pentecostal it may even smack of blasphemy: since the movement is nothing less than God's providential restoration of the "apostolic faith," one need look no further for sources than the New Testament itself. This perspective is also inclined to emphasize the discontinuity with what has preceded Pentecostalism and thus extract it from its immediate historical context.

We need not disparage entirely such claims. The emergence of Pentecostalism was part of an ongoing struggle to understand and make vital for our own time the meaning of the New Testament. As such it is not without insights of value for the rest of the church—though, until at least the rise of the Charismatic movement and its theological rearticulation of Pentecostal themes, these insights have not often been worked out or stated in terms likely to find easy acceptance elsewhere. It is nonetheless striking, for example, that the movement was reaffirming on the popular level the apocalyptic and eschatological elements of the Scriptures at roughly the same time that figures like Albert Schweitzer and Johannes Weiss were making on the level of academic theology a similar point about the neglect of such themes in nineteenth-century biblical scholarship.

We may, moreover, be warned by such concerns not to overemphasize the continuity of Pentecostalism with what went before. The perspective of hindsight makes many things clear—perhaps sometimes too clear. The search for "anteced-ents" and "roots" may uncover parallels and continuities to the overshadowing of novelty and discontinuity. The "new" in Pentecostalism, especially over against its immediate prede-cessors, cannot be denied, but this concern does not need to preclude the effort to gain a better historical understanding of the emergence of the theological and doctrinal claims of the movement.

But even if the validity of such a search is granted, the starting point for the story is not immediately obvious. The various Pentecostal themes may be traced back until they become less and less distinctively Pentecostal and begin to take the shape of similar themes in the more classical Christian traditions. In recent years a variety of starting points have been proposed. We should note them before choosing another that gathers these other proposals up into itself.

Some interpreters[1] have sought the roots of Pentecostal-ism in the Roman and Anglo-Catholic doctrine of confirma-tion, where there is a tendency to separate the reception of the Spirit from water baptism. This position is often argued from Acts 8:14–17, a key text for Pentecostals. The similarities to the Pentecostal case may be seen in such a recent advocate of the position as L. S. Thornton:

> In Galatians (4:6) . . . the phrase which recalls Pentecost is connected definitely with a second stage of initiation. "Because ye are sons, God sent forth the Spirit of his Son into your hearts." . . . the filial relation to God which is proper to our humanity was reestablished through our incorporation into the incarnate Son of God; and this took place in our baptism. . . . By that act of new creation, however, we are now fitted for a further stage of renewal, the indispensable corollary of that first beginning. The Spirit of the Son is the proper complement of that new sonship to which we have been admitted.[2]

It is difficult to read this and related passages without seeing some striking parallels to the Pentecostal separation of conversion and baptism of the Holy Spirit. The case for an Anglo-Catholic and Roman rootage of Pentecostal theology is perhaps strengthened in that these traditions have also tended to maintain a sense of continuation of the "miraculous" into the present day, not only within their sacramental systems, but also by affirming certain miracles of healing (often in relation to their understanding of sainthood) and by preserving ancient rites of exorcism and the laying on of hands for the sick.

Other interpreters have sought the roots of Pentecostalism in Puritanism, arguing that "a direct line of influence can be drawn from Puritan teaching on the Spirit."[3] Garth Wilson has advanced this position in his study "Puritan Doctrine of the Holy Spirit," claiming that intimations of Pentecostal doctrine may be found in Richard Sibbes, John Owen, Thomas Goodwin, Richard Baxter, and other Puritans who taught a "work of the Spirit" beyond regeneration and sanctification.[4] Thomas Goodwin, for example, spoke of a "sealing of the Spirit" on the basis of Ephesians 1:13–14 and correlated this with Pentecost to argue that "they must therefore receive him [the Holy Ghost] as a sanctifier before they can receive him as a Comforter" and to assert that "you that are believers, wait for a further promise of the Holy Ghost as a sealer. . . . you shall find, Acts 1:4, that the apostles were to wait for the promise of the Spirit; so do you."[5]

Such themes in Puritanism were often combined with a renewed emphasis on eschatology and the "latter-day glory" of the church—and these themes were radicalized in various forms of millenarianism on the fringes of the movement.[6] In this mix as well one can find intimations of basic Pentecostal teachings.

Another somewhat neglected but likely fruitful source of Pentecostal roots would be Pietism. German Pietism tended to break the Lutheran dialectic of *simul justus et peccator*[7] by emphasizing that in the grace of Christ one might "overcome" sin and the world—a common and crucial theme, as we shall see, in the years immediately preceding the emergence of Pentecostalism.[8] Likewise, when we turn to trace the rise of the doctrine of healing, we shall find that Pietism plays a crucial role.[9] And Jürgen Moltmann has observed that

as early as the seventeenth century, the age of orthodoxy
and absolutism, apocalyptic and chiliastic thought under-
went a quite remarkable renaissance in Protestant theology. It began in Holland and England and came into full
bloom in Wurtemburg and Saxony.[10]

He of course refers to the rise of Puritanism and Pietism.

THE METHODIST CONNECTION

But these more classical intimations of Pentecostalism
are to large extent parallels rather than direct or actual sources,
though some instances of indirect influence cannot be denied.[11] We shall begin our story with Methodism. This is in
part because it is clear that here we can pick up the story in
such a way as to demonstrate actual historical links and
developments that will climax in Pentecostalism. Methodism,
moreover, stands in a remarkable way at a point of confluence
of the three candidates just discussed. John Wesley, comments
John T. McNeill, was "vitally related to Anglicanism, Puritanism, and Pietism."[12]

Yet even this point of departure will seem strange to
those who know well both Methodism and Pentecostalism. It
is true that later advocates of the various themes isolated in the
last chapter would often attempt to claim Wesley for their
cause—that he taught premillennialism,[13] that he "was orthodox on divine healing,"[14] or that he distinguished between
"those who had been baptized in the Spirit and ordinary
Christians."[15] But as we shall see, all such claims are either
wrong or at least greatly overstated. And even though Methodism and the broader Evangelical Revival were major sources
of the conversion-oriented piety that found later expression in
Pentecostalism, one cannot easily collapse Methodist and
Pentecostal doctrines of conversion. Wesley was more inclined
to speak of "experiencing justifying grace," and even then his
understanding was highly qualified by his commitment to
Anglican ecclesiology and sacramental theology (to the point
of affirming baptismal regeneration)[16] and a highly complex
doctrine of salvation in which conversion was one of several
"moments."

On the other hand, it is not at all surprising that a great variety of Christian claims have been attributed to Wesley. Probably few figures in church history have generated more diverse judgments about their positioning among the Christian traditions. This is clearly revealed by the Wesley scholarship, which often appears to agree on very little. In the social arena, for example, Wesley has been blamed for undercutting the revolutionary potential of the English working class,[17] praised for his contributions to the Evangelical Revival as "the English counterpart to the 'democratic revolutions' of the eighteenth century,"[18] and championed for the "Wesleyan roots of Christian Socialism."[19] Theologically Wesley has been seen as a "reversion" to Catholicism within the Protestant tradition,[20] to have been but a "hair's breadth" from Calvinism,[21] as a true son of the Lutheran Reformation,[22] to have anticipated the experiential and ethical orientation of liberal theology,[23] to have been rooted primarily in the theology of the Eastern fathers,[24] as a form of synergistic tradition that reached back through the English Reformation to nominalism,[25] as a "proto-Barthian," at least in Christology,[26] and so forth. Ecclesiologically Wesley has been claimed for both high church[27] and low church[28] positions.

This diversity of opinion arises in part from the unsystematic, ad hoc character of the Wesleyan corpus and the fact that his thought developed historically in his efforts to channel the energies of Methodism between the Scylla of moralism and the Charybdis of antinomianism. But it also arises out of the catholicity of Wesley's sources and the fact that he blended themes that appear to be inconsistent into a fragile *gestalt* that seems at one time to provide the evidence of his genius and at another to be held together by little more than the sheer force of his personality and convictions. The result has been a sort of constitutional instability in which Methodism has slid from side to side or splintered into fragments, each preserving only certain parts and themes of the original Wesleyan vision. These tendencies were amplified when control was lost after Wesley's death, allowing Methodism to separate from Anglicanism, and they are especially significant in the greater freedom of the American scene.

This pattern of instability is perhaps clearest in Wesley's

ecclesiology. In abridging the Anglican "Thirty-nine Articles" into Methodism's "Twenty-five," Wesley kept the one on the church intact, but interpreted it to indicate things

> essential to a visible Church. First: Living faith; without which, indeed, there can be no church at all, neither visible nor invisible. Secondly: Preaching, and consequently hearing, the pure word of God, else that faith would languish and die. And, thirdly, a due administration of the sacraments—the ordinary means whereby God increaseth faith.[29]

Out of concern for the ecumenical potential of the Methodist stance, Colin Williams has suggested that in emphasizing these three points Wesley has attempted to hold together the accents of the "free church" tradition, classical Protestantism, and Catholicism.[30] Similarly, Donald Durnbaugh uses the axes of tradition, Word, and Spirit to develop a triangular diagram on which to place ecclesiologies. To him, "the middle ground is occupied by movements which are inherently instable"[31]— prime among them being Methodism with its tendency to fall back toward more classical forms of church life or, by contrast, be radicalized toward more "free church" or "pneumatically" oriented styles of church life.

Whatever one wishes to make of this element of instability within Methodism—to praise it as Wesley's genius in preserving a delicate balance or to deprecate it as inconsistent—one may perhaps be helped by this analysis to discern that Wesley attempted in many ways to stand at a point somewhere between the more classical Christian traditions (both Protestant and Catholic) and the more radical traditions. Because of Methodism's consequent tendency to affirm one side or another of this tension, it may be profitable to review three areas where this issue surfaces with particular reference to the themes of Pentecostalism: the "primitivistic" motif in Wesley, whether he may be appropriately called a "theologian of the Spirit," and his understanding of the gifts of the Spirit.

THE PRIMITIVISTIC MOTIF

The primitivistic note in Wesley invites immediate

comparison with the Pentecostal concern for the restoration of the "apostolic faith." Wesley clearly understood himself to be advocating the "old religion" or "true, primitive Christianity."[32] Something of the reason for this can be seen in a tract that had great influence on Wesley from his early years as a missionary in Georgia through the most formative years of the revival movement until he published a translation and extract in 1749. In Wesley's edition of *The Manners of the Ancient Christians* by Claude de Fleury, these are the opening words:

> As the Christian Religion is not an Invention of Men, but the Work of God, it received its full Perfection at the Beginning of it. For who can imagine, the Apostles were ignorant of any Truth necessary or useful to Salvation.[33]

Already nuances quite different from those of Pentecostalism are apparent. Wesley in fact shared his concerns—explicitly in early years—with the high church Anglican party of his era, whose major apologetic thrust was to ground the practices of Anglo-Catholicism in the first four centuries of the church. Indeed, through his experience in Georgia, Wesley's major concern was a rigorous restoration of the *practices* and church order of the early church. And in all of this Wesley seems not to mean so much the biblical period as the "ancients" to whom he appeals. It was the first three centuries of the church to which Wesley appealed, the ante-Nicene fathers and the pre-Constantinian church.[34] The shape of Wesley's primitivism was then in this sense somewhat more historically nuanced than the biblicistic appeal of Pentecostalism to the Book of Acts.

But Wesley's primitivism of the early years was to be profoundly transformed by his evangelical experience of 1738 and the surrounding events and influences. Luke Keefer, Jr., has suggested that Wesley's "ecclesiastical primitivism" was transformed into a form of "soteriological primitivism."[35] Similarly F. Ernest Stoeffler suggests that "henceforth his ecclesiology was informed by the soteriological interest which was the direct result of his own religious renewal under Pietist influence."[36] Wesley remained in many ways Anglican in his understanding of the church, according to Stoeffler, "yet, it is an understanding which is modified so as to make room for church-related Pietism's insistence upon reformation through restoration."[37]

This shift to a soteriological primitivism (which may also have shifted the norms relatively more toward Scripture among the ancient sources) brings Wesley closer to Pentecostalism, but the differences are still very significant. As we shall see shortly, Wesley was not primarily interested in the recovery of lost gifts of the Spirit of apostolic or patristic Christianity, but rather more of norms of behavior and conduct. The de Fleury extract quoted above continues with the words, "It is among the first Christians, therefore, that we must look for a Pattern of the most Perfect Life"—a sentence that well summarizes the nature of the primitivistic motif in Wesley.

A "THEOLOGIAN OF THE SPIRIT"?

But this shift to the soteriological under the impact of Wesley's Aldersgate experience and related influences raises an important question about the extent to which Wesley should be considered a "theologian of the Spirit." Several interpreters have proposed that Wesley is appropriately so designated, and the significance of the question in determining Wesley's relationship to Pentecostalism is obvious. Here again we are raising in another way the issue of Wesley's positioning to the more classical Protestant orientation to Christ and the Word as well as to the more radically, pneumatically oriented movements like Quakerism and Pentecostalism.

Again the divided state of the scholarship on the question indicates the complexity of the issue. A number of interpreters, especially those in the wake of the modern Holiness, Pentecostal, Charismatic movements, have claimed Wesley as essentially a "theologian of the Spirit."[38] A dissertation by Norman Laurence Kellett, for example, surveys the rise of Methodism under the title "John Wesley and the Restoration of the Doctrine of the Holy Spirit to the Church of England in the Eighteenth Century."[39] Others have, however, lamented Wesley's failure to link his soteriology to a vital doctrine of the Holy Spirit.[40]

Part of the disagreement is terminological, revolving

around what it would mean to be a "theologian of the Spirit."
Kellett's study, for example, turns out to be actually a study of
the revival of experiential or experimental Christianity in the
Evangelical Revival. While Wesley's shift to soteriology in
1738 and his consequent emphasis on experience no doubt
gave greater weight to themes related to the work of the Spirit,[41] it is not clear that this impulse was sufficiently strong to
pull Wesley out of the patterns of classical Protestantism with
their tendency to be Christocentric in shape.

There is a point at which Wesley does break into themes
of pneumatology more like the radical traditions. One major
source of the accusation that Wesley was an "enthusiast" was
his doctrine of assurance, which was rooted in an affirmation
of "perceptible inspiration."[42] Wesley rather consistently
taught that "the testimony of the Spirit is an inward impres-
sion on the souls of believers, whereby the Spirit of God
directly testifies to their spirit that they are the children of
God."[43]

Wesley realized that this teaching to a certain extent
placed him with the radicals, commenting that "if the Quakers
hold the same perceptible inspiration with me, I am glad; and
it is neither better nor worse for their holding it at all."[44] But
Wesley was quick to qualify this doctrine, insisting that such
experience in no way could establish doctrine, but was merely
"sufficient to *confirm* a doctrine which is grounded in
Scripture."[45] Wesley, moreover, refused to separate this "testimony of the Spirit" from the "fruit of the Spirit," exhorting,
"Let none ever presume to rest in any supposed testimony of
the Spirit, which is separate from the fruit of it."[46] As we shall
see, this emphasis on the fruit of the Spirit is very characteristic of Wesley and often serves to distinguish him from the
radicals.

But apart from this doctrine of assurance or the inward
testimony of the Holy Spirit and the heightened soteriological
orientation resulting from the emphasis on the experiential,
Wesley is strikingly Christocentric in his patterns of thought—
especially in contrast to later developments in the Holiness
movement and among Pentecostals. Both the moral ideal and
the shape of salvation are grounded firmly in Christ. When
Wesley wished to describe "one that is perfect" he often spoke

first of "one in whom is *the mind which was in Christ* and who
so walketh as He walked."[47] And Wesley incorporates the
Sermon on the Mount more fully into his vision of salvation
than most other Protestants working out of a Pauline soteriology[48] and similarly defines perfection frequently in terms of
Jesus' summary of the law.

Harald Lindstrom speaks of the "Christocentric align-
ment" of Wesley's doctrine of sanctification.[49] Even A. Skevington Wood, who wishes to speak of Wesley as a "theologian
of the Spirit," finally indicates the extent to which this
emphasis is carefully controlled. Wesley, writes Wood,

> realized that the specific task of the Holy Spirit is to
> glorify the Son and to apply the benefits of Christ's
> redemption. . . . Precisely because Wesley understood
> from Scripture this supportive role of the Spirit, his
> theology remains firmly Christocentric.[50]

WESLEY AND THE GIFTS OF THE SPIRIT

This same pattern of moving toward the themes of a more
radically Pneumatocentric position while remaining in a more
classical, Christocentric framework is evident in Wesley's
understanding of the gifts of the Spirit, a critical question of
Pentecostalism. In one sense Wesley was unsystematic and
incomplete in his treatment of the doctrine of the gifts. He was
inconsistent, sometimes returning to classically Protestant
conclusions, and at other times "developing beliefs in response to his own theological assumptions."[51] On the other
hand, Wesley argued ferociously against Conyers Middleton,
who was skeptical of patristic reports of the miraculous and
extraordinary gifts. Wesley insisted to the contrary that such
gifts and miracles were continued through the first three
centuries.[52]

Wesley seems to have been further convinced that
"spiritual coldness" was the cause of the decline of the gifts
and miracles after Constantine. Denying that the cause was not
"because there was no more occasion for them; because all the
world was become Christians," Wesley insisted rather that the
love of the Christians had "waxed cold"—"was turned
Heathen again and had only a dead form left."[53]

On the other hand, in spite of Wesley's concern to restore primitive Christianity and the special normativity he granted to the first three centuries, he actually showed very little interest in the question of spiritual gifts. The Methodists were, it must be admitted, often accused of "laying claim to almost every apostolic gift, in a full and ample manner, as they were possessed of old."[54] Wesley denied this while leaving space for a continuing miraculousness in the sense that "God now hears and answers prayer even beyond the ordinary course of nature."[55] Wesley's interest was fundamentally elsewhere:

> Whether these gifts of the Holy Ghost were designed to remain in the Church throughout all ages, and whether or no they will be restored at the nearer approach of the "restitution of all things," are questions which it is not needful to decide.[56]

As intimated above, Wesley's real interest was not with the gifts of the Spirit, but with the fruit of the Spirit. He regularly makes this distinction, insisting,

> Indeed I do not mean, that Christians now receive the Holy Ghost in order to work miracles; but they do doubtless now "receive," yea, are "filled with, the Holy Ghost, in order to be filled with the fruits of that blessed Spirit."[57]

Wesley felt that the extraordinary gifts were given only to the few. His concern was "what the Holy Spirit is to every believer, for his personal sanctification and salvation."[58]

WESLEY'S DOCTRINE OF SALVATION

Finally we come to what probably was the basic theme of Wesley's thought, his doctrine of salvation. Here the emphasis is on the restoration of the image of God through stages of the operation of grace. An extended passage from Wesley offers a concise summary of this process:

> Salvation begins with what is usually termed (and very properly) preventing grace; including the first wish to please God, the first dawn of light concerning his will, and the first slight transient conviction of having sinned

against him. All these imply some tendency toward life; some degree of salvation; the beginning of a deliverance from a blind, unfeeling heart, quite insensitive of God and the things of God. Salvation is carried on by *convincing grace,* usually in Scripture termed repentance; which brings a larger measure of knowledge, and a fuller deliverance from the heart of stone. Afterwards we experience the proper Christian salvation, whereby, "through grace," we "are saved by faith," consisting of those two grand branches, justification and sanctification. By justification we are saved from the guilt of sin, and restored to the favour of God; by sanctification we are saved from the power and root of sin, and restored to the image of God. All experience, as well as Scripture, show this salvation to be both instantaneous and gradual. It begins in the moment we are justified in the holy, humble, gentle, patient love of God on man. It gradually increases from that moment, as a "grain of mustard-seed, which, at first, is the least of all seeds," but afterwards puts forth large branches, and becomes a great tree; till, in another instant, the heart is cleansed from all sin, and filled with pure love to God and man. But even that love increases more and more, till we "grow up in all things into Him that is our Head"; till we attain "the measure of the stature of the fullness of Christ."[59]

Several points in this statement require some additional comment. First, we must notice the way in which Wesley's understanding of salvation goes beyond the forensic themes of justification to emphasize a strong doctrine of sanctification. A very characteristic feature of Wesley's thought is the twofold emphasis that is here expressed in reference to the "two grand branches" of salvation, "justification and sanctification." Albert Outler suggests that Wesley has developed a "therapeutic" motif implicit in Anglicanism, in which grace is viewed not primarily as a forensically based forgiveness but as a "healing" or "restorative" force,[60] so that, as Wesley put it above, "by sanctification we are ... restored to the image of God."

The Wesleyan doctrine of "entire sanctification" or "Christian perfection" is difficult to interpret and has been approached from various angles. One useful perspective is to view it as a form of "realized eschatology"[61] that expresses

Wesley's "optimism of grace" that balances out his "pessimism of nature."[62] Salvation for Wesley consists, therefore, of a reordering of fallen human existence in this life. Wesley himself put it, "Whatsoever else it imply, it is a present salvation. It is something attainable, yea, actually attained, on earth."[63] Or again, salvation

> is not a blessing which lies on the other side of death. . . .
> It is not something at a distance. It is a present thing, a blessing which through the free mercy of God ye are now in possession of.[64]

It is this vision that lies behind Methodism's controversial doctrine of Christian perfection. Wesley radically qualified the "perfection" to be expected. It did not imply "an exemption from ignorance, or mistake, or temptations,"[65] but it did include growth beyond "sin, properly so called, (that is, a voluntary transgression of a known law)."[66] Wesley sought to avoid the expression "sinless perfection," because it implied an inability to sin. He preferred to speak instead more positively of the "mind of Christ," total devotion to God, and love of God and neighbor:

> In one view, it is purity of intention, dedicating all the life to God. It is the giving God all our heart; it is one desire and design ruling all our tempers. It is the devoting, not a part, but all, our soul, body and substance to God. In another view, it is all the mind which was in Christ, enabling us to walk as Christ walked. It is the circumcision of the heart from all filthiness, all inward as well as outward pollution. It is a renewal of the heart in the whole image of God, the full likeness of Him that created it. In yet another, it is the loving God with all our heart and our neighbor as ourselves. Now take it in which of these views you please, (for there is no material difference).[67]

These claims are also qualified in Wesley by the teleological character of Christian perfection—by the extent to which this vision of the Christian life served as a goal to be struggled toward rather than the starting point that it became in much later "Wesleyan" thought. Several passages in the "Plain Account of Christian Perfection" grant that other Christian traditions expect an entire sanctification in death.[68] Wesley wondered, then, whether this state could be achieved earlier and gradually came to affirm, as he expressed in the 1767 summary appended to the "Plain Account,"

> I believe this instant generally is the instant of death, the moment before the soul leaves the body. But I believe it may be ten, twenty or forty years before.
>
> I believe it is usually many years after justification; but that it may be within five years or five months after it. I know of no conclusive argument to the contrary.[69]

These citations reveal the extent to which Wesley began to struggle with the goal of "perfection" as a climax to life. It was later "Wesleyan" thought that so easily moved this experience to the beginning of the Christian life and tied it so closely with the initiation into Christian experience.

There was also a similar ambiguity about whether the gradual or the instantaneous aspect of sanctification should be emphasized. Wesley argued that within the *process* of sanctification there was a "moment" of entire sanctification:

> If sin cease before death, there must, in the nature of the thing, be an instantaneous change, there must be a last moment wherein it does exist, and a first moment it does not.[70]

But for much of his life Wesley remained profoundly ambivalent about whether to give the priority to the "crisis" or the "process." Orville Walters has studied this issue and has argued that Wesley overcame this ambivalence about 1772, from that point emphasizing the instantaneous character of the second blessing, though it always preceded and was followed by process and gradual sanctification.[71]

THE MEANING OF THE "SECOND MOMENT"

About this time there arose the crucial question for understanding how Pentecostalism may be related to Methodism—a question that would trouble parts of the Wesleyan tradition for over a century. Once it was clear that Wesleyan thought would emphasize this "moment" of entire sanctification, the question arose as to whether it was appropriate to describe this experience as a baptism of the Holy Spirit understood in terms of images derived from the account of Pentecost in the New Testament.

Wesley himself, it appears, resisted this further development when it surfaced among his followers, especially his designated successor, John Fletcher, the saintly vicar of Madeley, and Joseph Benson, Fletcher's friend and later editor of Fletcher's collected Works.

This discussion must be reconstructed from only a few hints in the literature; key documents are no longer available.[72] It seems to have surfaced amid the more consuming issues of election and perfection of the Calvinistic controversy of the early 1770s. That controversy finally destroyed the coalition between the more Calvinistic wing of Methodism in the circles around George Whitefield and the more Arminian wing around Wesley and his co-workers. These struggles arose at Trevecca College in Wales, an institution supported by the Countess of Huntingdon, patron of Whitefield. Headmaster Joseph Benson was dismissed by the Countess for his Arminian views, an act that soon led to the resignation of President John Fletcher.

In a letter to Benson, Fletcher reported that Rev. Walter Shirley visited the college, and while there, "what you had written upon the 'baptism of the Holy Ghost' was taken to pieces." Apparently Benson by this time was maintaining that individuals should experience "perfection" in a "Pentecostal baptism of the Holy Ghost," because Shirley had argued against such a position that the "prophecy of Joel (Acts ii) had its fulfillment on the day of Pentecost."[73]

Wesley appears to have shared at least some of Shirley's convictions on this matter because a couple of weeks earlier he had encouraged Benson to "abstain from speaking of Universal Salvation and Mr. Fletcher's late discovery."[74] Benson was clearly tempted by the doctrine of "ultimate universal salvation," but the latter reference is obscure. John Telford, the editor of Wesley's Letters, suggests that it refers to Fletcher's doctrine of "receiving the Holy Ghost."[75] A few months earlier Wesley had objected to Fletcher's way of speaking of the event of entire sanctification. Though agreeing that Fletcher allowed "the whole thing which I contend for—an entire deliverance from sin, a recovery of the whole image of God, the loving God with all our heart, soul and strength," Wesley objected to the phrase "receiving the Holy Ghost," insisting that "the phrase in that sense is not scriptural and not quite proper; for they all 'received the Holy Ghost' when they were justified."[76]

A few years later Fletcher and Wesley seem to have sorted out their differences and had apparently agreed to disagree. As Wesley put it,

> It seems our views on Christian Perfection are a little different, though not opposite. It is certain that every babe in Christ has received the Holy Ghost, and the Spirit witnesses with his spirit that he is a child of God. But he has not obtained Christian perfection.[77]

Fletcher also grew more sophisticated about his own differences with Wesley, writing to Miss Mary Bosanquet, a Methodist preacher later to become his wife, that

> I do not rest the doctrine of Christian perfection on the *absence of sin,*—that is the perfection of a dove or a lamb; nor on the *loving God with all one's power,* for I believe all perfect Gentiles and Jews have done so; but on the *fullness* of that superior, nobler, warmer, and *more powerful* love, which the apostle calls the *love of the Spirit,* or *the love of God shed abroad by the Holy Ghost,* given to the Christian Believers, who, since the Day of Pentecost, go on to the perfection of the Christian dispensation.[78]

Though the above seems an explicit objection to Wesley's views, Fletcher makes the difference clear:

> You will find my views of this matter in Mr. Wesley's sermons on Christian Perfection and on Scriptural Christianity; with this difference, that I would distinguish more exactly between the believer baptized with the Pentecostal power of the Holy Ghost, and the believer who, like the Apostles after our Lord's ascension, is not yet filled with that power.[79]

Wesley and Fletcher shared much, but their differences were more than semantic and terminological. These hints of conflict reveal some fundamental divergences that underlay their commonality. In other times and other circumstances these subtle nuances could become accentuated and reveal more clearly a basic ambiguity inherited from the era of classical Methodism. We must make some effort to discern the fuller meaning of these subtle nuances before picking up the story of conflict on the American scene.

A CRUCIAL DIVIDE

Fletcher felt that the key to understanding his own thought was to be found in his doctrine of dispensations—a key point of difference from Wesley. Though his position is undeveloped, Wesley seems to reflect a more classically Protestant position that sees history divided fundamentally into two periods by Christ, or perhaps more exactly by the atonement effected in his death. Thus Wesley can speak of the "covenant of works" and the "covenant of grace" as the "Jewish dispensation" and the "Christian dispensation." The Holy Spirit, of course, plays an important role, as does Pentecost, but as the agent of Christ and subsidiary to him. This is to repeat the point above that even though Wesley placed great weight on the experiential appropriation of grace, he did so in a basically Christocentric framework.

Fletcher, however, saw history divided into three dispensations, each identified with a person of the Trinity, each characterized by a "grand promise of God."[80] The first of these is the "the dispensation of the Father," which looks forward to the "external manifestation of the Son." The "dispensation of the Son" is opened by John the Baptist and looks toward the "promise of the Father," or the effusion of the Spirit at Pentecost. The third dispensation, that of the Spirit, looks forward to the return of Christ.[81] These dispensations are not only a description of the movement of the Heilsgeschichte, or the stages of God's working within human history, but also—and perhaps even primarily—a description of the stages of spiritual growth and development through which each individual must pass.[82]

This doctrine of dispensations emphasizes the teleological movement of history in a way uncharacteristic of Wesley. Though Wesley referred to a climax of history, such as the final judgment, his eschatology was more oriented to questions of the person's death and destiny.[83] Eschatology in the sense of an expectation of the imminent return of Christ does not play the role in Wesley that many expect. Wesley, as we have already suggested, is primarily soteriologically oriented—his focus is on the appropriation of grace in this life and on the restoration of the image of God in preparation for death and eternal life. Fletcher, on the other hand, is much more interested in the promise of Christ's return and often speaks of such in the context of other discussions.[84]

Fletcher's pattern of dispensations accentuates the role of the Holy Spirit and the claim that the present age in some sense is especially characterized by the activity of the Holy Spirit. Because the "dispensation of the Holy Spirit is now in force," the "minister who preaches this dispensation cannot justly be esteemed an enthusiast."[85] This thrust of the dispensational pattern in Fletcher pushes Methodism further out of a Christocentric pattern of thought and closer to a Pneumatocentric one. Similarly, when the scheme of dispensations is used to interpret individual spiritual development, there is a tendency to separate the reception of the Holy Spirit from conversion in the way that began to trouble Wesley. Fletcher did not separate the Spirit from earlier stages, but did focus the role of the Spirit in a third stage inaugurated by the baptism of the Holy Spirit in such a way as to begin to raise these questions. When this scheme was later used by less-subtle minds, the tendency toward separation would be accentuated.

Part of what is at stake here is a shift in exegetical foundations. It is a remarkable fact that, in spite of Wesley's commitment to a "restoration" of the life of the early church, he only infrequently refers to the Book of Acts. This lack is especially noticeable in discussions of Christian perfection and entire sanctification. W. E. Sangster's study of the exegetical foundations of Wesley's thought at this point identifies thirty basic texts—one from Ezekiel, three from Matthew, ten from the Pauline literature, three from the Epistle to the Hebrews, one from the Book of James, two from the Gospel of John, and ten from the First Epistle of John.[86] The Book of Acts, along with any reference to Pentecost, is conspicuous by its absence.

Fletcher's formulation obviously, however, brings the Book of Acts into a new prominence. In fact, according to the index of biblical texts, the Book of Acts is cited more than any other biblical source in his collected *Works.* Thus we may detect between Wesley and Fletcher a significant shift in exegetical foundations, one that may even indicate a shift from a basically Pauline or Johannine orientation to a Lukan one. It would be easy to overemphasize these differences, but this perspective does provide some important clues about the deeper levels of the discussion.

Even the doctrine of dispensations itself may have some claim to being expressly rooted in Lukan theology. Redaction study of Luke and Acts is very much a storm center of discussion with few settled conclusions. It is worth noting, however, that Hans Conzelmann finds in *The Theology of St. Luke* a similar tripartite periodization of history: the period of Israel, the period of Jesus, and the period of the church and of the Spirit.[87] Conzelmann, of course, sees this as a *Heilsgeschichtliche* "de-eschatologization" in response to the "delay of the Parousia," whereas Fletcher in turning to this material reveals an intensification of eschatological orientation. But Conzelmann's redaction study is highly debated,[88] and some would find in Luke patterns more in line with the reading that Fletcher is implicitly giving the texts.[89]

Other interesting questions arise as well. J. E. Fison has suggested that "the Spirit in Acts is still pre-eminently ecstatic" and that "St. Paul's greatest contribution is to give priority to the ethical without the least abating one iota of the supernatural and eschatological character of His activity."[90] This claim has been disputed,[91] but it may nonetheless suggest that some of the emerging nuances in Fletcher over against Wesley may be rooted in the set of texts that each has given the prominent place. This is clearly true at some points—such as Fletcher's emphasis on "power" even in the snippets quoted above. Eduard Schweizer suggests in Kittel's *Wörterbuch* that Luke/Acts focuses on the Spirit and tends to use "δύναμισ [power] and πνεῦμα [spirit] almost as synonyms" and that

προφητεύειν [to prophesy] is for Luke quite central as the work of the Spirit. . . . Only on the margin do we find the formulae in which the Spirit is generally understood as dwelling continually in the individual or the community.[92]

We are not suggesting, of course, that Fletcher moved so far in this direction; he was too controlled by Wesleyan thought. But these distinctive themes do begin to appear in his thought, and under other circumstances those under his influence could pick up and intensify these themes, especially if the influence of more Wesleyan patterns should for a variety of reasons be weakened.

The study of that historical development is the major subject of this analysis, and a major result of the project is that in these shifts are to be found the historical roots of Pentecostal theology. These developments did not take place in early Methodism, in part because of Wesley's resistance and the controlling force of his motifs in that context. America provided the context for this transformation, and it is to that story that we must now turn.

NOTES

1. See James D. G. Dunn, "Spirit-Baptism and Pentecostalism," *Scottish Journal of Theology* 23 (November 1970): 397–407. Representative texts in this tradition are displayed by Bruner, *A Theology of the Holy Spirit*, in an "extended note," pp. 184–88.

2. L. S. Thornton, *Confirmation: Its Place in the Baptismal Mystery* (London: Dacre Press, A. and C. Black, 1954).

3. Dunn, "Spirit-Baptism and Pentecostalism," p. 398. Bruner suggests in *A Theology of the Holy Spirit* (p. 37, n. 5) that Puritanism would be a fruitful area for further study of Pentecostal antecedents.

4. Garth Wilson, "The Puritan Doctrine of the Holy Spirit: A Critical Chapter in the History of Doctrine" (Ph.D. diss., Toronto School of Theology, 1978).

5. Thomas Goodwin, *The Works of Thomas Goodwin*, vol. 1, containing an "Exposition of the First Chapter of the Epistle to the Ephesians" (Edinburgh: James Nichol, 1861), pp. 238, 247.

6. See Peter Toon, ed., *Puritans, the Millennium and the Future of Israel: Puritan Eschatology 1600 to 1660* (Cambridge, England: James Clarke, 1970), for discussion of these issues.

7. See this theme in C. John Weborg, "The Eschatological Ethics of Bengel," a paper presented to the Pietism Section of the American Academy of Religion, San Francisco, 29 December 1977. This paper has since been incorporated into a dissertation, "Johann Albrecht Bengel: Personal and

Ecclesial Piety and the Literature of Edification in the Letters to the Seven Churches in Revelation 2 and 3" (Ph.D. diss., Northwestern University and Garrett-Evangelical Theological Seminary, 1983).

8. Notice this theme even in the title of a dissertation by Edith Waldvogel, "The 'Overcoming Life': A Study in the Reformed Evangelical Origins of Pentecostalism" (Ph.D. diss., Harvard Divinity School, 1977).

9. See, for example, the comments on James 5:14−15 of John Albert Bengel, Gnomon of the New Testament, vol. 5, 7th ed. (Edinburgh: T. and T. Clark, 1877), pp. 39−41, and Endre Zsindely, Krankheit und Heilung im älteren Pietismus (Zurich: Zwingli Verlag, 1962).

10. Jürgen Moltmann, Hope and Planning (New York: Harper and Row, 1968), p. 185.

11. This is especially true, as we shall see below, of Pietism.

12. Chapter entitled "Evangelicalism" in John T. McNeill, Modern Christian Movements, rev. ed. (New York: Harper Torchbooks, 1968), p. 91.

13. See, for example, Nathaniel West, John Wesley and Premillennialism (Louisville: Pentecostal Publishing, 1894). The name of Wesley was frequently included among the lists of premillennial antecedents promulgated at "prophecy conferences" and among other advocates of premillennialism in the late nineteenth century.

14. W. B. Godbey, Spiritual Gifts and Graces (Cincinnati: God's Revivalist Office, 1895), p. 37.

15. W. J. Hollenweger, The Pentecostals (London: SCM Press; and Minneapolis: Augsburg, 1972), p. 21.

16. See, for example, John Chongnahm Cho, "John Wesley's View on Baptism," Wesleyan Theological Journal 7 (Spring 1972): 60−73.

17. See E. P. Thompson, The Making of the English Working Class (New York: Pantheon, 1964), passim.

18. Bernard Semmel, The Methodist Revolution (New York: Basic Books, 1973), p. vii.

19. Robert Hughes III, "The Wesleyan Roots of Christian Socialism," Ecumenist 13 (May-June 1975): 49−53.

20. Maximin Piette, John Wesley in the Evolution of Pentecostalism (London: Sheed and Ward, 1937).

21. George Croft Cell, The Rediscovery of John Wesley (New York: Henry Holt, 1938).

22. See the work of Franz Hildebrandt in Christianity According to the Wesleys (London: Epworth, 1955) and From Luther to Wesley (London: Lutterworth, 1951).

23. See George Eayrs, John Wesley: Christian Philosopher and Church Founder (London: Epworth, 1926), and Umphrey Lee, John Wesley and Modern Religion (Nashville: Cokesbury, 1936).

24. See the now-famous extended footnote 26 on pages 9−10 of the introduction to Albert C. Outler, ed., John Wesley (New York: Oxford University Press, 1964).

25. See Albert C. Outler, "Methodism's Theological Heritage," in Paul M. Minus, Jr., ed., Methodism's Destiny in an Ecumenical Age (Nashville: Abingdon, 1969), pp. 44−70.

26. John Deschner, *Wesley's Christology, An Interpretation* (Dallas: Southern Methodist University Press, 1960), not surprisingly, originally a dissertation under Karl Barth.

27. Especially in the wake of the nineteenth-century Oxford Movement and as a part of recent Anglican/Methodist merger discussions in Britain. See for the former "an Old Methodist," *John Wesley in Company with High Churchmen*, 4th ed. (London: John Hodges, 1871); for the latter perhaps A. B. Lawson, *John Wesley and the Christian Ministry* (London: SPCK, 1963).

28. Especially in the context of American Methodism deeply influenced by American revivalism and finding its most radical expression in the revivalistic Holiness tradition that emerged from Methodism in the late nineteenth century. See, for example, W. H. Fitchett, *Wesley and His Century: A Study in Spiritual Forces* (New York: Eaton and Mains, 1906). For a more recent effort to relate Wesley to the "left-wing" ecclesiologies, see Howard A. Snyder, *The Radical Wesley and Patterns for Church Renewal* (Downers Grove, Ill.: InterVarsity, 1981), incorporating material from his 1977 Ryan Lectures, "John Wesley and the Radical Protestant Traditions," at Asbury Theological Seminary.

29. "An Earnest Appeal to Men of Reason and Religion" (1744), sect. 77, now available in a critical edition in the new Oxford edition of Wesley's *Works*, vol. 11, ed. Gerald R. Cragg (Oxford: Clarendon, 1975).

30. See Colin Williams, *John Wesley's Theology Today* (Nashville: Abingdon, 1960), ch. 9 and appendix.

31. *The Believer's Church: The History and Character of Radical Protestantism* (New York: Macmillan, 1968).

32. "A Letter to a Roman Catholic" (1749), sect. 15, available in a variety of editions and also in Outler, *John Wesley*, p. 498. Such expressions are, however, common in Wesley.

33. John Wesley, *The Manners of the Ancient Christians Extracted from a French Author*, 2d ed. (Bristol: Felix Farley, 1749).

34. See Outler, *John Wesley*, pp. 9–10.

35. Luke Keefer, Jr., in a seminar paper entitled "The Primitivistic Note in John Wesley" (Spring 1975), an advanced study for "John Wesley, A Disciple of Early Christianity" (Ph.D. diss., Temple University, 1982).

36. F. Ernest Stoeffler, "Tradition and Renewal in the Ecclesiology of John Wesley," in Bernd Jaspert and Rudolf Mohr, eds., *Traditio-Krisis-Renovatio aus theologischer Sicht* (Marburg: N. G. Elwert Verlag, 1976), p. 305.

37. Ibid., p. 306.

38. For this claim, made from various perspectives and with differing nuances, see, for example, Robert G. Tuttle, Jr., speaking from the Charismatic movement within the United Methodist tradition, in his unpublished papers prepared for the United Methodist Commission on the Charismatic Movement. Hints of his position appear in *The Partakers* (Nashville: Abingdon, 1974) and further in *John Wesley: His Life and Thought* (Grand Rapids: Zondervan, 1978); from more within the Methodist mainstream, Lycurgus M. Starkey, Jr., *The Work of Holy Spirit: A Study in Wesleyan Theology* (New York: Abingdon, 1962); from within the American Holiness movement, Charles W.

Carter, *The Person and Ministry of the Holy Spirit: A Wesleyan Perspective* (Grand Rapids: Baker, 1974); and from within British "Evangelical Methodism," A. Skevington Wood, "John Wesley, Theologian of the Spirit," *Theological Renewal* 6 (June-July 1977): 26–34.

39. Norman Laurence Kellett (Ph.D. diss., Brandeis University, 1975).

40. W. E. Sangster, for example, notes Wesley's failure to "link the doctrine [of Perfect Love] enough (as Paul does) with the Cross and the Holy Spirit" in *The Path to Perfection* (New York: Abingdon-Cokesbury, 1943). A similar perspective is affirmed by Herbert McGonigle, "Pneumatological Nomenclature in Early Methodism," *Wesleyan Theological Journal* 8 (Spring 1973): 61–72. This position, with which this study is basically aligned, has been vigorously disputed by Timothy L. Smith in a series of essays written after this analysis was composed and partially in response to public hints of its results. His work is best summarized in "The Doctrine of the Sanctifying Spirit in John Wesley and John Fletcher," *Preacher's Magazine* 55 (September-November 1979): 16–17, 54–58. An amplification of this essay has appeared as "How John Fletcher Became the Theologian of Wesleyan Perfectionism, 1770–1776," *Wesleyan Theological Journal* 15 (Spring 1980): 68–87. Smith relies on more general references to the work of the Holy Spirit and a more general use of "Pentecostal imagery"—neither of which is denied in this study—to argue that the Spirit is more central and determinative than this analysis allows. Smith, however, fails to establish that the instances to which he points are as *characteristic* of Wesley as he implies. The ensuing debate on these questions is surveyed by Rob L. Staples, "The Current Wesleyan Debate on the Baptism with the Holy Spirit" (privately circulated paper, March 1979), and by Thomas A. Langford in *Practical Divinity: Theology in the Wesleyan Tradition* (Nashville: Abingdon, 1983), pp. 141–43. Both authors tend to concur with the reading given in this study.

41. This would appear to be the point of William Arnett's response to McGonigle in "The Role of the Holy Spirit in Entire Sanctification in the Writings of John Wesley," *Asbury Seminarian* 29 (April 1974): 5–23. The question is not whether Wesley had a soteriological role for the Holy Spirit—he obviously does—but whether the role given to the Holy Spirit is such that it becomes the theological fulcrum on which his thought turns.

42. The major study of this doctrine is Arthur S. Yates, *The Doctrine of Assurance, with Special Reference to John Wesley* (London: Epworth, 1952).

43. "The Witness of the Spirit; Discourse II," sect. 5, para. 1, in Edward H. Sugden, ed., *Wesley's Standard Sermons* (London: Epworth, 1921), 2:357.

44. Letter to "John Smith," dated 25 March 1747, in John Telford, ed., *The Letters of the Rev. John Wesley, A.M.* (London: Epworth, 1931), 2:90.

45. "The Witness of the Spirit; Discourse II," sect. 5, para. 2, in the Sugden edition of the *Sermons*, 2:357–58.

46. Ibid., para. 3, p. 358.

47. In the preface to John and Charles Wesley, *Hymns and Sacred Poems* (Bristol: Felix Farley, 1742), as reprinted in G. Osborn, ed., *The Poetical Works of John and Charles Wesley* (London: Wesleyan Methodist Conference Office, 1869), 2:46.

48. Fourteen of the basic forty-four Sermons of Wesley—along with the *Explanatory Notes on the New Testament*, the doctrinal standard of Methodism—are devoted to an exposition of the Sermon on the Mount and follow immediately upon the Sermons on the New Birth.

49. Harald Lindstrom, *Wesley and Sanctification* (London: Epworth, 1950), p. 152.

50. Wood, "John Wesley, Theologian of the Spirit," p. 26.

51. James Gordon King, Jr., "A Brief Overview of Historic Beliefs in Gifts of the Spirit," p. 14. This unpublished paper was read at the 1977 meeting of the Society for Pentecostal Studies and anticipates a dissertation in progress at New York University.

52. See Wesley's letter to Dr. Conyers Middleton, dated 4 July 1749, in the Telford edition of Wesley's *Letters*, 2:312–88, responding to Middleton's *Free Inquiry into the Miraculous Powers Which Are Supposed to Have Subsisted in the Christian Church* (London: Manby and Cox, 1749).

53. Sermon 89, "The More Excellent Way," introduction, para. 2, in Thomas Jackson, ed., *The Works of the Rev. John Wesley A.M.* (London: John Mason, 1829), 7:27.

54. This from William Warburton, Bishop of Gloucester, *The Doctrine of Grace; or, The Office and Operations of the Holy Spirit Vindicated from the Insults of Infidelity and the Abuses of Fanaticism* (1762), as reported by Richard Green, *The Works of John and Charles Wesley: A Bibliography* (London: C. H. Kelly, 1869), p. 123.

55. See Wesley's response "to Dr. Warburton, Bishop of Gloucester," dated 26 November 1762, in the Telford edition of Wesley's *Letters*, 4:325–84. The quotation is from p. 344 in this edition.

56. Sermon 4, "Scriptural Christianity," introduction, para. 3, in the Sugden edition, 1:93.

57. "A Farther Appeal to Men of Reason and Religion," pt. 5, sect. 28, in the Jackson edition of Wesley's *Works*, 8:107.

58. Sermon 141, "The Holy Spirit," pt. 3, in the Jackson edition of Wesley's *Works*, 7:514.

59. Sermon 85, "On Working Out Our Own Salvation," pt. 2, sect. 1, in the Jackson edition of Wesley's *Works*, 6:509.

60. See Albert Outler, *Theology in the Wesleyan Spirit* (Nashville: Tidings, 1975), especially pp. 52ff.

61. See the use of this term in David Cubie, "Perfection in Wesley and Fletcher: Inaugural or Teleological," *Wesleyan Theological Journal* 11 (Spring 1976): 26.

62. These terms are used by E. Gordon Rupp, *Principalities and Powers* (London: Epworth, 1952), ch. 5.

63. Sermon 1, "Salvation by Faith," pt. 2, sect. 1, in the Sugden edition, 1:41.

64. Sermon 50, "The Scripture Way of Salvation," pt. 1, sect. 1, in the Sugden edition, 2:444–45.

65. Sermon 35, "Christian Perfection," pt. 1, sect. 9, in the Sugden edition, 2:156.

66. This distinction (between sins "properly so called" and sins "improperly so called") is important for Wesley. The reference is from "A Plain Account of Christian Perfection," sect. 19, in the Jackson edition of Wesley's *Works*, 11:396.

67. "Plain Account," sect. 27, in the Jackson edition of Wesley's *Works*, 11:444.

68. See the discussion of this question in Cubie, "Perfection in Wesley and Fletcher," pp. 22–37.

69. "Brief Thoughts on Christian Perfection," appended to the "Plain Account of Christian Perfection," in the Jackson edition of Wesley's *Works*, 11:446.

70. "Minutes of Several Conversations," in the Jackson edition of Wesley's *Works*, 8:329.

71. Orville S. Walters, "The Concept of Attainment in John Wesley's Christian Perfection," *Methodist History* 10 (April 1972): 12–29.

72. Every effort has been made to locate these materials, but searches of the British Methodist archives and correspondence with Frank Baker, foremost bibliographer of the Wesleys, have failed to turn up more than is fragmentarily available in the published biographies and editions of the *Letters*.

73. Letter of John Fletcher to Joseph Benson, dated 22 March 1771, reprinted in Luke Tyerman, *Wesley's Designated Successor* (London: Hodder and Stoughton, 1882), pp. 179–80.

74. Letter of John Wesley to Joseph Benson, dated 9 March 1771, reprinted in the Telford edition of Wesley's *Letters*, 5:228.

75. This proposal of Telford has been disputed by Timothy L. Smith, "The Doctrine of the Sanctifying Spirit in John Wesley and John Fletcher" and "How John Fletcher Became the Theologian of Wesleyan Perfectionism, 1770–1776," but on the apparently theological grounds that Wesley could not have meant this because he had earlier casually used the expression "filled with the Spirit" in correspondence with Fletcher without critique. This assumes that the use of such expressions as "filled with the Spirit" must necessarily imply the use of Pentecostal imagery and a doctrine of the baptism of the Holy Spirit. The necessity of this assumption is not at all obvious. Therefore I have continued to follow Telford.

76. Letter of John Wesley to John Fletcher, dated 28 December 1770, reprinted in the Telford edition of Wesley's *Letters*, 5:214–15.

77. Letter of John Wesley to John Fletcher, dated 22 March 1775, reprinted in the Telford edition of Wesley's *Letters*, 6:146.

78. Letter of John Fletcher to Mary Bosanquet, dated 7 March 1778, reprinted in Tyerman, *Wesley's Designated Successor*, p. 411.

79. Ibid.

80. This understanding of dispensations is spelled out most fully in Fletcher's *Portrait of St. Paul*, reprinted in *The Works of the Reverend John Fletcher* (reprint, Salem, Ohio: Schmul Publishers, 1974). In the secondary literature the best treatment of this question appears in John Allan Knight, "John William Fletcher and the Early Methodist Tradition" (Ph.D. diss., Vanderbilt University, 1966), especially pp. 176–90. Some of the relevant material is incorporated into Knight's essay, "John Fletcher's Influence on the

Development of Wesleyan Theology in America," *Wesleyan Theological Journal* 13 (Spring 1978): 13–33.

81. This outline is from Fletcher, *The Portrait of St. Paul*, pp. 166–69.

82. Ibid., pp. 170–73.

83. Thus the *Compend of Wesley's Theology*, ed. Robert W. Burtner and Robert E. Chiles (New York: Abingdon, 1954), properly presents Wesley's thought at this point by focusing on questions of "human destiny," "eternal life," and so on. See also the similar perspective in William Strawson, "Wesley's Doctrine of the Last Things," *London Quarterly and Holborn Review* 28 (July 1959): 240–49.

84. See, for example, Fletcher's discussion in *An Equal Check*, in Fletcher's *Works*, 2:262–64, or his *Letter on the Prophecies*, 4:238–49.

85. Fletcher, *The Portrait of St. Paul*, p. 181.

86. Sangster, *The Path to Perfection*, ch. 5, pp. 37–52.

87. Hans Conzelmann, *The Theology of St. Luke* (New York: Harper and Brothers, 1960), p. 150.

88. This debate is summarized by E. Earle Ellis, *Eschatology in Luke* (Philadelphia: Fortress, 1972).

89. See especially Fred O. Francis, "Eschatology and History in Luke–Acts," *Journal of the American Academy of Religion* 37 (March 1969): 49–63. Francis emphasizes the significance of the prophecy in Joel for the interpretation of Luke in places as an "eschatological meditation upon Joel."

90. J. E. Fison, *The Blessing of the Holy Spirit* (London: Longmans, Green, 1950), p. 121.

91. For example, by J. H. E. Hull, *The Holy Spirit in the Acts of the Apostles* (Cleveland: World, 1968), p. 170.

92. Gerhard Friedrich, ed., *Theological Dictionary of the New Testament*, tr. Geoffrey W. Bromiley (Grand Rapids: Wm. B. Eerdmans, 1968), 6:407–8.

174 The Cleansing Wave

PHOEBE PALMER

MRS. J. F. KNAPP

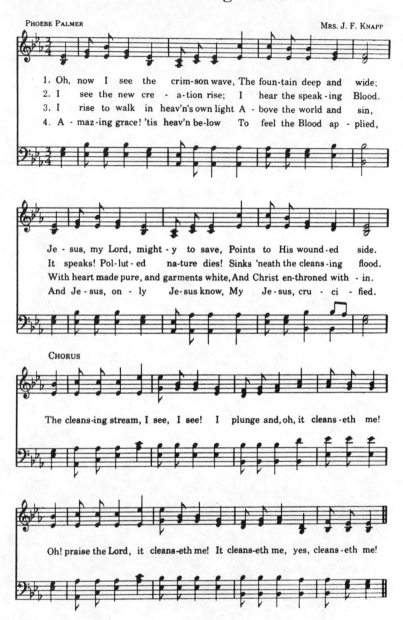

1. Oh, now I see the crim-son wave, The foun-tain deep and wide;
2. I see the new cre - a-tion rise; I hear the speak-ing Blood.
3. I rise to walk in heav'n's own light A - bove the world and sin,
4. A - maz-ing grace! 'tis heav'n be-low To feel the Blood ap - plied,

Je - sus, my Lord, might - y to save, Points to His wound-ed side.
It speaks! Pol-lut - ed na-ture dies! Sinks 'neath the cleans-ing flood.
With heart made pure, and garments white, And Christ en-throned with - in.
And Je - sus, on - ly Je-sus know, My Je - sus, cru - ci - fied.

CHORUS

The cleans-ing stream, I see, I see! I plunge and, oh, it cleans-eth me!

Oh! praise the Lord, it cleans-eth me! It cleans-eth me, yes, cleans-eth me!

CHAPTER III

THE AMERICAN REVIVAL
OF CHRISTIAN PERFECTION

Methodism was to find its real destiny in America. Already by mid-nineteenth century, Philip Schaff was to recognize that "in America [the Methodist Movement] has had, perhaps, of all sections of the church, next to Puritanism, the greatest influence on the general religious life."[1] This is in itself a remarkable fact, because by the time of the American Revolution, Methodism in America was still an unorganized marginal sect with barely a foothold in the New World. But by 1820 the Methodists had grown abreast of the rapidly growing Baptists in membership and were well on their way to becoming the largest Protestant denomination in the United States in the nineteenth century. By 1840 Methodists outnumbered the Baptists by a ratio of ten to six and by "a similar ratio the combined membership of Presbyterian, Congregational, Episcopal, Lutheran, and Reformed churches,"[2] the great Protestant shapers of colonial America.

The reasons for this astounding growth of Methodism are manifold. The Wesleyan movement hit America at the point of its greatest vigor. Her evangelists and circuit riders, their forces easily expanded by the incorporation of lay persons and new converts, spread throughout the country and proved themselves especially adapted to the expanding frontier as the West was being settled. And the Arminian and perfectionist motifs of Methodism, both explicit and implicit, were a congenial background to express and add fuel to the optimistic expansionism of the era. Under such conditions, Methodism so grew in influence that interpreters of nineteenth-century America are inclined to speak of "the Methodist Age in America."[3] What happened then among the Methodists was, therefore, of broader cultural significance than is sometimes assumed.

But the Methodist Age in America means more than the growth of a particular denomination into the country's largest; it means that to a great extent Methodism set the tone for many other groups. Methodist ideas and practices permeated many other denominations, especially in the Reformed camp. The Great Awakenings of the eighteenth century added an additional factor to the erosion of Puritan Calvinism and contributed to what has been called the "Arminianizing of American Theology."[4] This impulse, which climaxed in the rise of revivalism, coalesced with burgeoning Methodism to lay the foundations of the evangelical religious and cultural synthesis that was to dominate pre–Civil War America. Thus Timothy L. Smith can describe the dominant religious force in the United States on the eve of the Civil War as a coalition of "revivalistic Calvinism" and "Evangelical Arminianism"—a coalition dominated by Methodist-like ideas, including the doctrine of Christian perfection.[5]

The most influential of the Calvinist revivalists of the era came to be the controversial Charles Grandison Finney, advocate of a new style "New Measures" revivalism. Richard Carwardine has argued that the emergence of this pattern of revivalism should be seen primarily as the permeation of Presbyterian and Congregational circles by Methodist ideas and practices. Among these were the use of the "anxious bench," the encouragement of women to speak and pray in "promiscuous assemblies," extemporaneous preaching more oriented to the emotions, and the push toward Arminian theology—all the filtering into the dominant culture of the motifs and usages of Methodism.[6] The climax of the process may be seen in Finney's adoption of near-Wesleyan views on sanctification and the consequent development of "Oberlin perfectionism" in the 1830s.

But our real interest is in the vicissitudes of the Wesleyan doctrine of Christian perfection on the American scene.

Methodism crossed the Atlantic in the midst of the theological developments described in the previous chapter, and in so doing found better soil for the cultivation of its peculiar doctrine—though not immediately.

The matter is debated,[7] but it seems fair to say that in early years "Christian perfection was a respected but not dominant feature of the [Methodist] preaching of this period."[8] John Peters has suggested that the frontier context encouraged more "salvation" preaching among the Methodists. A survey of the literature confirms these conclusions. Though always a matter of concern for early Methodists, there is a sense in which preaching of the second blessing is especially adapted to the spiritual condition of second-generation Christians.

THE RISE OF THE HOLINESS REVIVAL

But it is not necessary to resolve this question to recognize, especially in the 1830s, a rising tide of emphasis on Christian perfection that produced the "Holiness crusade," a neglected but important feature of nineteenth-century American religious life.[9] An early harbinger of what was to come was a little book entitled *The Christian's Manual; a Treatise on Christian Perfection, with Directions for Obtaining That State,* published in 1825 by the Methodist Episcopal Church.[10] The author was Timothy Merritt, a prominent New England minister, stationed at the time in Boston. "The doctrine of Christian perfection was his favorite theme and he was a living example of it."[11] This concern led in 1839 to his founding the *Guide to Christian Perfection,* destined to become under later editors the dominant organ of the Holiness Revival, especially as it found expression within the confines of Methodism.

Meanwhile in New York, physician's wife Phoebe Palmer and her sister Sarah Lankford came into the experience of sanctification. Phoebe, for whom this experience provided the assurance that others found in conversion, was to become the major figure of the Holiness Revival—first as primary leader of the "Tuesday Meeting for the Promotion of Holiness" that met in the Palmer home for most of sixty years, then as editor of the magazine that Merritt had founded (rechristened the *Guide to Holiness*), and finally as an itinerant evangelist who traveled widely both on the North American continent and in the Old World. The Palmers' parlor meetings, not unlike the Charismatic home gatherings of our own day, were widely imitated and generated by the end of the century a vast network of Holiness meetings. The Palmer meeting, started in 1835, was opened to men in 1839 and became a center of the renewal of a version of the Wesleyan doctrine of Christian perfection that touched Methodist bishops and leaders and extended its influence far beyond denominational lines.

At the same time, Reformed revivalism was turning in a similar direction. The theme of "Holiness" permeated the literature of the era. Nathaniel Taylor's emerging "New Divinity" convictions at Yale led naturally to a concern for holiness and sanctification.[12] Edward Beecher, whose father, brother, and sisters are perhaps better known, published Six Sermons on "the Nature, Importance, and Means of Eminent Holiness throughout the Church" that were carried in the American National Preacher.[13] And the more prominent Charles G. Finney began to turn to the Wesleyan tradition for clues to achieving the experience, picking up the topic before personally experiencing the "blessing," in his widely influential Lectures to Professing Christians, first published in the New York Evangelist but then collected in book form in 1837.[14]

This question had emerged the year before in a meeting at Oberlin College when a student had asked President Asa Mahan a troubling question: "When we look to Christ for sanctification, what degree of sanctification may we expect from him? May we look to him to be sanctified wholly, or not?"[15] This question propelled Mahan and Finney, Oberlin's professor of theology, on a search for entire sanctification that culminated in their finding the "blessing" and the emergence of Oberlin perfectionism, a teaching promulgated variously in the Oberlin Evangelist and Mahan's influential exposition, The Scripture Doctrine of Christian Perfection.[16]

Oberlin perfectionism was basically Wesleyan in character, though influenced by its context (explicitly or implicitly) in the Calvinist New Divinity to give greater weight to the "moral law" (reflecting Mahan's moral philosophy and tendency toward Kantianism) and "free will" (especially in Finney, who emphasized that the call to perfection implies the ability to achieve it). George Peck, editor of the *Methodist Quarterly Review* and author a few years later of a similar study, *Scripture Doctrine of Christian Perfection*,[17] concluded in a review of Mahan's book that

> though it is not to be maintained that he expresses himself Methodistically upon all the points of this great doctrine, we are satisfied that the *thing* which we mean by *Christian Perfection* is truly set forth in that work.[18]

Mahan's book had been published by H. V. Degen, second editor of the Methodist-rooted *Guide to Christian Perfection*, and warm relations and interaction between Oberlin and the Palmers over the next decade testify to the affinities felt. The constellation of authorities in the Holiness Revival is indicated somewhat negatively by an oft-repeated statement that in the circles surrounding the *Guide*, "not Wesley, not Fletcher, not Mahan, not Upham, but the Bible, the Holy Bible, is the first and last, and in the midst always."[19]

The culture was ripe for the explosion of books and periodicals that carried the doctrine and experience throughout the Protestant world in America. The revival of 1857—58 especially "spread abroad the ideals of the Holiness and Perfectionist movements"[20] and marked the high point of the broad cultural impact of the movement before its disintegration into a variety of diverse expressions later in the century.

In the 1840s Horace Bushnell fell under the influence of these currents, in particular the writings of Congregationalist Thomas Upham, and his later work shows the implicit impact.[21] At the same time Presbyterian W. E. Boardman was being drawn in this direction. His *Higher Christian Life*[22] was published at the height of the 1858 revival and provided a new terminology that enabled it to become perhaps "the first popular treatment on this subject that won its way amongst all denominations."[23] British Methodist Mark Guy Pearse was to comment that through Boardman's work, "the despised doctrine of the early Methodists has become the glorious heritage of all denominations."[24] Baptist A. B. Earle and others carried the experience into that denomination after his sanctification in 1859.[25] Physician Charles Cullis, to whom we shall turn in a later chapter, carried similar themes into the Episcopal Church.[26]

NEW DIRECTIONS IN THEOLOGY

Though these later currents show an increasing variety of expression and terminology, the antebellum formulation of Christian perfection and entire sanctification remained basically Wesleyan in character. The American context, however, soon began to shape Methodist thought in new directions. The general impact on broader themes of theology has been analyzed several times. Robert Chiles has traced the changing nuances involved in the Americanization of Methodist theology in terms of subtle shifts from "revelation to reason," from "sinful man to natural man," and from "free grace to free will."[27] The growing emphasis on "moral agency" and "free will" was somewhat accentuated in this period by interaction with the New Divinity mediated through the revivalist currents and Oberlin perfectionism.

The doctrine of entire sanctification also took on new nuances. Most noticeable was a tendency to resolve the Wesleyan tension between crisis and process by a growing emphasis on the instantaneous character of the second blessing as a "second definite work of grace." To a certain extent this development had already taken place in England, not only in the later Wesley, but in particular in the work of Adam Clarke, whose influential commentary on the Bible was published first in America between 1811 and 1825.[28] A posthumous collection of Clarke's writings was published in 1835 as *Christian Theology*. Therein Clarke protested that

> in no part of the Scripture are we to seek holiness
> *gradatim*. We are to come to God as well for an instanta-
> neous and complete purification from all sin, as for an
> instantaneous pardon. Neither the *seriatim* pardon, nor
> the *gradatim* purification, exists in the Bible. It is when
> the soul is purified from all sin that it can properly grow
> in grace, and in the knowledge of our Lord Jesus Christ.[29]

This emphasis not only resolves the tension in Wesleyan thought in favor of crisis, but also undercuts the teleological character of Wesley's teaching to move entire sanctification to an earlier point in Christian experience. It becomes the presupposition rather than the goal of normal Christian existence. H. Ray Dunning has suggested that in Clarke these shifts are accompanied by a tendency to cast "the meaning of sanctification in terms of 'salvation from sin' rather than perfection in love."[30]

Similar tendencies are revealed in the thought of Phoebe Palmer, known for her "altar theology" that stressed the immediate availability of the second blessing. In her own spiritual struggle she came to see "that holiness, instead of being an attainment beyond her reach, was a state of grace in which every one of the Lord's redeemed ones should live."[31] Appealing to the text that "the altar . . . sanctifieth the gift," she argued that once "consecration" had taken place, the believer should "exercise faith" and claim entire sanctification even if no accompanying emotion brought assurance.[32] This teaching tended to evaporate the spiritual struggle more characteristic of eighteenth-century Methodism and encouraged immediate appropriation of the experience. After all, "as it has been purchased for you, it is *already* yours. If you do not now receive it, the delay will not be on the part of God, but wholly with yourself."[33]

Such themes accelerated the movement in Clarke toward de-emphasizing the teleological character of Christian perfection, making it an experience more closely tied to Christian conversion and initiation.

The Oberlin teaching was more complex at this point. Emerging as it did amidst the New Divinity thrust toward Arminianism, early Oberlin theology placed greater stress on the possibility of perfection than on the precise means by which it might be achieved,[34] though most of the Oberlin faculty affirmed some sort of second experience. The matter was further complicated by the doctrine of the "simplicity of moral actions" that good moral actions were inherently perfect because the "coexistence of sin and holiness, as of two opposite moral states, is impossible."[35] This and other developments tended to fragment the Oberlin School. Mahan moved increasingly toward Methodism and continued to play a role in the development of Holiness theology, while Finney increasingly pulled back from Wesleyan formulations.

But there is a more profound level at which Finney's revivalist style gave support to the developments manifested in Palmer and others of the American revival of sanctification. This is more easily seen by contrasting Finney's sense of immediacy and pragmatism with themes of the eighteenth-century awakenings. His insistence on the availability of salvation "now" and his exalting of human agency in effecting revival undercut the concern of Jonathan Edwards and his followers to speak of revival more as a "work of God" and conversion as a "miracle" to be granted in God's own time.[36] In the words of William Warren Sweet, "Finney made salvation the beginning of religious experience in contrast to the older revivalism which made conversion the end."[37] This is precisely the difference between Wesley and Palmer and indicates the extent to which the new nuances in sanctification resulted from the contextualization of Wesleyan thought within American revivalism.

These developments were a necessary prelude to what would follow. Once "crisis" overwhelms "process" to make sanctification primarily an event occurring at a definite point in time—that is, when sanctification has been largely absorbed into entire sanctification—and once the teleological thrust of Christian perfection is transmuted into an initiatory experience that usually follows rapidly on conversion, the stage has been set for the reemergence of the Pentecostal formulation of entire sanctification. This emergence became widely evident at mid-century, though intimations of the shift appeared earlier.

The reason why this shift did not take place earlier is perhaps best explained by the fact that the American revival of entire sanctification was in part carried by the broader perfectionist impulse rooted in the culture. Early writings tend to emphasize the ideas of perfection over other possible expressions. We have seen this already in the titles of the *Guide to Christian Perfection* and Asa Mahan's *Scripture Doctrine of Christian Perfection*, as well as in the subtitle to Timothy Merritt's *The Christian's Manual*. We have also mentioned *The Scripture Doctrine of Christian Perfection Stated and Defended* by George Peck, editor of the *Methodist Quarterly Review*.[38] Peck's brother Jesse was also to argue for Christian perfection in his book *The Central Idea of Christian-*

ity,[39] though by 1856 this book was to show the increasing preference for the Holiness terminology reflected in the change of title to the *Guide to Holiness*. And Phoebe Palmer, of course, reflects this latter pattern in most of her writings before the late 1850s.

THE EMERGENCE OF PENTECOSTAL IMAGERY

No doubt the impact of Oberlin Perfectionism also contributed to blunting the possible impact of Fletcher's patterns of thought and thus postponed the turn to Pentecostal sanctification that was to characterize the late nineteenth century. But the sources of the revival, and even of Oberlin perfectionism, were Wesley *and* Fletcher, as repeated references make clear. The works of Fletcher and Benson were issued in this country, and compendia like *The Christian's Manual* excerpted Fletcher alongside Wesley.

Probably more important for the popular development of the doctrine was an item like the wisely disseminated spiritual autobiography of Hester Ann Rogers, who was very close to Fletcher and occasionally used Pentecostal imagery to describe sanctification.[40] Other similar uses of Pentecostal language occur on occasion in the early Methodist literature in America,[41] though usually in a more general manner without specific reference to the experience of sanctification. In both the *Oberlin Evangelist* and the *Guide to Holiness*, the vocabulary is generally used to refer to a more general "awakening" or "revival," of which Pentecost is seen as the great archetype, or to refer to the special "anointings" of the Christian or minister.

There was a special burst of Pentecostal language at Oberlin in the wake of the discovery of entire sanctification. Timothy Smith has shown that Finney moved in this direction in a series of lectures published in the *Oberlin Evangelist* in 1839 and 1840.[42] But Pentecostal imagery was not used in his more formal and widely distributed *Views of Sanctification*,[43] nor in his volumes of systematic theology published a few years later. Indeed, A. M. Hills, a Congregationalist student of Finney who would pen the first systematic theology of the Church of the Nazarene, was to lament later on that "Finney failed to connect the obtaining of sanctification with the baptism of the Holy Ghost"—though "sometimes he almost got the truth."[44] Much later, in 1871, Finney would address the Oberlin Council of Congregationalism on the "Baptism of the Holy Spirit," but only after the doctrine had become widespread and without the characteristic Holiness themes of the earlier period.[45]

Other Oberlin faculty were more explicit in their emphasis on the Holy Spirit in sanctification and much more likely to associate the experience with Pentecost. Henry Cowles in 1840 prepared two short sermons on the "baptism with the Holy Ghost" for the *Oberlin Evangelist.* The second of these concluded that

> the plan of salvation contemplates as its prime object, the
> sanctification of the church; and relies on the baptism of
> the Holy Spirit as the great efficient power for accomplish-
> ing the work.[46]

A later work of Cowles was to be entitled *On Being Filled with the Holy Ghost.*[47]

But perhaps more interesting are the writings of John Morgan, who contributed two essays on the question to the first volume (1845) of the *Oberlin Quarterly Review.* The first of these, entitled "The Holiness Acceptable unto God," so impressed Finney that he incorporated it into the first edition of his systematic theology (1847).[48] A second essay, "The Gift of the Holy Spirit," argued, however, that "the baptism of the Holy Ghost, then, in its Pentecostal fullness was not to be confined to the Primitive Church; but is the common privilege of all believers."[49] Morgan also insisted that "the baptism of the Spirit is the peculiar privilege of the saints" and not to be confused with "the influence of the Spirit of God by which sinners are converted."[50]

These two essays also reflect the continuing problem of integrating themes of sanctification and perfection into the accounts of Pentecost. The former essay illustrates the themes of Holiness without special emphasis on the work of the Holy Spirit. In the latter essay on the Holy Spirit, themes of perfection give way to an emphasis on the "enduement from on high."

But the broader impact of these Oberlin discussions was

not great, especially at that time, though there was some tendency after the Civil War to reach back and reappropriate some of the Oberlin literature. Timothy Smith has pointed to some isolated parallels, perhaps derived from the Oberlin discussions, among Methodists in the early 1840s.[51] With the waning of Oberlin's impact on the emerging Holiness movement and the rise of Phoebe Palmer, these fell into the background, though occasionally in the Methodist literature and in the *Guide to Holiness,* the Pentecostal imagery and even the identification of entire sanctification with Pentecost do occur. The broader impact of the doctrine of Pentecostal sanctification may be dated largely from about the time of the revival of 1857–58.

THE TURN TO PENTECOSTAL RHETORIC

The way for this shift was well prepared. Building on the restorationism implicit in the very idea of revival, a concern to recover the vitality of the primitive church was growing. Illustrative of this was a much-discussed "premium essay" by Baptist Henry C. Fish, which was published in 1855 by the Congregational Publishing House in Boston under the title *Primitive Piety Revived.* Primarily a call to such themes as "simplicity of purpose,—consecration to God,—a scriptural faith,—self denial for Christ,—earnestness,—individualism [i.e., individual responsibility],"[52] this essay helped to pave the way for the awakening of 1858 and won its author an honorary doctorate from the University of Rochester.[53] In it Fish sought "a return of the scene of apostolic days, especially those of the ever memorable Pentecost," asking "*why may we not anticipate the return of the Pentecostal seasons?* Why may not Christians *now* be 'filled with the Holy Ghost,' as were they in primitive times?"[54]

Fish, of course, did not have in mind the framework of Wesleyan thought or its newer Holiness versions, but his work does indicate the broad, rising interest in Pentecost and its characteristic themes that were a natural result of the restorationist push of revivalism. But even more explicitly Pentecostal in imagery and orientation was another very popular book published the next year (1856) and destined to go through eighteen editions within the next three years. *The Tongue of Fire*, written by British Methodist William Arthur and later to be adopted as a Chautauqua text, also looked forward to a general revival that would restore Pentecost in his time. Much more subtle than much that would follow, *The Tongue of Fire* was primarily concerned with the effects on the church of a "new Pentecost," but because of its Wesleyan background implicitly conveyed for many the idea of Pentecostal sanctification. Arthur's book concludes with a prayer:

> And now, adorable Spirit, proceeding from the Father and the Son, descend upon all the Churches, renew the Pentecost in this our age, and baptize thy people generally—O, baptize them yet again with tongues of fire! Crown this nineteenth century with a revival of "pure and undefiled religion" greater than that of the last century, greater than that of the first, greater than any "demonstration of the Spirit" even yet vouchsafed to men![55]

The revival of 1857–58 could hardly help but appear to be the answer to such entreaties. Looking back on the event a couple of years afterward, the *Guide to Holiness* would comment that "one of its cheering results is, that *since it commenced a deeper interest has been felt among God's people, of every denomination, on the subject of Holiness.*"[56] This development took place amidst a plethora of Pentecostal imagery used to describe the impact of the revival. One journal reported that "revivals now cover our very land, sweeping all before them as on the day of Pentecost. Ministers seem baptized with the Holy Ghost, and speak with new power and earnestness."[57] Another contemporary report was entitled *Pentecost, or the Work of God in Philadelphia, A.D. 1858.*[58] It is little wonder that in such a context the rising Holiness currents should turn increasingly to Pentecostal themes to proclaim their distinctive message, a pattern that was to dominate the rest of the century as the movement continued to break beyond Methodist confines to suffuse much of late nineteenth-century revivalism.

Reasons for this shift are complex, and the overwhelming of Holiness thought by the more Pentecostal formulation of Fletcher must be related to a number of factors, cultural and theological.[59] And we must note the increasing complexity of the context of these changes.

The revival of 1858 may have been the last great "awakening" of a "Christian America" that would shape in a determinative way a whole culture. The Civil War era marks the beginning of the collapse of the antebellum Evangelical consensus. The struggles over slavery not only split the major denominations, but also produced new fragmentation (such as, within Methodism, the anti-slavery Wesleyan Methodist Connection and the Free Methodist Church, groups that would later be swept largely into the growing Holiness movement). New scientific knowledge and theories, such as new datings of geology and the claims of Darwin's theory of evolution, forced new tensions to the fore that would finally result in the acrimonious divisions of the fundamentalist/modernist controversy early in the next century. Immigration, especially Catholic and later Jewish, shook the foundations of the dream for a "Christian America" (Protestantly conceived, of course) and forced new questions of pluralism.

The forces of secularization gained momentum and forced many, especially those attempting to preserve intact the antebellum Evangelical styles, into a defensive and reactionary stance. Industrialization and urbanization complicated the social context and accentuated class differences in the society that had almost yielded to the Jacksonian and Evangelical thrust toward egalitarianism.

Churches began to fragment according to class lines. The upward social mobility of Methodism in mid-century, for example, was clearly a factor in precipitating many splits, including the Holiness movement, attempting to maintain greater contact with the masses. And in all of this the nineteenth-century patterns of sect formation were given greater intensity.

All these factors, and others more theological and exegetical, conspired to support a major transformation in Wesleyan thought where any effort was made to preserve that tradition intact.

First, the broader cultural optimism and push toward perfectionism that had reawakened interest in Wesleyan themes subsided even before the Civil War. Life was seen to be more complex, and evil more entrenched than anticipated. Early advocates of "Christian perfection," such as editors Timothy Merritt or Henry Degen of the *Guide to Christian Perfection*, the founders of the anti-slavery Wesleyan Methodist Connection, and the early leaders and theologians at Oberlin College all supported a constellation of values that included commitment to revival styles, Christian perfection, abolitionism, pacifism, feminism, and often an imminent millennium as the climax of this perfectionist impulse.

The gathering storm clouds of impending civil war were already in the 1840s forcing heartrending struggles on questions such as the appropriateness of civil disobedience while federal and state legislatures adopted fugitive slave laws that seemed to defend the hated institution of slavery. The growing specter of violence forced a choice between abolitionism and pacifism. The dissolution of the cultural supports for a doctrine of Christian perfection gave impetus for ways to re-express in new ways the doctrine and experience that had become so important.

Second, Donald Scott has traced a "devotional transformation" during the 1830s and 1840s as the churches turned from public responsibility to private devotion, or "from Reform to Refuge." He suggests that by the 1850s the "churches had become protected and withdrawn islands of piety."[60] Surely shifts in Holiness thought reflect some of these broader shifts. The early 1840s change of title from the *Guide to Christian Perfection* to the *Guide to Holiness* indicates publicly a reordering of priorities and nuances that mirrors to a certain extent these broader currents. The growing influence of the parlor meetings of Phoebe Palmer, who eschewed involvement in the acrimonious debates and struggles over such social issues as slavery (though her work did give added impulse to more philanthropic styles of social engagement),[61] was carried to some extent by these currents.

There is a sense, then, in which the turn to a more experiential and "spiritual" mood of Holiness prepared the way for the more Pentecostal style, and the latter may well be viewed as an extension and radicalization of that earlier shift, perhaps accentuated by the apocalyptic experience of the Civil War.

It is also tempting to speculate about the significance of class structures and their impact on the development of Holiness currents, but that is an insufficiently explored question. A graph of the socioeconomic status of advocates of Holiness would probably show a dip after the Civil War between the antebellum beginnings in the cities of Boston and New York (where doctor's wife Phoebe Palmer entertained professors and bishops in her Tuesday Meetings in a home staffed with domestic help) and the twentieth-century upward social mobility of the membership of such denominations as the Church of the Nazarene. Though such patterns cannot be rigidly universalized, it is clear that Holiness churches from the Free Methodist Church founded in 1860 to the Church of the Nazarene dating from the turn of the century found their ministry especially among the poor and lower middle classes and increasingly in the central cities.[62]

The report of the first fourteen camp meetings (1867–72) of the National Camp Meeting Association for the Promotion of Holiness carries a chapter by George Hughes sketching the "state of the church" in 1867 that required this new movement. This chapter reveals not only the growing splits over formalism, the preaching of sanctification, and other themes, but also the class and cultural differences between churches oriented to the poor or the upper classes, diverging worship and institutional styles, and so forth.

The Holiness currents were increasingly, though not exclusively, the carriers of the experiential fidelity to the doctrine of the entire sanctification. One of the most striking differences in mood between the antebellum advocates of Christian perfection, especially those at Oberlin College, and the postwar proclaimers of Pentecostal sanctification is the earlier sense of "ability" and the latter search for "power."

It may well be that the late nineteenth century saw the decline of confidence, at least in some circles, in the ability of human effort to cope with growing social complexity and a consequent growing search for the "power" either to cope or to sustain one through to better times. The Pentecostal formulation of entire sanctification may have played an important role in the "empowering" of the "powerless" beyond the more obvious "spiritual" power its advocates sought. And it may be possible to detect a radicalization of these themes correlated with the downward social mobility of the late nineteenth-century Holiness converts. Such factors may also help to explain the modulation and moderation of Holiness themes by those movements carried along by the search for Holiness but unwilling to adopt the more radical ideas of perfection and eradication of "inbred sin."[63] At least some observers of the scene have noticed a correlation between social class and the radicalization of Holiness ideas.

But such cultural and historical factors do not void the theological issues at stake. Later interpreters, especially those in the wake of the doctrine of Pentecostal sanctification, were troubled not so much by the identification as by why it had taken so long. Theirs is "the problem of Wesley's apparent reluctance to use the term 'baptism in the Spirit' in relationship to Sanctification"[64] and why this remained the dominant position until the mid-nineteenth century. Charles Brown, a major twentieth-century theologian in the Church of God (Anderson, Indiana), a Holiness body, suggested that "the early Wesleyan theologians were so misled by the technical theologians that they failed to put proper emphasis on the baptism of the Holy Spirit."[65] More recently, Timothy Smith has seen in the rise of Pentecostal sanctification the recovery of an appropriate balance of divine and human agency that was threatened, especially at Oberlin, by the emphasis in free will and human agency.[66] For such theologians this identification was the resolution for which the Wesleyan tradition had been reaching since the 1770s.

At least two other theological factors in the shift are revealed in the literature. It is possible to discern in the late nineteenth century a radical turn to themes of the Spirit and the "spiritual" that took different shape in different contexts—in the rise of spiritualism, in the emergence of Christian Science and its deprecation of the material, in the rise of philosophical idealism in America, and so forth. In more orthodox theological circles this development took the form of an increasing emphasis on the doctrine of the Holy Spirit. At the end of the century C. I. Scofield, the famous dispensational editor of the *Scofield Bible*, was to point out,

We are in the midst of a marked revival of interest in the
Person and work of the Holy Spirit. More books, booklets,
and tracts upon that subject have issued from the press
during the last eighty years than all the previous time
since the invention of printing. Indeed, within the last
twenty years more has been written and said upon the
doctrine of the Holy Spirit than in the preceding eighteen
hundred years.[67]

From this perspective, the shift in Wesleyan thought to
Pentecostal sanctification may be seen as the particular form
this rising interest in the Holy Spirit took within the more
narrow confines of late nineteenth-century Holiness thought.

But certain apologetic advantages may also have helped
to accelerate the adoption of this new position. The very idea
of perfection was always controversial. Innumerable Methodist
sermons on Christian perfection had followed a pattern set by
Wesley in carefully distinguishing "in what sense Christians
are *not perfect*" before attempting a positive delineation of the
goal that Wesley would hold before his hearers.[68]

This apologetic problem was intensified when the experience of entire sanctification spread beyond Methodism into
other theological contexts, especially Reformed, as it did in the
wake of the revival of 1857–58. In those contexts the
vocabulary of Pentecost subordinated themes of perfection in
such a way as to have a claim for some to be more *prima facie*
biblical. Thus in 1874 Daniel Steele, having two years before
left the presidency of Syracuse University to return to the
pastorate, would describe in the *Guide to Holiness* his own
entire sanctification as a baptism of the Spirit and advise all
Christians to

cease to discuss the subtleties and endless questions
arising from entire sanctification or Christian perfection,
and all cry mightily to God for the baptism of the Holy
Spirit. This is certainly promised to all believers in Jesus.

O that every minister and layman would enquire the way
to the upper room in Jerusalem, and there abide till
tongues of fire flame from their heads.[69]

But whatever the reason, it is clear that this shift did take
place and that it swept in its path nearly all those in various

camps who continued to teach a doctrine of the higher
Christian life. The story of the triumph of the Pentecostal
formulation of John Fletcher will constitute the next chapter.

NOTES

1. Philip Schaff, *America: A Sketch of its Political, Social and Religious
Character* (New York: Charles Scribner, 1855), critical edition edited by Perry
Miller (Cambridge: Harvard University Press, Belknap Press, 1961), p. 137.

2. Winthrop S. Hudson, "The Methodist Age in America," *Methodist
History* 12 (April 1974): 11.

3. Ibid. Antecedent uses of this expression are cited by C. C. Goen, "The
'Methodist Age' in American History," *Religion in Life* 34 (Autumn 1965):
562–72.

4. See, for example, James E. Hamilton, "Academic Orthodoxy and the
Arminianizing of American Theology," *Wesleyan Theological Journal* 9
(Spring 1974): 52–59.

5. Timothy L. Smith, *Revivalism and Social Reform in Mid-Nineteenth-
Century America* (New York: Abingdon, 1957), pp. 32–33.

6. Richard Carwardine, "The Second Great Awakening in the Urban
Centers: An Examination of Methodism and the 'New Measures,' " *Journal of
American History* 59 (September 1972): 327–40.

7. This material has been surveyed by Allan Coppedge, "Entire
Sanctification in Early American Methodism: 1812–1835," *Wesleyan Theological Journal* 13 (Spring 1978): 34–50.

8. John Leland Peters, *Christian Perfection and American Methodism*
(New York: Abingdon, 1956), p. 97.

9. See Timothy L. Smith's survey of these developments in Emory
Stevens Bucke, ed., *The History of American Methodism*, 3 vols. (New York:
Abingdon, 1964), 2:608–27. Of the several longer treatments, the most useful
for the questions at hand is Melvin E. Dieter, *The Holiness Revival of the
Nineteenth Century*, Studies in Evangelicalism, no. 1 (Metuchen, N.J.:
Scarecrow Press, 1980).

10. Anonymous, *The Christian's Manual; a Treatise on Christian
Perfection, with Directions for Obtaining That State* (New York: N. Bangs and
J. Emory for the Methodist Episcopal Church, 1825). This volume consists of
excerpts primarily from Wesley and secondarily from Fletcher.

11. Abel Stevens, *A Compendious History of American Methodism*
(New York: Carlton and Porter, 1863), p. 371.

12. Timothy L. Smith, "The Doctrine of the Sanctifying Spirit: Charles
G. Finney's Synthesis of Wesleyan and Covenant Theology," *Wesleyan
Theological Journal* 13 (Spring 1978): 93.

13. Edward Beecher, "Six Sermons," *American National Preacher* 10
(June and July 1835): 193–224.

14. This development is sketched in ch. 7, "The Holiness Revival at
Oberlin," in Smith, *Revivalism and Social Reform*, pp. 103–13. See also James

H. Fairchild, "The Doctrine of Sanctification at Oberlin," *Congregational Quarterly* 18 (1876): 237–59.

15. Asa Mahan, *The Scripture Doctrine of Christian Perfection* (Boston: D. S. King, 1839), p. 188.

16. Ten editions of this book appeared within a decade, as well as later editions even into the twentieth century. The fullest treatment of these themes may be found in Barbara Zikmund, "Asa Mahan and Oberlin Perfectionism" (Ph.D. diss., Duke University, 1969). See also Benjamin B. Warfield's essays on Oberlin in the *Princeton Theological Review* (1921), later gathered into vol. 2 of *Perfectionism* (New York: Oxford University Press, 1931) and reprinted in a one-volume edition by the Presbyterian and Reformed Publishing Co., 1958.

17. George Peck, *The Scripture Doctrine of Christian Perfection Stated and Defended* (New York: Lane and Sandford, 1842).

18. *Methodist Quarterly Review* 23 (April 1841): 307–8.

19. I have not been able to locate the original publication of this comment, variously attributed to a "Congregational paper" and the *Guide to Holiness*. It is here taken from George Hughes, *Fragrant Memories of the Tuesday Meeting and the Guide to Holiness* (New York: Palmer and Hughes, 1886), pp. 38ff. Thomas Upham was a Congregationalist professor of moral philosophy at Bowdoin College who experienced sanctification under Phoebe Palmer's influence and gave popular expression to the doctrine in a series of books drawing more explicitly on Catholic mysticism and Quietism. See George Peck, "Dr. Upham's Works," *Methodist Quarterly Review* 28 (April 1846): 248–65, and an essay in the Oxford edition of Warfield's *Perfectionism*.

20. Nelson R. Burr, *A Critical Bibliography of Religion in America*, Religion in America (Princeton: Princeton University Press, 1961), 3:165. Smith, *Revivalism and Social Reform*, traces these currents, as does Dieter, *The Holiness Revival*.

21. See Mary E. (Bushnell) Cheney, *Life and Letters of Horace Bushnell* (New York: Charles Scribner's Sons, 1880), pp. 190–93. Among the many Holiness celebrations of this fact, see S. A. Keen, "Dr. Bushnell, the Saint," *Divine Life and Bible Expositor* 21 (September 1893): 77–80.

22. William E. Boardman, *The Higher Christian Life* (Boston: Henry Hoyt, 1858). This book was published in both Britain and America and went through several editions.

23. Mark Guy Pearse, preface to Mary M. Boardman, *Life and Labors of the Rev. W. E. Boardman* (New York: D. Appleton, 1887), p. vii.

24. Ibid., pp. v–vii.

25. A. B. Earle, *Bringing in the Sheaves* (Boston: James H. Earle, 1870). His teachings may be found especially in *The Rest of Faith* (Boston: James H. Earle, 1876).

26. William E. Boardman, *Faith Work Under Dr. Cullis in Boston* (Boston: Willard Tract Repository, 1874), and William H. Daniels, ed., *Dr. Cullis and His Work* (Boston: Willard Tract Repository, 1885).

27. See Robert E. Chiles, *Theological Transition in American Methodism* (New York: Abingdon, 1965); Leland H. Scott, "Methodist Theology in America in the Nineteenth Century" (Ph.D. diss., Yale University, 1955), summarized under the same title in *Religion in Life* 25 (Winter 1955–56): 87–

98; and David Clark Shipley, "The Development of Theology in American Methodism in the Nineteenth Century," *London Quarterly and Holborn Review* 134 (July 1959): 249–64.

28. Adam Clarke, *The Holy Bible . . . with a Commentary and Critical Notes*, 6 vols. (New York: Ezra Sargent, 1811–25). This set became the exegetical standard for Methodism and has been kept in print in various editions since its original publication.

29. Adam Clarke, *Christian Theology*, ed. Samuel Dunn (New York: Carlton and Porter, 1835), pp. 207–8. See the discussion of this development in John L. Peters, *Christian Perfection and American Methodism*, pp. 103–7.

30. H. Ray Dunning, "Nazarene Ethics as Seen in a Theological, Historical and Sociological Context" (Ph.D. diss., Vanderbilt University, 1969).

31. Phoebe Palmer, *The Way of Holiness, with Notes by the Way* (New York: Lane and Tippett, 1845), p. 33. By 1867 the Palmers were able to issue the "fiftieth edition" of this work.

32. See the summary of this in Palmer, *The Way of Holiness*, pp. 60ff.

33. Phoebe Palmer, *Faith and Its Effects* (New York: Published for the author, 1852), p. 53.

34. See the early pages of Asa Mahan, *Scripture Doctrine of Christian Perfection*, or the lectures on Christian perfection in Charles G. Finney, *Lectures to Professing Christians* (Oberlin, Ohio: E. J. Goodrich, 1879). The latter volume was originally published in New York in 1837.

35. William Cochran, "Simplicity of Moral Actions," *Oberlin Evangelist* 4 (16 March 1842): 1. This is the second part of an essay continued from the previous issue (2 March 1842).

36. On these differences, see William G. McLoughlin, *Modern Revivalism* (New York: Ronald Press, 1959), especially p. 85, fn. 37.

37. William Warren Sweet, *The American Churches: An Interpretation* (New York: Abingdon-Cokesbury, 1947), p. 126.

38. George Peck, *The Scripture Doctrine of Christian Perfection Stated and Defended* (New York: Carlton and Porter, 1842).

39. Jesse T. Peck, *The Central Idea of Christianity* (Boston: Henry V. Degen, 1856).

40. Hester Ann Rogers, *Account of the Experience of Hester Ann Rogers* (New York: J. Emory and B. Waugh, 1831), p. 35. Note also the description of after-dinner conversations of Fletcher under the entry for 24 August 1781, pp. 111ff. This volume appeared in many nineteenth-century editions.

41. For other illustrations of this development, see Coppedge, "Entire Sanctification in Early American Methodism," pp. 45f., and Timothy Smith, "The Doctrine of the Sanctifying Spirit," pp. 106ff.

42. Smith, "The Doctrine of the Sanctifying Spirit," pp. 100ff.

43. Charles G. Finney, *Views of Sanctification* (Oberlin, Ohio: James Steele, 1840).

44. A. M. Hills, *Life of Charles G. Finney* (Cincinnati: God's Revivalist Office, 1902), p. 226.

45. This may be reflected in Finney's appendix to British editions of Asa Mahan's *Baptism of the Holy Ghost* (London: Elliot Stock, n.d.).

46. *Oberlin Evangelist* 2 (1840): 93.

47. Henry Cowles, *On Being Filled With the Holy Ghost* (Oberlin, Ohio: J. M. Fitch, 1848).

48. This was also reprinted as a pamphlet, 2d ed. (Oberlin, Ohio: J. M. Fitch, 1847), and more recently as a small paperback (Minneapolis: Bethany Fellowship, 1967).

49. *Oberlin Quarterly Review* 1 (August 1845): 115. This essay was later published separately with an introduction by Finney (Oberlin, Ohio: E. J. Goodrich, 1875).

50. *Oberlin Quarterly Review* 1 (August 1845): 95–96.

51. See his "Christian Perfection and American Idealism, 1820–1900," *Asbury Seminarian* 31 (October 1976): 7–34.

52. Henry C. Fish, *Primitive Piety Revived; or, the Aggressive Power of the Christian Church* (Boston: Congregational Board of Publication, 1855).

53. Smith, *Revivalism and Social Reform*, p. 49.

54. Fish, *Primitive Piety Revived*, pp. 244–45.

55. William Arthur, *The Tongue of Fire; or, the True Power of Christianity* (New York: Harper and Brothers, 1856), p. 354.

56. *Guide to Holiness* 37 (April 1860): 124.

57. An unidentified report quoted in Warren Candler, *Great Revivals and the Great Republic* (Nashville: Publishing House of the M. E. Church, South, 1924), pp. 197–98.

58. *Pentecost; or, the Work of God in Philadelphia, A. D. 1858*, prepared by the Young Men's Christian Association (Philadelphia: Parry and McMillan, 1859). Compare the title chosen by Russell E. Francis, "Pentecost: 1858, A Study in Religious Revivals" (Ph.D. diss., University of Pennsylvania, 1948).

59. A helpful survey of the forces at work in the late nineteenth century is found in Arthur M. Schlesinger, Sr., "A Critical Period in American Religion," *Massachusetts Historical Society Proceedings* 64 (October 1930–June 1932): 523–46; reissued under the same title with an introduction by Richard Wolf (Philadelphia: Fortress, 1967).

60. Donald M. Scott, *From Office to Profession: The New England Ministry, 1750–1850* (Philadelphia: University of Pennsylvania Press, 1978), ch. 8, entitled "From Reform to Refuge: The Devotional Transformation," pp. 133–47. The quote is found on page 147.

61. Smith, *Revivalism and Social Reform*, pp. 211–12.

62. See the documentation for this in Donald W. Dayton, *Discovering an Evangelical Heritage* (New York: Harper and Row, 1978), especially ch. 9.

63. These issues are raised by George M. Marsden, *Fundamentalism and American Culture: The Shaping of Twentieth Century Evangelicalism, 1870–1925* (New York: Oxford University Press, 1980), and Robert Mapes Anderson, *Vision of the Disinherited: The Making of American Pentecostalism* (New York: Oxford University Press, 1979).

64. The title of a section on this question by Charles W. Carter, *The Person and Ministry of the Holy Spirit: A Wesleyan Perspective* (Grand Rapids: Baker, 1974), pp. 178–81. Carter struggles with this question because, in spite of the subtitle of his book, his work actually represents the position of late nineteenth-century Holiness theology rather than the Wesleyanism that he claims. Carter's response to an early report of the conclusions of this study

may be found in an extended footnote on pages 188–89 of the original hardcover edition.

65. Charles Ewing Brown, *The Meaning of Sanctification* (Anderson, Ind.: Warner, 1945), pp. 114–15.

66. Smith, "Christian Perfection and American Idealism," especially pp. 21ff. See also his preface to Charles G. Finney, *The Promise of the Spirit* (Minneapolis: Bethany Fellowship, 1980).

67. C. I. Scofield, *Plain Papers on the Doctrine of the Holy Spirit* (New York: Fleming H. Revell, 1899), preface, p. 9.

68. See Wesley's Sermon 35 on "Christian perfection" in Edward H. Sugden, ed., *Wesley's Standard Sermons* (London: Epworth, 1921), 2:147–77.

69. Daniel Steele, "Baptism of the Spirit," *Guide to Holiness* 20 (February 1874): 38. Steele's later writings reveal more ambivalence about this identification. His *Defense of Christian Perfection* (New York: Hunt and Eaton, 1896), a response to James Mudge's attack on the instantaneous element in entire sanctification in *Growth in Holiness Toward Perfection; or, Progressive Sanctification* (New York: Hunt and Eaton, 1895), clearly recognizes Wesley's reluctance to identify sanctification with Pentecost. Notice also an element of vacillation at the various points at which the question arises in the collection of *Steele's Answers* (Chicago: Christian Witness, 1912).

59   "Back to Pentecost"

Dedicated to Rev. C. J. Fowler, Pres't, National Holiness Association.

Mrs. C. H. M.   Mrs. C. H. MORRIS.

1. "I will not leave you com - fort-less," But if I go a - way,
2. Church of the Liv - ing God a - rise The full-ness to re - ceive;
3. God's skies are full of Pen - te-costs, For you, for me, for all;
4. Then quick - ly "back to Pen - te-cost," That bless - ed up - per room;

Will send the Ho - ly Com - fort - er, Your roy - al Guest for -
Un - til the lost in ev - 'ry place, Shall feel the need of
Then let us hum - bly, bold - ly press, Our her - i - tage in
And pray the might - y Lord of Hosts, To send on us the

CHORUS.

ev - er-more, A - bid - ing day by day.
sav - ing grace, And shall on Christ be-lieve.
Christ pos - sess, That pow'r from heav'n may fall.
Ho - ly Ghost, And tar - ry till he come.

Has he come to you, to

you, to you? Has the Com - fort-er come to you? .... The Lord will re-
to you?

prove the world of sin, When the Com-fort-er comes to you. ....
to you.

Copyright, 1900, by H. L. Gilmour, Wenonah, N. J.

CHAPTER IV

THE TRIUMPH
OF THE DOCTRINE
OF PENTECOSTAL
SPIRIT BAPTISM

After the Civil War the revivalist traditions were increasingly marginalized within the American culture. The late nineteenth century also saw massive sect formation, much of it along the lines of the Holiness withdrawal or expulsion from the larger Methodist mainstream, but similar patterns were also manifested in parallel traditions. What is notable for our purposes is the extent to which these revivalist currents, whether within or without the mainstream churches, were dominated in this period by one variation or another of a doctrine of Pentecostal baptism in the Holy Spirit—though still at this point, of course, without the practice of glossolalia.

Thus far we have traced the rise of Pentecostal imagery as it was focused in the perfectionist wing of antebellum revivalism. Now we must trace the articulation of an explicit doctrine of the baptism of the Holy Spirit and catalog its variations as it suffused late nineteenth-century revivalism.

The first books to develop a full and self-conscious doctrine of Pentecostal sanctification apparently appeared in the wake of the revival of 1857–58. Phoebe Palmer, the motivating force behind the burgeoning Holiness Revival within Methodism, seems to have moved in this direction just before the outbreak of the revival—perhaps under the influence of William Arthur, who was touring this country and correcting the proofs of *The Tongue of Fire* in 1855.[1] At any rate, her reports from western New York in the fall of 1856 show this development,[2] as do her reports to the *Guide to Holiness* during her four years of evangelism in Great Britain from 1859 to 1863. Toward the end of 1859 she reported, for example, from Newcastle that

> at our afternoon meetings, "Holiness to the Lord," or, in other words, the full baptism of the Holy Spirit, as received by the one hundred and twenty disciples on the day of Pentecost, is set forth as the absolute necessity of all believers of every name. Hundreds, composed of various sects, and from miles distant, crowd to these meetings; and, when Dr. P[almer] gives the invitation to all who are resolved with unyielding faith to claim the grace at once, the communion-rail, which will accommodate about sixty persons, is generally surrounded.[3]

In 1859 Phoebe Palmer issued *The Promise of the Father*. Subtitled a "Neglected Specialty of the Last Days," this book used, in effect, the latter rain argument to defend the ministry of women. By giving an understanding of "preaching" along the lines of "prophecy," the book supports the ministry of women (and obviously her own ministry) by appeal to the prophecy of Joel, quoted in Acts 2, that "I will pour out my Spirit upon all flesh, and your sons and *your daughters* shall prophesy"—a text reproduced on the title page. The whole book reverberates with the themes on Pentecost, claiming that "a recognition of the full baptism of the Holy Ghost, as a grace to be experienced and enjoyed in the present life, was the distinguishing doctrine of Methodism."[4] And the latter half of the book is a description of her work of Holiness evangelism and the *Guide to Holiness*, as well as a call to enter the experience. The old themes are present, of course, but there is a new emphasis on the characteristic vocabulary of the Pentecost account—a concern for "power," the expected "prophecy," and so forth.

The next and crucial development would appear to be a volume appropriately entitled *The Baptism of the Holy Ghost* by Asa Mahan, former president of Oberlin College, and published in 1870 by the Palmers. Mahan had become the president of Adrian College in 1859, which was then sig-

nificantly under the control of the abolitionist and perfectionist Wesleyan Methodists but later to pass to the Methodist
Protestants. Apparently this book was germinating for six to
eight years, before publication, as lectures at Adrian that
became the occasion of three periods of revival. Yet, when
Mahan offered the book to the Palmers, they were reluctant
and, fearing controversy, suggested a Calvinistic publisher.

But Mahan wished a Methodist publisher, as he had had
for his *Scripture Doctrine of Christian Perfection*, and argued
that the Presbyterians were not yet ready to publish such
works. Insisting that the issue was being widely discussed
beyond Methodism, Mahan pressed for the importance of its
publication, and the Palmers finally relented.[5] Mahan's predic-
tion that as a result of the book a "new interest in the whole
subject will be excited" proved correct; within a dozen years
he could report that "it has been very extensively circulated in
America, in Great Britain and in all missionary lands; and has
been translated into the German and Dutch languages."[6]

Mahan understood in *The Baptism of the Holy Ghost* that
"the doctrine of entire sanctification is presented in a form old
and yet new."[7] But the context of this development is more
Reformed than Methodist—not only in the illustrations used
and the broader biblical base developed, but also in the extent
to which the themes of "cleansing from sin" are largely
relegated to a single discourse. Indeed, the "consequences" of
the "baptism" are described primarily in terms of "*perma-
nence and power*," or more elaborately as (1) a quickening of
our "*natural powers*"; (2) "a vast accumulation of *moral* and
spiritual power—power to endure, and power to accomplish";
(3) "*soul-transforming apprehensions of Truth*"; (4) "*absolute
assurance of hope*"; (5) more intimate "*fellowship with the
Father, and with his Son Jesus Christ*"; (6) a "deep and
permanent spiritual blessedness"; and (7) a "unity of the
Spirit" among believers.[8]

By 1870 the foundations had been laid for the future
developments. The determinative explications of the doctrine
had been published in both Methodist and Reformed circles.
From this point on, the teaching of a Pentecostal baptism of the
Holy Spirit would profoundly suffuse most branches of at least
conservative revivalism, though not always in exactly the same

form. There were, in fact, three variations in the doctrine that must be traced: the mainstream Holiness teaching of Pentecostal sanctification, a more radical Holiness variation that split this experience into two separate works of grace, and finally the form that became dominant in the more nearly Reformed circles by suppressing the more distinctively Wesleyan themes to teach the baptism of the Spirit as a "second, definite work" of grace subsequent to salvation but for the purpose of "enduing with Power for service."

THE SHIFT TO PENTECOSTAL SANCTIFICATION

In the years after the Civil War, the Holiness movement increasingly adopted the Pentecostal formulation of entire sanctification. The most important institution of the Methodist-dominated yet interdenominational segment of the movement was the National Camp Meeting Association for the Promotion of Holiness, which called its first camp meeting at Vineland, New Jersey, in July 1867. The call to the event hoped "to realize together a Pentecostal baptism of the Holy Ghost."[9] Sermons at the Vineland meeting included one on Acts 1:8 ("ye shall receive power, after that the Holy Ghost is come upon you") by Benjamin M. Adams, a founder of the National Camp Meeting Association. In this sermon, themes of "power" overwhelm traditional Wesleyan themes, though the latter are also present.[10] And the report of the first fourteen such meetings held during the following five years was significantly entitled *Days of Power in the Forest Temple.*

The report of the sixteenth camp meeting was entitled *A Modern Pentecost* and describes a sermon on Acts 1:8 by William H. Boole in which "empowerment" predominates in his advocacy of an "electric baptism." Boole claimed that "the baptism of the Holy Ghost is a positive, specific, conscious instantaneous experience. Here we stand or fall—Methodism stands or falls. Our church has taught no other doctrine from the beginning."[11] The Pentecostal themes are emerging in this context during this period, though muted—no doubt in part because this was the most classically oriented wing of the Holiness movement and thus implicitly the most determined by the original Wesleyan themes.

But the seeds had been planted and would grow throughout the rest of the century as the Holiness tradition pulled more and more away from Methodism and early, more conservative leadership was eclipsed. The 1890s probably reveal the climax of these developments and the most intense outburst of Pentecostal themes. By this time S. A. Keen of Ohio was holding innumerable "Pentecostal Services" in scores of Methodist Annual Conferences and published in 1895 his teachings as *Pentecostal Papers; or the Gift of the Holy Ghost.*[12] Methodist H. C. Morrison, the major figure behind the institutions known today as Asbury College and Asbury Theological Seminary in Kentucky, changed the title of his magazine in 1897 from the *Methodist* to the *Pentecostal Herald* and in 1900 summarized his teaching in *The Baptism with the Holy Ghost,* a pamphlet that circulated in the tens of thousands and was translated into Chinese and Japanese.[13]

Such tendencies were perhaps more accentuated among the more sectarian strands of the movement that were to produce new denominations by the end of the century. Quaker Seth Cook Rees, a figure prominent in the founding of both the Pentecostal Church of the Nazarene and the Pilgrim Holiness Church, would sketch his vision in the *Ideal Pentecostal Church* in 1897.[14] The biography of his wife was entitled *Hulda A. Rees, the Pentecostal Prophetess.*[15] Their colleague Martin Wells Knapp would write *Lightning Bolts from Pentecostal Skies.*[16] The same publisher issued a series of paperbacks as the "Pentecostal Holiness Library," most of which reveal a Pentecostal fixation. And so on.

In January 1897, the *Guide to Holiness and Revival Miscellany* substituted for the final phrase in its title the words *Pentecostal Life* in response to

> the signs of the times, which indicate inquiry, research and ardent pursuit of the gifts, graces, and power of the Holy Spirit. "The Pentecostal idea," is pervading Christian thought and aspiration more than ever before . . . and we hope this year to contribute something toward a better understanding of the fact—that this is, "THE DISPENSATION OF THE HOLY GHOST."[17]

The inside front cover of that issue announced a new edition of that "great pentecostal gift," Asa Mahan's book *The Baptism of the Holy Ghost,* that "truly magnificent work of Dr. Mahan on the great theme of the period."

From this point to its demise not quite four years later, the magazine fairly reverberated with the Pentecostal theme. Sermons were published in a column entitled the "Pentecostal Pulpit," women's reports under "Pentecostal Womanhood," testimonies as "Pentecostal Testimonies"—everything from camp meetings to choirs were "Pentecostal" while private devotions were held in the "Pentecostal closet." This is but an extreme illustration of what was generally true in most strands of the Holiness movement by the 1890s.

Even the more conservative (now renamed) National Association for the Promotion of Holiness seems to have fallen into line. President Charles J. Fowler issued in 1900 a book entitled *Back to Pentecost,* in which he claimed to

> mean by Pentecost what the New Testament means by it—
> what Methodism has always meant by it—we mean that
> work of grace one needs after his regeneration, and may
> have, and what is known in theology as ENTIRE SANCTI-
> FICATION.[18]

By this time the formulations of Fletcher had virtually overwhelmed the more Wesleyan explication of entire sanctification. The Holiness movement tried to maintain the content of Wesley in the new formulations, but could not. The Pentecostal formulation had its own power that pulled in new directions.

FLETCHER REDIVIVUS

The turn toward Pentecost brought to the fore Fletcher's doctrine of the dispensations. Hints of this occur already in Asa Mahan, who, though he preferred to speak of "two covenants" in *Christian Perfection,* spoke of "old and new dispensations." Methodist Edward Davies's book, *The Gift of the Holy Ghost: The Believer's Privilege* (1874)—which was read far beyond the confines of his own denomination— devoted a whole chapter to a "Brief History of the Three

Dispensations" and included an appendix by Daniel Steele on "The Three Dispensations" reprinted from the *Advocate of Christian Holiness*. The latter is essentially a summary of Fletcher's treatment of the topic in *The Portrait of St. Paul*.[19]

Similar essays appeared increasingly throughout the rest of the century so that by the 1890s the pattern was so well established that Phineas Bresee, later to become a major founder of the Church of the Nazarene, would begin his National Camp Meeting Association sermon, "The Baptism with the Holy Ghost," with the statement that "the dispensation of the Holy Ghost was ushered in soon after the ascension of Jesus, by His coming upon the apostles and disciples in sanctifying and filling power."[20]

This shift to Pentecostal vocabulary also brought to the fore various pneumatological themes. This may be seen in Mahan's emphasis on spiritual gifts and the gift of prophecy or Phoebe Palmers's very frequent references to prophecy.[21] In early years "prophecy" tended to be interpreted more naturalistically as preaching or testifying, but with the change there is a discernible tendency toward the more supernaturalistic and "ecstatic." Mahan, it is true, would warn that "no careful reader of the Scriptures at the present time confounds the gift or promise of the Spirit with any *miraculous endowments*,"[22] but by the turn of the century attention had expanded to include the more "supernatural" gifts of healing and miracles. Seth Cook Rees would argue that "signs and miracles have reappeared with every Holy Ghost revival."[23] Those who stayed closest to the Wesleyan tradition emphasized the *ethical* consequences and the "graces" rather than the gifts of the Spirit, but the push was increasingly toward the "spiritual gifts *and* graces"[24]—especially where the fascination with Pentecost was most intense.

"POWER" OR "HOLINESS"?

But perhaps the most difficult problem was still with integrating the "perfection" and "cleansing" motifs brought from the Wesleyan tradition with the theme of "power" dominant in the Pentecost texts that were now receiving more attention. Often the "power" themes merely overwhelmed the "holiness" themes, as we have suggested at various points already. The mainstream Holiness movement tried valiantly to preserve the classical themes in the midst of the new changes in vocabulary and rhetoric.

One answer—evident, for example, in Phoebe Palmer—was to equate the two, suggesting that "holiness *is* power,"[25] that "holiness possesses an almightiness of power that will raise any sinking church,"[26] that "purity and power are identical."[27] More typical was the effort to maintain that Pentecost brought both "holiness and power," the title of perhaps the most important book of Congregationalist A. M. Hills, who had studied at Oberlin with Finney and later held college presidencies for the Church of the Nazarene as he became the first systematic theologian of the denomination.[28] In the words of H. C. Morrison, "the baptism with the Holy Ghost purifies believers' hearts and empowers them for service."[29]

This position usually involved distinguishing between the negative and positive aspects of the same "work," the formulation that became normative in many Holiness contexts. Thus Nazarene theologian E. P. Ellyson later reflected a consensus by quoting his denomination's *Manual* to the effect that entire sanctification

> is wrought by the baptism with the Holy Spirit and comprehends in one experience the cleansing of the heart from sin and the abiding, indwelling presence of the Holy Spirit, empowering the believer for life and service.[30]

Or this double pattern could be developed more elaborately and somewhat differently, as by theologian Russell R. Byrum of the Church of God (Anderson, Indiana):

> The Bible teaches, not only two works of grace—the first commonly described as conversion, and the second a later special work of God in the heart—but it also clearly teaches a double phase of each of these experiences. The first work, conversion, includes both justification and regeneration, which are different in their very nature though both are received at the same time. . . . the second work includes, not only a perfect cleansing of the heart from inherited depravity, but also the baptism of the Holy Ghost.[31]

THE "THREE BLESSINGS" TEACHING

But this consensus was not easily won or maintained, and the careful wording reflects a self-conscious polemic against a variant position that, though anticipated earlier, arose primarily just before the turn of the century. A party that found the synthesis above too easy argued instead for three works or "blessings" in which the second work of the dominant Holiness position was broken into two separate blessings. This party, however, was not the fanatical fringe that it appeared to be to Holiness leaders then and since. It pointed to the fundamental difficulty in expressing Wesleyan theology in Pentecostal dress—one that has surfaced, as we have seen, each time the attempt was made. The ongoing struggle with this problem was clearly revealed in the literature long before the 1890s, when the "three blessing heresy" came to wider notice.

The question arose as early as 1856 in the *Guide to Holiness*. An unidentified "J. D." asked,

> Does entire holiness, entire sanctification, a clean heart, perfect love, or full salvation, etc. necessarily imply the full baptism of the Holy Ghost? May not a soul enjoy the blessing of entire holiness, and still live short of the fulness of the Spirit?[32]

"J. D." appealed to Fletcher's doctrine of dispensations and quoted Fletcher to the effect that "we must not be content to be only cleansed from sin; we must be filled with the spirit."[33] These questions in the *Guide to Holiness* seem to have arisen at least in part in response to the empirical observation that many who claimed to be "entirely sanctified" seemed to lack the appropriate "spiritual power." Others as well had personal experience that seemed to support such a separation. Thus Arthur S. Clibborn, destined to become a son-in-law of William Booth, founder of the Salvation Army, was to write Asa Mahan, by then the British editor of *Divine Life*:

> By degrees light broke again out of the darkness, and I became more and more surrendered to Christ and weaned from *self* and the world. After a time of entire consecration (about four years from the former call) in which I was

> made willing to become a fool for Christ—to renounce
> self, the world, reputation, all to Him, and gave *myself* to
> His service, I received a Baptism of the Spirit.[34]

Others placed so great an emphasis on the cleansing as preparation for the baptism that at least an ordering if not an actual separation was implied. Thus Baptist Holiness evangelist A. B. Earle was once asked in a Holiness conference: "May not a person have a clean heart without the baptism of the Holy Ghost?" Earle replied that "a clean heart is preparatory for the baptism of the Holy Ghost."[35]

Asa Mahan seems to have toyed with such distinctions as well and seems on occasion to speak of entire sanctification and the baptism of the Holy Ghost as two doctrines or experiences, not one. In *Divine Life* he suggested the metaphor of emptying a vessel and filling it to indicate that "purity is one thing, power is quite another." The significance seems to have been to emphasize the ordering, that "the former, as an immutable condition precedent, always comes before the latter," so that seekers of the baptism would not "forget to pray in faith for the inward purification indispensable to the reception of this unspeakable gift."[36]

Similarly Methodist Asbury Lowrey, American editor of *Divine Life,* unhesitatingly answered yes to the question, "May we have a dispensation of the Holy Ghost after sanctification, and supplementary to that grace, a dispensation greater or more powerful than necessarily belongs to the state of a pure heart?" Lowrey argued that the

> work of the Holy Ghost, up to the point of entire
> sanctification, is *renovating,* the baptism is *qualifying.*
> The first purges and refines; the second empowers. The
> first works in and restores the image of God in the heart;
> the second works out, and touching society, hallows the
> world. The first purifies and makes a saint; the second
> anoints and makes a priest and king mighty through God,
> to the pulling down of strongholds.[37]

Lowrey's crowning argument of the need for the sanctified to receive the baptism was the model of Christ, who was "holy, harmless, undefiled, and separate from sinners and yet He sought and received the baptism of the Spirit."[38] Turn-of-the-century Holiness evangelist George D. Watson also on occasion came close to this position and similarly used the example of Christ to refute those like Phoebe Palmer who argued that "holiness is power."[39]

Other persons were inclined to make a distinction on the basis of the words of John the Baptist regarding Christ, that "he shall baptize you with the Holy Ghost, and with fire" (Matt. 3:11). From this the Rev. Edwin Pope concluded in *Divine Life* that "the baptism of fire is a different baptism from that with the Holy Ghost, a baptism for which the baptism with the Holy Ghost is preparatory."[40]

Similar questions agitated a number of persons in the *Way of Faith,* published by J. M. Pike in Columbia, South Carolina, after 1890. Probably the most important person to adopt these views was Baptist Benjamin Harden Irwin, key figure on the way to Pentecostalism by virtue of his work in founding the Fire-Baptized Holiness Church.[41] Irwin left few writings[42] and projected his teaching in person or through several small tracts. He taught that

> so far as the sin question is concerned, it is forever settled
> in the two works of grace—forgiveness and cleansing. The
> baptism with the Holy Ghost and with fire, special
> anointings, undergirdings, and deep inner illuminat-
> ings.[43]

But though Irwin appears to be speaking of one baptism, it nevertheless had two parts, and Irwin fell into a pattern of piling spiritual experience upon spiritual experience. This was spelled out much later in the constitution of the Fire-Baptized Holiness Church, where after articles on justification and sanctification, the following two are found:

> We believe also that the baptism of the Holy Ghost is
> obtainable by a definite act of appropriating faith on the
> part of the fully cleansed believer (Acts 1:5; 2:1–4, 38;
> Luke 11:13, Acts 19:6).

> We believe also that the baptism with fire is a definite,
> scriptural experience, obtainable by faith on the part of
> the Spirit-filled believer (Matt. 3:11; Luke 3:16; Rev. 15:2;
> Psa. 104:4; Acts 2:1–4; Heb. 12:29; Ezek. 1:4–14; 10:2–7;
> Isa. 33:14; 6:1–8).[44]

Irwin, however, was already promoting by this time additional baptisms of "dynamite," lyddite," and "oxidite."[45] But by 1900 he was discovered in "open and gross sin" and was deposed, and his excesses were discarded with him.

Theologically more interesting, however, was yet another circle of persons who began to advocate three blessings. Simon P. Jacobs, Methodist president of the Southwestern Holiness Association, understood the "unorthodox" doctrine of Pentecostal sanctification to be a late development and argued,

> If purity of heart and the Pentecostal baptism of the Holy Spirit are identical or inseparable experiences, then no one before Pentecost ever had a pure heart. But such is not the case. This is clear to any Bible reader. Purity of heart was enjoyed both under the Mosaic and Patriarchal dispensations. In fact, all writers on holiness quoted from the Old Testament, both the doctrine and witnesses of complete purity of heart.
>
> All will concede that our Lord lived in perfect purity thirty years before he received the *personal* indwelling Holy Spirit (Luke III: 21, 22).
>
> Therefore such indwelling of the Holy Ghost, or the baptism of the Holy Ghost, and perfect heart-purity are neither identical nor inseparably connected.
>
> It follows, then, that one being cleansed from all sin (I John 1:7) is not thereby necessarily baptized with the Holy Ghost.[46]

Somewhat similar in concerns was R. C. Horner, a maverick Canadian evangelist claimed as founder by three small denominations.[47] Having written a refutation of Jeremiah Boland's attack on Wesley and second blessing theology in the Methodist Episcopal Church, South,[48] Horner knew his Wesley and was quite clear on his failure to connect sanctification with Pentecost:

> Wesley taught that holiness was salvation from inbred sin, and he knew that the disciples were not told to wait for cleansing. He collected and quoted prayers that had been offered up for the entire sanctification of God's people, but did not intimate that any of these prayers were answered on the day of Pentecost.[49]

One might say that Horner understood Wesley better than the mainstream Holiness movement. His resistance to a Pentecostal elaboration of entire sanctification allowed him to preserve more original Wesleyan themes in his explication of Holiness, though there is a tendency to emphasize the instantaneous aspect of the sanctification in a manner characteristic of the American movements. Horner's basic theological statement, the two volumes of *Bible Doctrines*,[50] also more closely approximates Wesleyan thought in its emphasis on the whole elaborate process of grace from prevenient through repentance and justification, sanctification, and entire sanctification—up to the point where he begins to develop the characteristic themes of Pentecost as a consequence of his "third blessing" commitments.

Horner had come to this third experience in a search for "soul-winning power" after "perfect love made me groan for power to reach the perishing masses and lead them to Jesus." For him this

> extra gift for soul winning has been the aggressive element in my experience. It brought all the dormant powers of my soul into activity and energized all my faculties for efficiency in the vineyard of the Lord.[51]

Much of the argumentation of Simon P. Jacobs related above was adopted by the Hornerites to argue against the doctrine of Pentecostal sanctification.[52] Horner was committed to arguing his case with other leaders of the Holiness movement on the basis of the biblical and historical sources. Mainstream Holiness leaders strained to prove that the disciples had not been sanctified before Pentecost,[53] while Horner argued, on the other hand, that the disciples showed signs of entire sanctification before Pentecost and that the forty days of tarrying for the Spirit were in fact one long "Holiness revival."[54] And since he found it impossible to deny that Wesley lacked spiritual power, Horner also faced the problem of discerning in Wesley his own pattern of spiritual experience. This he resolved by picking up the suggestion of Canadian Methodist scholar Nehemiah Burwash that Wesley had been "entirely sanctified when he supposed that he had been converted" and extended the analysis to conclude that "when he received what he called 'entire sanctification,' it must have been the baptism of the Holy Ghost, as they received it on the day of Pentecost."[55]

In anticipation of what will follow, we should also notice that the work of both B. H. Irwin and R. C. Horner, the two most prominent advocates of the "third blessing" teaching, was accompanied by "demonstrations of the Spirit" and physical phenomena more extreme than found in other parts of the Holiness movement. To this extent they both represent a further radicalization of broader Holiness and even Methodist tendencies. Irwin was controversial not only for his teaching on the baptism of fire but also for the fact that "shouting, dancing in the Spirit, falling into trances, and many other manifestations, characterized his meetings."[56] The testimonies included in reports of annual Pentecost Festivals held in Canada by R. C. Horner reveal a more restrained, but still intense, pattern.[57] "Physical manifestations—prostration, ec-stasy, immediate laughter—were common" in Horner's early work among the Methodists and contributed to the censure that accelerated his separation from them.[58] Horner and his followers responded as usual with an appeal to early Method-ist practice with publications such as *Wesley on Prostration* or *Demonstrations of the Spirit*.[59]

THE REVIVALIST DOCTRINE OF THE "BAPTISM OF THE HOLY SPIRIT"

But there was also a third late nineteenth-century varia-tion on the doctrine of the baptism of the Holy Spirit that appealed more to the better-known revivalists of the era, especially those who claimed more fidelity to the Reformed theological tradition. This variation increasingly suppressed the Methodistic elements present in early articulations of the doctrine in favor of the "empowering for service" motifs. In this form the doctrine of the baptism with the Holy Spirit suffused late nineteenth-century revivalism in a way that has largely gone unnoticed.

Again the roots of this development are to be found in the Oberlin theology. While Mahan moved increasingly toward Methodism, Finney appears to have moved away from themes of entire sanctification after an initial period in the 1840s that

might be described as more Wesleyan. Finney's mature views
on the subject may apparently be found in an appendix to the
British edition of Mahan's *Baptism of the Holy Ghost*. This
essay of four chapters entitled "The Enduement of Power"
uses the usual Pentecostal imagery to encourage the seeking of
"the enduement of power from on high" defined exclusively as
the "indispensable condition of performing the work" Christ
set before the church in the Great Commission. There is no
reference to a "sanctification" or "cleansing" in the Pentecostal experience—though there is some concern that the period
of preparation and "tarrying" should include "consecration."[60] This is the form of the doctrine that is found in the
teaching of such successors of Finney's evangelism as Dwight
L. Moody, R. A. Torrey, and J. Wilbur Chapman.

A crucial year for Moody was 1871. His hall in Chicago
was destroyed by the Great Fire, and he was about to be
launched into an international career. In the midst of this, two
women, recently "sanctified" and later to be known as Free
Methodists, began to "get a burden" for Moody, feeling that
"he lacked what the apostles received on the day of Pentecost."[61] When they approached Moody with a report of their
prayers, he invited them to pray with him regularly on Fridays.
Their prayers brought a great hunger to Moody's soul—he
"began to cry out as I never did before. I really felt that I did
not want to live if I could not have this power for service."[62]
Resolution of this struggle was to come while Moody paced the
streets of New York as he was about to leave for England.

It is not clear when this experience began to influence
Moody's preaching. Holiness folk, of course, watched his
preaching carefully for hints of his position with regard to
their own distinctive claims. Observers of his work in Britain
in the early 1870s noticed that he did not "give any very
special prominence to the subject of entire holiness" and "was
heard" to say that "he did not believe in a 'second blessing.'"
They were relieved, however, later to receive reports that
Moody "had altered his views"—supposedly in connection
with the perusal of the autobiography of Charles G. Finney—
and was "now setting forth very earnestly the baptism of the
Holy Spirit as the privilege of all Christ's people."[63] Such
observers may have seen too much in these reports, however.

The accompanying transcribed sermon from America expresses the whole structure of the "Pentecostal baptism of the Holy Ghost" but primarily as an "enduement of power" though there is reference to the "entire cleansing" and getting "empty of sin" involved.

If such reports are accurate, the cleansing themes appear to have soon dropped out. An 1877 report of Moody's "Doctrinal Discourses" includes one entitled "The Baptism of the Holy Spirit for Service" that begins as follows:

> In some sense, and to some extent, the Holy Spirit dwells with every believer; but there is another gift, which may be called the gift of the Holy Spirit for service. This gift, it strikes me, is entirely distinct and separate from conversion and assurance. God has a great many children that have no power, and the reason is, they have not the gift of the Holy Ghost for service.[64]

And a similar position is present, though perhaps in somewhat modulated form, in Moody's widely distributed book, *Secret Power*, first published in 1881.[65]

Moody had a sure instinct for avoiding controversy and kept his public statements, some have suggested, deliberately vague, especially on disputed issues. He certainly shied away from the characteristic vocabulary of the Holiness movement and was reluctant to speak in public of his experience of 1871, though he sometimes relented in private. But his teaching of a special "Pentecostal enduement of power for service" seems to have been a relatively constant theme of his preaching and apparently "did not significantly change between the mid-1870s and the late 1890s."[66]

If Moody was vague and reticent about these themes, his successor was just the opposite; they dominated the ministry of Reuben A. Torrey,[67] who reveals a startling narrowing of focus on the "Baptism with the Holy Spirit." Torrey was quite clear that one of the major reasons "why God used D. L. Moody" was that "*he had a very definite enduement with power from on high, a very clear and definite Baptism with the Holy Ghost*" and stressed that Moody, when sending Torrey out to preach, would usually insist on two sermons: "Ten Reasons Why I Believe the Bible to Be the Word of God" and

"The Baptism With the Holy Ghost."[68] Moody's death was to come in 1899, the year Moody Bible Institute opened with Torrey at its head. But clearly, by the mid-1890s Torrey was becoming known for such works as *How to Obtain Fullness of Power*[69] and *The Baptism With the Holy Spirit*.[70] The teaching of the latter work is summarized in four propositions that constantly recur in Torrey's writings:

1. . . . that *there are a number of designations in the Bible for this one experience . . . baptized with the Holy Ghost . . . filled with the Holy Ghost . . . endued with power from on high . . . the Holy Spirit fell on them . . . the gift of the Holy Ghost . . . and received the Holy Ghost. . . .*

2. . . . that *the Baptism with the Holy Spirit is a definite experience of which one may know whether he has received it or not. . . .*

3. *The Baptism with the Holy Spirit is a work of the Holy Spirit separate and distinct from His regenerating work. . . .*

4. *The Baptism with the Holy Spirit is always connected with testimony and service.*[71]

This last proposition was directed specifically against "a line of teaching, put forward by a very earnest but mistaken body of people, that has brought the whole doctrine of the Baptism with the Holy Spirit into disrepute." The disputed teaching was that "this Baptism with the Holy Spirit is the eradication of the sinful nature," or in other words, the doctrine of Pentecostal sanctification. Torrey would grant that "it is indeed the work of the Holy Spirit to cleanse from sin," but this was not the "Baptism with the Holy Spirit."[72]

In making such statements Torrey very likely had in mind A. M. Hills, his Yale classmate and the preacher of his ordination sermon. These two men had served their first pastorates near each other and had assisted each other in spiritual quest, but by 1900 they had found themselves in intensely opposed camps on the meaning of the doctrine of the baptism of the Holy Spirit. Hills affirmed Torrey's first three propositions, and the two men differed only on the fourth. Torrey claimed that the effect of the baptism of the Holy Spirit was "empowering for service," while Hills insisted on "holiness and power." For Hills anything less was *Pentecost Rejected,* his own refutation of Torrey.[73]

But Torrey was to be eclipsed as a revivalist in the early twentieth century by J. Wilbur Chapman, educated at Oberlin and spiritually enlivened under the ministry of Moody in 1878.[74] His own commitment to the themes we have been tracing may be seen in his 1894 book, *Received Ye the Holy Ghost?* which was dedicated to Moody.[75] Chapman developed in this book all the themes of the Moody/Torrey tradition except that he suggests that "every child of God has received the baptism of the Spirit" and that Pentecost illustrates a later "infilling." Chapman the next year would write an introduction to a similar book by the Rev. Ford C. Ottman entitled *Have Ye Known the Holy Ghost?*[76] Ottman was later Chapman's biographer.

All these illustrations indicate the extent to which the turn-of-the-century revivalist movements were deeply suffused with a doctrine of the Holy Spirit baptism and the extent to which these figures approached their public through books on these themes.

THE KESWICK MOVEMENT

But before moving on, we should also notice a parallel and interconnected development, the rise in the late nineteenth century of the so-called Keswick movement and teaching. "Keswick" was the form Holiness and "higher life" teaching took in Britain, primarily among Anglican Evangelicals, though its influence was destined to be much larger.[77] The work of such figures as Charles Finney; Asa Mahan; W. E. Boardman; Hannah Whitall Smith and her husband, Robert Pearsall Smith; Charles Cullis; and others[78] led to the "Union Meeting for the Promotion of Scriptural Holiness" at Oxford in 1874[79] and in the next year the gathering of eight thousand people at a "Convention for the Promotion of Scriptural Holiness in Brighton."[80] These and other forces coalesced into a movement that culminated in a series of annual conventions held in tents in Keswick, England, beginning in 1875. These conventions became a major center of late nineteenth-century

Evangelical spirituality, closely associated with missions, especially the China Inland Mission and its imitators.

The Keswick theology occupied territory somewhere in between the American Holiness movement and the American revivalists just surveyed.[81] Over against Torrey and Moody, the Keswick teaching was more concerned with the second blessing as an answer to sin, but on the other hand, it shied away from the perfectionism of the American Holiness teaching. The major difference between the latter two may be seen in the epithets that they hurled at each other: the Holiness teachers were "eradicationists," while the Keswick teachers were "suppressionists" with regard to the sinful nature. The Keswick teaching was not so precise as that of the other groups and does not fall into the patterns we have identified; even the definiteness of the "second experience" was often qualified and subdued.

Nor is there a consistent pattern on the doctrine of the Spirit. Mahan led well-attended seminars on the baptism of the Holy Spirit at both the Oxford and the Brighton meetings.[82] But these teachings apparently soon fell into the background, and more characteristic was a call to the "fullness of the Spirit" or the "Spirit-filled life" in a more restrained and often Christocentric pattern less characteristic of the American developments.

Keswick, however, was imported back into the United States by Moody, who brought into his Northfield Conventions in the early 1890s such figures as F. B. Meyer, a Londoner who returned five times within the decade; Andrew Murray, the Dutch Reformed minister from South Africa; H. W. Webb-Peploe, an Anglican clergyman; and G. Campbell Morgan, a Baptist from England. These figures had much in common with American figures usually labeled "Keswick" such as A. B. Simpson, the Presbyterian founder of the Christian and Missionary Alliance, and A. J. Gordon, the Baptist New Englander whose work is known today primarily through Gordon College and Gordon-Conwell Theological Seminary.

On the American scene, this coalescing of British Keswick and American revivalism produced an important constellation of figures (especially Simpson; Gordon; Torrey; and though not American, Andrew Murray)[83] who emphasized our common themes, though only A. B. Simpson went so far as to advocate a four-fold gospel.[84] Simpson was inclined to present "the Lord Jesus Christ in a four-fold ministry as Saviour, Sanctifier, Healer and Coming King."

THE LAST HARBINGERS: SIMPSON AND GORDON

With the emergence of this pattern we have come close to the *gestalt* of theological claims that constitutes Pentecostalism. The rest of this study will concern itself with tracing the rise of Simpson's latter two themes, the emphases on divine healing and the second coming of Christ. But before doing that, we need to glance a little more closely at Simpson's and Gordon's teachings on the Holy Spirit.

Simpson's exposition of sanctification in 1890 is difficult to classify. The experience is described in terms of "separation from sin," "dedication to God," "conformity to the likeness of God and to the will of God," and "love to God and all mankind." There is little emphasis on a second blessing, but Simpson uses language that implies a moment of "consecration" or "complete surrender" that results in a "personal indwelling of Jesus."[85] This also involves a special indwelling of the Holy Spirit that is compared to Pentecost. Just as "when the tabernacle was finished the Holy Ghost came down and possessed it," so too, "He that came down in power upon the disciples at Pentecost comes to you and me when we are fully dedicated to Him, as really as though we should see Him come fluttering down in visible form from yonder upon our shoulder."[86]

A. J. Gordon's teachings show a greater direct influence from Oberlin. John Morgan is cited in the preface to *The Two-Fold Life* as a major influence, and Finney's work and conversion are cited, including references to a baptism of the Holy Ghost in a discussion of "power for sonship and power for service." Arguing from a "fresh study of the Acts of the Apostles" and "new experience in revival work," Gordon concludes that

> the Scriptures seem to teach that there is a second stage in spiritual development, distinct and separate from conver-

sion; sometimes widely separated in time from it, and sometimes almost contemporaneously with it—a stage to which we rise by a special renewal of the Holy Ghost, and not merely by the process of gradual growth.[87]

But by the mid-1890s both authors had followed the tendency of most "higher life" movements to give greater emphasis to a special role of the Holy Spirit. Gordon's widely distributed book *The Ministry of the Spirit* appeared in 1894. In an introduction F. B. Meyer suggests that if the book's truths "be well wrought into the mental and spiritual constitution of God's servants . . . the age would close with a world-wide Pentecost."[88] And Gordon's exposition in this book places the greater emphasis on the Spirit and develops a doctrine of consecration in that context rather than the other way around. After a discussion of Pentecost, Gordon suggests that though "the baptism in the Holy Ghost was given once for all on the day of Pentecost," it does "not follow therefore that every believer has received this baptism."[89] The "gift of the Spirit" is "a subsequent operation; it is an additional and separate blessing" whose purpose is "our qualification for the highest and most effective service in the church of Christ."[90] Though there is a tendency to move toward the Moody/Torrey pattern, Gordon, like the Keswick tradition in general, still preserves more themes of sanctification in his formulation.

Similar tendencies may be detected in Simpson, who devoted two years to preaching the Holy Spirit and produced in 1895 and 1896 two volumes entitled *The Holy Spirit; or, Power from on Higher.* Here the shift is even more radical especially in the second volume on the New Testament. After a chapter on the significance of Jesus' own baptism, Simpson treats the baptism with the Holy Spirit and its manifold consequences. Then the parable of Jesus about the wise and foolish virgins is interpreted in terms of two different types of Christians distinguished by the baptism of the Spirit. "The apostles before Pentecost, the apostles after Pentecost, represent this difference."[91] The parable of the pounds is interpreted to teach the "Pentecostal enduement of power for service."

The point of all this is that by the mid-1890s almost every branch of the Holiness and "higher life" movements of the nineteenth century, as well as the revivalism of the period in general, was teaching a variation of some sort or another on the baptism of the Holy Spirit, though with some significant differences in nuance and meaning. The pervasiveness of the Pentecostal themes is further illustrated by the publishing of a series of very popular revival hymnals under the title *Pentecostal Hymns* during the last decade of the nineteenth and the first decade of the twentieth centuries. At least six such hymnals were published and widely used throughout these movements.

It is thus no accident that Pentecostalism emerged when it did. All that was needed was the spark that would ignite this volatile tinder. But before turning to that, we must quickly trace the rise of divine healing and the premillennial emphasis on the imminence of the second coming of Christ. The next two chapters will be devoted to this task.

NOTES

1. "Preface to the new American edition" (New York: Harper and Brothers, 1880).

2. Richard Wheatley, *The Life and Letters of Mrs. Phoebe Palmer* (New York: W. C. Palmer, Jr., 1874), pp. 312–17, 326–27. See also the letters collected in Phoebe Palmer, *The Promise of the Father* (Boston: H. V. Degen, 1859), pp. 191ff.

3. These reports are collected as *Four Years in the Old World* (New York: Foster and Palmer, Publishers, 1866), p. 107, reprinting a letter dated 12 October 1859.

4. Palmer, *The Promise of the Father*, p. 55.

5. This information is taken from two 1870 letters (exact dates not clear) from Asa Mahan to Phoebe Palmer among the Palmer papers, Drew University Library.

6. Asa Mahan, *Autobiography, Intellectual, Moral and Spiritual* (London: T. Woolmer, 1882), p. 414.

7. In the Mahan/Palmer correspondence cited in footnote 5 above.

8. Asa Mahan, *The Baptism of the Holy Ghost* (New York: Palmer and Hughes, 1870), pp. 52ff.

9. George Hughes, *Days of Power in the Forest Temple: A Review of the Wonderful Work of God at Fourteen National Camp-Meetings from 1867 to 1872* (Boston: J. Bent, 1873; reprint, Salem, Ohio: Allegheny Wesleyan Methodist Connection, 1975), p. 55.

10. A. McLean and J. W. Eaton, eds., *Penuel; or, Face to Face with God* (New York: W. C. Palmer, Jr., 1869), pp. 59–69.

11. Adam Wallace, ed., *A Modern Pentecost* (Philadelphia: Methodist Home Journal Publishing House, 1873; reprint, Salem, Ohio: Convention Book Store, H. E. Schmul, 1970), p. 83.

12. S. A. Keen, *Pentecostal Papers; or the Gift of the Holy Ghost* (Cincinnati: Published for the author, 1895). This was published in many successive editions.

13. H. C. Morrison, *The Baptism with the Holy Ghost* (Louisville: Pentecostal Herald Press, 1900). This is still in print.

14. Seth Cook Rees, *The Ideal Pentecostal Church* (Cincinnati: M. W. Knapp, Revivalist Office, 1897).

15. Byron J. Rees, *Hulda A. Rees, the Pentecostal Prophetess* (Philadelphia: Christian Standard, 1898).

16. Martin Wells Knapp, *Lightning Bolts from Pentecostal Skies; or, Devices of the Devil Unmasked* (Cincinnati: Revivalist Office, 1889).

17. "Pentecost—What Is It?" *Guide to Holiness* 66 (January 1897): 37.

18. Charles J. Fowler, *Back to Pentecost* (Philadelphia: Christian Standard, 1900), p. 7.

19. E. Davies, *The Gift of the Holy Ghost: The Believer's Privilege* (Reading, Mass.: E. Davies, 1874), ch. 2 and appendix.

20. Phineas F. Bresee, "Baptism with the Holy Ghost," in *The Double Cure; or, Echoes from National Camp-Meetings* (Boston and Chicago: Christian Witness, 1894), p. 326. The abridged reprint of this book (Salem, Ohio: Convention Book Store, 1965) does not include this sermon.

21. Mahan, *The Baptism of the Holy Ghost*, pp. 46–47, and especially Phoebe Palmer, *Four Years in the Old World* and *The Promise of the Father*, *passim*.

22. Mahan, *The Baptism of the Holy Ghost*, p. 113.

23. *The Ideal Pentecostal Church*, p. 78. See also the chapter entitled "Pentecostal Gifts" in Knapp, *Lightning Bolts from Pentecostal Skies*, pp. 80–85.

24. See W. B. Godbey, *Spiritual Gifts and Graces* (Cincinnati: God's Revivalist Office, 1895; reprint, Hobe Sound, Fla.: Hobe Sound Bible College, 1975).

25. Palmer, *The Promise of the Father*, p. 206, and *Four Years in the Old World*, p. 395.

26. Palmer, *Four Years in the Old World*, p. 395.

27. Phoebe Palmer, *Pioneer Experiences; or, The Gift of Power Received by Faith, Illustrated and Confirmed by the Testimonies of Eighty Living Ministers, of Various Denominations* (New York: W. C. Palmer, Jr., 1868), p. vi.

28. A. M. Hills, *Holiness and Power for the Church and the Ministry* (Cincinnati: Revivalist Office, 1897), a veritable catalog of competing views on this question in the nineteenth century. The preface carries an address in Oberlin, Ohio, his home during a period of itinerant evangelism. See also his *Cleansing Baptism* (Manchester, England: Star Hall, n.d.).

29. Morrison, *The Baptism with the Holy Ghost*, p. 31, the fourth of six propositions expounded in this pamphlet.

30. E. P. Ellyson, *Doctrinal Studies* (Kansas City, Mo.: Nazarene Publishing House, 1936), p. 106.

31. Russell R. Byrum, *Holy Spirit Baptism and the Second Cleansing* (Anderson, Ind.: Gospel Trumpet, 1923; reprint, Guthrie, Okla.: Faith Publishing House, n.d.), p. 18.

32. "J. D.," "Entire Sanctification and the Fulness of the Spirit," *Guide to Holiness* 29 (April 1856): 97.

33. Ibid., p. 98.

34. Arthur S. Clibborn, "Testimony," *Divine Life* 5 (December 1881): 114.

35. "Enquiries Answered," *Divine Life* 1 (15 June 1877): 35.

36. Asa Mahan, "Questions Answered," *Divine Life* 6 (December 1882): 109–10.

37. Asbury Lowrey, "Is The Baptism of the Holy Ghost a Third Blessing?" *Divine Life* 3 (September 1879): 47.

38. Ibid.

39. George Douglas Watson, *The Secret of Spiritual Power* (Boston: Christian Witness, 1894; reprint, Noblesville, Ind.: Newby Book Room, n.d.), p. 3.

40. Edwin Pope, " 'With fire' as well as 'with the Holy Ghost,' " *Divine Life* (October 1885): 95.

41. On Irwin, see the work of Vinson Synan, *The Old-Time Power* (Franklin Springs, Ga.: Advocate Press, 1973), a history of the Pentecostal Holiness Church, especially ch. 5, and *The Holiness-Pentecostal Movement in the United States* (Grand Rapids: Wm. B. Eerdmans, 1971), ch. 3. See also the thesis by Craig Fankhauser, "The Heritage of Faith: An Historical Evaluation of the Holiness Movement in America" (M.A. thesis, Pittsburg [Kansas] State University, 1983), especially ch. 6.

42. His two most important statements appear to be in tracts, *The Baptism of Fire* and *Pyrophobia*. The former, a description of his own experience, first appeared in the *Way of Faith* 6 (13 November 1895): 2, and in the *Way of Faith* 7 (28 October 1896): 2.

43. *Pyrophobia*, p. 2.

44. *Constitution and General Rules of the Fire-Baptized Holiness Church* (Royston, Ga.: Live Coals Press, 1905), p. 3.

45. See Vinson Synan, *The Old-Time Power*, p. 93, and also a mocking of this pattern by A. M. Hills, "Fanaticism Among Holiness People," *Holiness Advocate* (1 April 1903): 5.

46. S. P. Jacobs, "Receiving the Holy Spirit," *Canadian Methodist and Holiness Era* 2 (13 September 1893): 146, apparently "selected" from *Divine Life* and later to be reprinted by the Canadian Methodists with an essay by R. C. Horner under the title *Power for Service* (Toronto: William Briggs, n.d.), pp. 3–18. See also the book-length expansion of such discussions in S. P. Jacobs, *The Real Christian* (n.p.: S. P. Jacobs, 1899).

47. On Horner, see Brian R. Ross, "Ralph Cecil Horner: A Methodist Sectarian Deposed, 1887–1895," *Journal of the Canadian Church Historical Society* 19 (March-June 1977): 94–103, and Harold William Pointen, "The Holiness Movement Church in Canada" (unpublished B.D. thesis, Emmanuel College of Victoria University, 1950).

48. R. C. Horner, *Notes on Boland; or, Mr. Wesley and the Second Work of Grace* (Boston and Chicago: McDonald and Gill, 1893; also Toronto: William Briggs, 1893).

49. Ralph C. Horner, *Pentecost* (Toronto: William Briggs, 1891), p. 138.

50. R. C. Horner, *Bible Doctrines* (Ottawa: Holiness Movement Publishing House, 1909). Compare the somewhat less-Wesleyan expression of this movement by Wilfred Flower, *The Promise of the Father; or, The Theology of the Third Blessing*, with an introduction by R. C. Horner (Ottawa: Holiness Movement Publishing House, 1906; reprint, Brockville, Ont.: Christian Standard Publishing House, 1931).

51. *Ralph C. Horner, Evangelist: Reminiscences from His Own Pen, also Reports on Five Typical Sermons* (Brockville, Ont.: Published for Mrs. A. E. Horner by Standard Church Book Room, n.d.), pp. 13–14.

52. See, for example, W. J. Nesbitt, "Holiness and Power," *Holiness Era* 7 (20 April 1898): 60.

53. See such refutations of the Hornerite teachings as Peter Wiseman (who came out of the Holiness Movement Church), *Entire Sanctification Before Pentecost: Is It Methodistic and Scriptural?* (Chicago: Christian Witness, 1934); John R. Church (from the Methodist Episcopal Church, South), *Which Is Right? One- Two- or Three-Works of Grace?* (Louisville: Pentecostal Publishing, n.d.); and Charles V. Fairbairn (a Canadian Methodist who became a Free Methodist bishop), *Purity and Power; or, the Baptism with the Holy Ghost* (Chicago: Christian Witness, 1930).

54. See Horner, *Bible Doctrines*, especially vol. 2.

55. Horner, *Pentecost*, p. 140.

56. Synan, *The Old-Time Power*, p. 84.

57. I have seen Ralph C. Horner's *Feast of 1905, Feast of 1907*, and *Feast of 1909* (Ottawa: Holiness Movement Publishing House, 1905, 1907, and 1909), each concluded with "testimonies" and "experiences" of participants.

58. See Ross, "Ralph Cecil Horner," especially p. 99.

59. R. C. Horner, *Wesley on Prostration, etc.* (Toronto: William Briggs, 1889), a collection of passages of Wesley's journals and letters on "prostration, shouting and laughing" as they occurred under the ministry of Wesley; and W. B. Burns, *Demonstrations of the Spirit* (Ottawa: Holiness Movement Publishing House, 1908), an abridgment of an earlier work by G. W. Henry, *Shouting: Genuine and Spurious* (Oneida, N. Y.: Published and bound by the author, 1859).

60. Charles G. Finney, "The Enduement of Power," appended to Asa Mahan, *The Baptism of the Holy Ghost* (London: Elliot Stock, n.d.), especially pp. 231–34.

61. These women were "Sister Hawxhurst" and "Auntie Sarah Cooke." The latter's account of the event may be found in Sarah A. Cooke, *The Handmaiden of the Lord; or, Wayside Sketches* (Chicago: S. B. Shaw, 1900), pp. 42–43, as "Mr. Moody's Pentecost."

62. These words are from "Mr. Moody, in relating the incident years after," as reported by his son William R. Moody, *The Life of Dwight L. Moody* (New York: Fleming H. Revell, 1900), p. 147. The most extended account is in J. C. Pollock, *Moody: A Biographical Portrait of the Pacesetter in Modern Mass Evangelism* (New York: Macmillan, 1963), pp. 84–91.

63. "Mr. D. L. Moody on the Baptism of the Holy Spirit," *King's Highway, a Journal of Scriptural Holiness* (London) 8 (1879): 66.

64. W. H. Daniels, ed., *Moody: His Words, Work, and Workers* (New York: Nelson and Phillips, 1877), pp. 396–403.

65. D. L. Moody, *Secret Power; or The Secret of Success in Christian Life and Christian Work* (Chicago: Fleming H. Revell, 1881).

66. Stanley N. Gundry, *Love Them In: The Proclamation Theology of D. L. Moody* (Chicago: Moody, 1976), p. 154.

67. The differences between Moody and Torrey may be most easily grasped by a close comparison of addresses on successive days of the 1894 Northfield Conferences: D. L. Moody, "The Anointing of the Holy Spirit for Service," and R. A. Torrey, "The Baptism with the Holy Spirit," in D. L. Pierson, ed., *Northfield Echoes* (East Northfield, Mass.: Conference Book Store, 1894), pp. 323–28 and 329–39.

68. This is in chapter 7 of R. A. Torrey's widely circulated booklet, *Why God Used D. L. Moody* (Chicago: Moody Bible Institute, 1923; reprint, Monroeville, Pa.: Banner Publications, n.d.), pp. 55–63.

69. R. A. Torrey, *How to Obtain Fullness of Power* (New York: Fleming H. Revell, 1897).

70. R. A. Torrey, *The Baptism With the Holy Spirit* (New York: Fleming H. Revell, [c. 1895 and 1897]).

71. Ibid., pp. 9–14.

72. Ibid., p. 15.

73. A. M. Hills, *Pentecost Rejected and the Effect on the Churches* (Cincinnati: God's Revivalist Office, 1902).

74. See William G. McLoughlin, Jr., *Modern Revivalism* (New York: Ronald Press, 1959), pp. 377ff., and Ford C. Ottman, *John Wilbur Chapman* (New York: Doubleday, Page, 1920).

75. J. Wilbur Chapman, *Received Ye the Holy Ghost?* (New York: Fleming H. Revell, 1894).

76. Ford C. Ottman, *Have Ye Known the Holy Ghost?* (Albany: Evangelistic Publishing, 1895).

77. On this movement, see David D. Bundy, *Keswick: A Bibliographic Introduction to the Higher Life Movements*, Occasional Bibliographical Papers of the B. L. Fisher Library, no. 3 (Wilmore, Ky.: B. L. Fisher Library, Asbury Theological Seminary, 1975). The standard interpretation is Steven Barabas, *So Great Salvation: The History and Message of the Keswick Convention* (Westwood, N.J.: Fleming H. Revell, 1952). A representative collection of convention addresses may be found in Herbert F. Stevenson, *Keswick's Authentic Voice* (Grand Rapids: Zondervan, 1959), though more detail is regularly available in the annual *Keswick Week.*

78. The most recent sketch of these interconnections is in Dieter, *The Holiness Revival of the Nineteenth Century*, ch. 4, summarized as "From Vineland and Mannheim to Brighton and Berlin: The Holiness Revival in Nineteenth Century Europe, *Wesleyan Theological Journal* 9 (Spring 1974): 15–27.

79. Reported in *Account of the Union Meeting for the Promotion of Scriptural Holiness Held at Oxford August 29 to September 7, 1874* (distrib-

uted by a number of publishers in the USA, including the Willard Tract Repository, Fleming H. Revell, and others).

80. *Record of the Convention for the Promotion of Scriptural Holiness Held at Brighton, May 29 to June 7, 1875* (Brighton: W. J. Smith; London: S. W. Partridge, 1875).

81. See Barabas, *So Great Salvation*, and Bishop Handley C. G. Moule et al., *Holiness by Faith: A Manual of Keswick Teaching* (London: Religious Tract Society, 1904) for this teaching.

82. These discussions are reflected in the reports above, though they provide no actual texts revealing Mahan's teaching at this time.

83. For further bibliography and lists of the works of these figures, see Bundy, *Keswick*, and part 3 on the "Keswick Movement" in Charles E. Jones, *A Guide to the Study of the Holiness Movement* (Metuchen, N.J.: Scarecrow Press, 1974), pp. 485–511.

84. See A. B. Simpson's exposition of these themes in *The Four-Fold Gospel* (New York: Christian Alliance Publishing, 1890), reprinted 1925 with an introduction by Frederic H. Senft, or an early exposition as "The Fullness of Jesus" in G. P. Pardington, *Twenty-Five Wonderful Years, 1889–1914: A Popular Sketch of the Christian and Missionary Alliance* (New York: Christian Alliance Publishing, 1914), ch. 3.

85. Simpson, *The Four-Fold Gospel* (1925 ed.), pp. 33, 46.

86. Ibid., pp. 39–40.

87. A. J. Gordon, *The Two-Fold Life; or, Christ's Work for Us and Christ's Work in Us* (New York: Fleming H. Revell, 1895), p. 12.

88. A. J. Gordon, *The Ministry of the Spirit* (New York: Fleming H. Revell, 1894), pp. ix–x.

89. Ibid., p. 67.

90. Ibid., pp. 69–70.

91. A. B. Simpson, *The Holy Spirit; or, Power from on High* (New York: Christian Alliance Publishing, 1895–96), 2:43.

270. Blessed Be the Great Atonement.

A. B. S.　　　　　　　　　　　　　　　　　　A. B. SIMPSON.

1. Bless-ed be the glo - rious tid - ings To a suff'ring world re-vealed;
2. Je - sus ev - er welcomed the sufferers, To His mer - cy who ap-pealed;
3. Bless-ed be the sa - cred anoint-ing, By the Ho - ly Spir - it sealed;

Je - sus has atoned for our sick-ness, And by His stripes we are healed.
Still He bids us bring Him our sick-ness, For by His stripes we are healed.
Je - sus lay Thine own hand up - on us, For by Thy stripes we are healed.

CHORUS.

Bless - ed be the great a - tone - ment, To a suff-'ring world re - vealed;

Bless-ed be the great Phy - si - cian, For by His stripes we are healed.

4 Saviour, mid the arrows of Satan,
　Be our refuge and our shield;
Safely shall we walk through all danger,
　For by Thy stripes we are healed.

5 Jesus to Thy glory forever,
　All our members we would yield;
Never let us cease to remember,
　That by Thy stripes we are healed.

CHAPTER V

THE RISE OF THE DIVINE HEALING MOVEMENT

Perhaps even more characteristic of Pentecostalism than the doctrine of the baptism of the Spirit is its celebration of miracles of divine healing as part of God's salvation and as evidence of the presence of divine power in the church. The roots of this teaching are complex and difficult to trace, in part because of the problems of distinguishing the superstitions of popular piety, the tendency of Christians in all times and places to pray for relief from distress and misfortune, and a variety of developed doctrines of the possibility of divine healing in direct response to the faith of the believer. But using clues from the historical sources we have discovered with regard to the development of the doctrine of Pentecostal Spirit baptism, we may outline the rise of this doctrine and understand how it emerged from the same revival of perfectionist themes.

We cannot resolve here the many complicated questions about how to understand the permanent validity of the motif of healing in the Christian tradition. Pentecostalism, however these questions may be answered, understood itself to be restoring a lost concern of the early church.

Debates about the exact nature and role of healing in the early church will no doubt continue for some time. Morton Kelsey,[1] relying to great extent on the work of Evelyn Frost,[2] argues that the early church was characterized by an emphasis

115

on healing that was variously related to the positive valuation of the body reflected in the prevalence of the doctrine of the resurrection of the body, a "realistic" doctrine of the atonement that stressed Christ's victory over the powers and evil forces that impinge on human life, and a model of redemption that highlighted the therapeutic effects of grace, especially as appropriated through the sacraments. Such themes apparently faded in the wake of the Constantinian church as miracles of healing were relegated more to signs of exemplary sainthood and the transformation of the anointing of the sick into the sacrament of extreme unction. Kelsey, concerned to reestablish certain Platonist themes in modern Jungian dress, places special emphasis on the rise of the Aristotelian and modern world views more closed to models of divine intervention outside the natural order of events.

The Protestant polemic against alleged Catholic "superstition" and a related concern to pare back the number of the sacraments contributed to this tendency. It did not help Martin Luther, for example, that one of the crucial texts appeared in the Book of James:

> For Christ did not make anointing with oil a Sacrament, nor do St. James' words apply to the present day. For in those days the sick were often cured through a miracle and the earnest prayer of faith, as we see in James and Mark 6.[3]

There is some suggestion that Luther altered this opinion toward the end of his life.[4] Later advocates of healing doctrines have often pointed to an incident in which Philip Melanchthon was restored to health after Luther's own prayers; but there is little doubt that the thrust of Luther's thought, which was to help set the tone for much of Protestantism, was to minimize themes of divine healing.

The Reformed tradition has, if anything, more easily relegated the gift of healing to another age. John Calvin, commenting on extreme unction and James 5:14–15, for example would insist that

> James spake for that same time when the church still enjoyed a blessing of God . . . but we experience otherwise. . . . the Lord is indeed present with his people in

every age; and he heals their weaknesses as often as necessary, no less than that of old; still he does not put forth these manifest powers, nor dispense miracles through apostles' hands. For that was a temporary gift and also quickly perished.[5]

If anything, this "dispensational" assignment of healing to the apostolic era became more rigid and the assumed position of the Reformed tradition. Thus Puritan John Owen distinguished between ordinary and extraordinary gifts, relegating the latter to the time of revelation:

The reason of these extraordinary operations in extraordinary cases seems to have been the encouragement of that great faith which was then stirred up in them that beheld those miraculous operations; which was of singular advantage unto the propagation of the gospel; for the *magical* superstition of the Roman church, sundry ways endeavouring to imitate those inimitable acts of sovereign divine power, hath been a dishonour to Christian religion.[6]

The extreme development of this position took place probably in the nineteenth-century "Old School" Calvinism of Benjamin B. Warfield, who used this doctrine, as we have already indicated, to attack various of the pre-Pentecostal healers at the turn of the century.[7]

WESLEY AND DIVINE HEALING

Our survey of the rise of the doctrine of the Pentecostal baptism in the Spirit directed our attention more to the perfectionist and Methodist traditions, especially the figure of John Wesley. Here too we must turn in that direction, and again we find the evidence ambiguous.

Wesley was deeply influenced by Puritanism, but also was in tension with it. Moreover, through his parents Wesley was a product of the high church Anglican tradition with its tendency to preserve a doctrine of the miraculous. He was also concerned, as we have seen, with restoring the faith and practice of the ante-Nicene church. Perhaps even more conflict-producing would be the impact of Quakerism[8] and

Pietism, to which we shall turn in a moment. We have already indicated Wesley's ambivalence in seeking to restore the supernatural work of the Holy Spirit in the early church while resisting gifts and "supernatural operations" for grace and ethical transformation. Here we must probe more deeply into Wesley's relationship to subsequent teachings on healing.

Self-conscious advocates were later to claim that "John Wesley was orthodox on divine healing"[9]—though the story that was most often marshalled to support that claim was one in which Wesley's headache and his horse's lameness were "healed" instantaneously to permit him to "go on and preach the gospel." But the picture is much more complex, and it is difficult to discern the shape that his convictions would have taken at a later time. Wesley was not above the superstitions of his own age and reported spiritual phenomena that would probably be discounted today, such as Jeffery, the poltergeist that inhabited the Epworth rectory, and other psychic experiences.[10] Wesley's notorious but widely distributed *Primitive Physic*[11] also appears quaint and even superstitious by modern medical standards, though one could argue that in its own age Wesley's guidebook used the best of contemporary medical science alongside more popular folk remedies. And though Wesley was critical of self-serving doctors and their failure to provide care for the poor, it is noteworthy that he in no sense opposed medical science.

Yet it is true, as Morton Kelsey and other advocates are quick to point out, that Wesley's *Journal* often mentions events that would today count as miraculous healings.[12] In this, however, even apart from the way in which such experiences might be understood from a more modern perspective, we should note the level of Wesley's own reticence and ambivalence about such themes. Far from the intense advocacy of modern faith healers was Wesley's more detached attitude, illustrated, for example, in the following journal entry of 20 December 1742:

> When I came home they told me the physician said he did not expect Mr. Meyrick would live till the morning. . . . A few of us immediately joined in prayer (I relate the naked fact); before we had done his sense and his speech

returned. Now he that will account for this by natural
causes has my free leave; but I choose to say this is the
power of God.[13]

Challenged on this and similar reports, Wesley replied, "But
what does all this prove? Not that I claim any gift above other
men, but only that I believe that God now hears and answers
prayer even beyond the ordinary course of nature."[14]

But as we shall see, probably more important for what
would follow was Wesley's emphasis on what we have called a
"therapeutic" model of grace and salvation. Grace was the cure
for the disease of sin, and the two-fold nature of the Wesleyan
view of salvation (justification *and* sanctification) was often
described as the "double cure." Wesley's strong sense of the
present power of God to restore the fallen creation cast a new
light on his concern for physical health (evidenced not only in
the *Primitive Physic* but also in his work for health care and
dispensaries for the poor) and would eventually help raise
more insistent questions about the extent to which healing and
restoration of health would be included in the benefits of grace
to be expected in this life. If, indeed, we might be fully
restored spiritually to the full image of God, to what extent
might physical restoration also be expected, since disease is
ultimately to be traced to the sin of Adam?

These questions were not directly pursued by Wesley
with the intensity with which they would be probed in the
next century. Raising these questions requires that a few more
themes be added to the mix. And to trace these we must turn
first to Pietism.

THE INFLUENCE OF PIETISM

Pietism may have been one of the most important forces
in the rise of the doctrine of divine healing.[15] It was very likely
also a force that shaped Wesley's thought at this point.
Pietism's biblical realism and pastoral orientation combined
with a belief in the continuation of miracles produced a
doctrine of healing through prayer and faith. This may be seen
in several of the comments of John Albert Bengel in his
Gnomon of the New Testament, that popular commentary that

became the major source of Wesley's *Explanatory Notes on the New Testament.* On Mark 16:17 Bengel remarks:

> Even in our day, faith has in every believer a hidden power of a miraculous character: every effect resulting from our prayers is really miraculous, even though that miraculous character be not apparent; although in many, both on account of their own feebleness, and on account of the unworthiness of the world,—not merely because [as some say] the Church, being once planted, needs not the continuance of miracles, though no doubt the early miracles of the New Testament have "made" for the Lord Jesus "an everlasting name" (comp. Isa. lxiii.12), that power does not exert itself in our day. Signs were in the beginning the props and stays of faith: now they are also the object of faith. At Leonberg, a town of Wirtemberg [A.C. 1644, thirteenth Sunday after Trinity], a girl of twenty years of age was so disabled in her limbs, as hardly to be able to creep along by the help of crutches; but whilst the Dean [Raumeier was his name] was, from the pulpit, dwelling on the miraculous power of Jesus' name, she suddenly was raised up and restored to the use of her limbs.[16]

On James 5:14–15, Bengel comments that "the only design of that *anointing* originally was miraculous healing" and that

> it even seems to have been given by God with this intent, that it might always remain in the Church, as a specimen of the other gifts: just as the portion of Manna laid up in the ark was a proof of the ancient miracle.[17]

Both these statements are reproduced in abridged form in Wesley's *Explanatory Notes.*

Such themes in Pietism were restrained and not the dominant motifs, but they were present and manifested themselves at various points that began to include an interest in demon possession and exorcism.[18] For our purpose the most significant manifestation of these themes was in the work of Johann Christoph Blumhardt, a "latter day" Pietist of the nineteenth century.

Blumhardt is known by his battle cry "Jesus is Victor" (appropriated by Karl Barth and others in contemporary theology), which expressed his sense of the ongoing victorious struggle of Christ with evil forces and sin in the world. He argued that fundamentally "sin is the cause of sickness" and therefore that "the forgiveness of sins and healing stand in an inner relationship to one another."[19] This constellation of convictions led Blumhardt to expect healing, or at least improvement of health, in response to the gospel. His sense of the reality and power of evil also allowed him to entertain ideas of demon possession, and he became a center of controversy over the case of Gottliebin Dittus, a young woman of Möttlingen, whose "possession" was overcome under the ministry of Blumhardt and led to the theme "Jesus is Victor."[20]

Blumhardt's *Kampf* in Möttlingen was widely reported and brought him to the attention of many who sought his help. Such demands and his own interest led him in 1852 to Bad Boll, a Württemberg spa, where he established a community for those seeking spiritual and physical help.[21] Meanwhile a similar home was emerging under the ministry of Dorothea Trudel of the Swiss village of Männedorf on Lake Zürich—in spite of local resistance, including prosecution and fines, to her claims of healing and miracles.[22] Reports of the work of Trudel (and her successor, Samuel Zeller) and Blumhardt began to circulate during the 1850s through the English-speaking world, where developments of another sort had drawn new attention to the "prayer of faith."

DEVELOPMENTS IN ENGLAND AND AMERICA

In England, the work of George Müller, an early member of the developing sect of Plymouth Brethren, was attracting international attention. Combining the orphanage work of Pietist August Hermann Francke (1663–1727) of Halle, Germany, and the emerging "faith work" principles of Johannes Evangelista Gossner (1773–1858) of Berlin,[23] Müller (who was born in Prussia and studied at Halle) founded in Bristol, England, in 1835 the orphanage for which he and his methods were to become widely known.[24] Concerned about the extent to which Christian institutions depended on "*unconverted persons of rank or wealth*" and an emphasis on (exaggerated) reports of success for support, Müller vowed never to seek funds, but rather to work "*by prayer and faith*," believing that

God would supply their needs. The stories that circulated about the orphanage often emphasized that in each frequent extremity, the Lord provided exactly what was needed, often down to the very cent required at the very moment that disaster was imminent. Müller advocated "importunity in supplication" and confidence in expecting answers to prayer, insisting that his was no special gift of faith, but the common experience available to all Christians.

In America, evangelist Charles G. Finney was beginning to advocate "prevailing" or "effectual prayer." One of the controversial "new measures" of his revivalism was the practice of prayer for the conversion of specific sinners or "mere professors of religion." Characteristic of his style was the conviction that any failure to achieve revival was due to human failure rather than God's mysterious and inscrutable will (as had been the more normal conviction in the Great Awakenings of the previous century). Similarly with prayer, Finney insisted that in order to "prevail in prayer," one must "pray for a definite object," "pray in faith," and "expect to obtain the blessing." Among Finney's illustrations was a story of the Jesuit missionary Francis Xavier, who so fervently prayed for a sick man that he recovered.

Finney was convinced that such "faith *always obtains the object.*" Failure to get an answer indicated that one was out of the will of God—or not really praying "in faith." Such a position led Finney to suggest that Christ prayed in the Garden merely that he should not die *before* going to the cross and that Paul had not really prayed "in faith" in asking to be relieved of his "thorn in the flesh."[25] But Finney did not shrink from such conclusions in spite of the accusations of his opponents that this put prayer on a "cause-and-effect basis" that permitted "manipulation of God."

"HEALING BY FAITH"

With these developments, the stage had been set for Charles Cullis, an Episcopalian homeopathic physician in Boston who did "more than any other man to bring healing by faith to the attention of the church in the last century."[26] The death of his wife awakened in Cullis a spiritual quest for "a better heart and a better channel for my earnings." Part of this had to do with the truth of the Bible and the extent to which "I might appropriate the promises to myself." Cullis responded with the vow that "I will take every precept and promise in the Bible as my own, just as if my own name, Charles Cullis, was written in every one of them." Soon after, on 19 August 1862, his reading 2 Thessalonians 2:13 raised for Cullis the question of entire sanctification and he "prayed God to sanctify me wholly by the Spirit, and destroy all selfishness and unbelief in my heart."[27]

The call to his new work came about two years later when Cullis began to think of founding a "home for indigent and incurable consumptives" committed to the "faith principles" of George Müller. By the end of the century this new work had grown to include an extensive publishing program, a deaconess school, homes for spinal and cancer cases, a church, several city rescue missions, a program of foreign missions, a college for blacks in Virginia, and other activities.

As we have seen, Cullis became a major leader of the broader Holiness movement in the wake of the revival of 1857–58. His work was permeated with a call to the "higher spiritual experience" of entire sanctification, especially in a Tuesday "consecration meeting." His Willard Tract Repository became a major publisher of Holiness literature in the 1870s and 1880s. His (significantly named) Faith Training College, announced in 1876, included among its first faculty, besides Cullis himself as president, such Holiness leaders as W. E. Boardman, A. B. Earle, Daniel Steele, and William McDonald. The object of his journal *Times of Refreshing*, founded in 1879, was "to present Jesus as a full and perfect savior," a goal met in part by reporting Holiness conventions and activities.

Faith Cures, published in 1879, tells how Cullis moved toward the doctrine of faith healing. For

> several years my mind had been exercised before God as to whether it was not his will that the Work of Faith in which he had placed me, should extend to the cure of disease, as well as the alleviation of the miseries of the afflicted.[28]

The key text in James 5:14–15 prompted Cullis to enquire among "earnest Christians" about "instances of answers to prayer for the healing of the body." In the midst of this search a book about Dorothea Trudel fell into his hands. He immediately put out his own expanded version of the book[29] and in 1873 made his own pilgrimage to Männedorf, then announced in his annual report "the call of the Lord which had come to him to use his faith in praying for the healing of the sick"[30] and included testimonies of those healed under his ministry. The work was expanded and was advocated by Cullis in a series of conventions in such centers as Framingham, Massachusetts; Old Orchard, Maine; and finally at Intervale, New Hampshire, where new buildings had to be constructed to handle the crowds.

The significant role of the Holiness doctrines in radicalizing and facilitating the rise of the "faith cure" is even more clearly illustrated by those who followed Cullis in this work. Presbyterian W. E. Boardman, whose *Higher Christian Life* played such a role in spreading Holiness doctrines beyond Methodism and whose *Faith-Work* publicized the work of Charles Cullis, described the development of his own experience in the following words:

> More than thirty years ago, ten years after my conversion, the Lord Jesus graciously revealed Himself to me as always with me, my Saviour from my sins, and brought me to accept Him and rest in Him each moment for present deliverance and constant keeping in perfect peace, as truly as He before had revealed Himself to me and brought me to accept Him, as my sin-bearing and pardoning Saviour. The new light that then opened upon my soul was marvelous . . . and one of the things that came to me with great force and sweetness was the office work of our gracious Lord as the Healer.[31]

Dr. Robert McKilliam, a surgeon who read the manuscript of Boardman's book, *"The Lord That Healeth Thee,"* added a footnote to the text, noting

> an interesting order of manifestations of Himself by the Lord to His child. First, as the sin-bearing and pardoning Saviour; next in the ever-abiding presence as the Deliverer

from present sin in its power, and as the keeper of the
heart in perfect peace; and lastly, as the Deliverer from all
the consequences of sin, and from all the heritage of sinful
flesh—disease, &c [etc.]. Something like this, I believe,
will always be found in the experiences of those who are
going in to prove the fulness of God in Christ.[32]

Boardman, therefore, concluded that healing through
faith is "itself part and parcel of the Gospel"[33]—of the
redemption to be sought in Christ. The crucial biblical text for
Cullis had been James 5:14–15; for Boardman it was Psalm 3,
especially verses 2 and 3: "Bless the LORD, O my soul, and
forget not all his benefits: who forgiveth all thine iniquities:
who healeth all thy diseases" (KJV). Especially important was
the Hebrew parallelism in verse 3, which Boardman understood to bring together "forgiveness" and "healing." The
restoration motifs of the Wesleyan tradition are here being
extended. "Our completeness in Him cannot be actualized
until our faith welcomes Him in whom dwells the All-fulness,
as our Fulness of life and health in the body as well as in the
soul."[34]

Though he moved to England, Boardman maintained
contact with Cullis and other leaders of the American healing
currents, most of whom he invited to an International Confer-
ence on Divine Healing and True Holiness in London in 1884.
Shortly before that, Boardman had established with Mrs.
Michael Baxter and Charlotte C. Murray a home, "Bethshan,"
that eventually required a six-hundred-seat hall to serve the
Wednesday afternoon meetings for holiness and healing. Mrs.
Baxter was the wife of the editor of the influential *Christian
Herald* and herself wrote on the question of healing.[35]

Healing and holiness were even more closely connected
in the work of Episcopalian Carrie Judd Montgomery, who
through the influence of Mrs. Edward Mix, a black woman,
turned quickly to Dr. Cullis and became part of the network of
those advocating faith healing. As Carrie F. Judd she founded
Faith Rest Cottage in Buffalo in 1882 and in 1880 authored *The
Prayer of Faith*, which saw many private editions. It was also
published in this country by Fleming H. Revell, the dominant
publisher associated with the Moody revivals, and in England
by the *Christian Herald* and was translated into at least four

European languages. After her marriage to George Montgomery
she moved to San Francisco and then to Oakland to found the
Home of Peace and finally was swept into Pentecostalism in
the wake of the Azusa Street Revival.

Carrie Judd Montgomery's magazine, *Triumphs of Faith,*
"a monthly journal devoted to faith-healing and to the
promotion of Christian Holiness," reveals closer identification
with the Methodistic wing of the Holiness movement in
America. The opening editorial is reminiscent of the altar
theology of Phoebe Palmer:

> Very simple and plain is our part in the obtaining of God's
> promised blessings, and this *laying hold by faith* is much
> easier of accomplishment than most of us are willing to
> believe. Our part is simply to reckon our prayer as
> answered, and God's part is to *make faith's reckonings
> real.* This is by no means a question of *feeling* faith, but of
> *acting* faith. . . .
>
> If we will constantly reckon our evil nature dead, we shall
> feel no more need of giving it our attention, and God will
> make faith's reckonings real to us. . . .
>
> And to my dear invalid readers, let me say that what is
> true of this precious spiritual healing is likewise true of
> physical healing by the "Great Physician." Christ bore our
> sickness as well as our sins, and if we may reckon
> ourselves free from the one, why not from the other?[36]

These columns also carried one of the most systematic
developments of the analogy of spiritual and physical healing
under the series title *Gospel Parallelisms: Illustrated in the
Healing of Body and Soul* by R. L. Stanton, a former president
of Miami (Ohio) University and a moderator of the general
assembly of the Presbyterian Church. Montgomery later issued
these articles in book form, and they became an important
defense of the doctrine of healing through faith. Stanton
argued that "the atonement of Christ lays a foundation equally
for deliverance from sin and for deliverance from disease; that
complete provision has been made for both."[37] Stanton
appealed to the same Hebrew parallelism that lay at the root of
Boardman's thought—though this time as found in Isaiah
53:3–5 and quoted in Matthew 8:16–17—to argue that "the

healing of the sick was one of the blessings which Christ's atonement was designed to provide for."[38]

Here we see again that "in order to [achieve] the full renovation of man, it is essential that the remedy provided should contemplate his bodily healing as truly as his soul-cure."[39] Such argument leads to the restorationist claims that

> when the primitive faith and practice of the Church shall be restored throughout Christendom, of putting the "healing of the sick" and "preaching the Kingdom of God" on the same plane of duty and privilege, the Church may expect "the Lord working with them," and confirming the word with "signs following"; even restoring the Church's lost faith and power to its ancient measure.[40]

"HEALING IN THE ATONEMENT"

These developments in the doctrines of healing set the stage for one further teaching, that of "healing in the Atonement." In this matter two figures who held a very prominent place are the same pair with whom we ended the previous chapter: A. B. Simpson and A. J. Gordon.

In 1881, under the ministry of Charles Cullis at Old Orchard, Simpson, then serving the Thirteenth Street Presbyterian Church in New York City, became convinced of "divine healing" (as he preferred to call it) though several previous experiences had prepared him for it.[41] A few years later, perhaps at Boardman's convention in London, Simpson would describe this as one of three great epochal religious experiences in his life:

> Some twenty-seven years ago, I floundered for ten months in the waters of despondency, and I got out of them just by believing in Jesus as my Saviour. About twelve years ago I got into another deep experience of conviction, and I got out of that by believing in Jesus as my Sanctifier. After years of teaching from and waiting on Him, the Lord Jesus Christ showed me four years ago that it was His blessed will to be my complete Saviour for body as well as soul.[42]

Simpson opened the Berachah Home ("House of Blessing") in 1884 and started a "Friday Meeting" that crowded the

auditorium of New York City's Gospel Tabernacle. Through
these activities and other work at such places as Old Orchard,
Simpson became second only to Charles Cullis as a leader of
the growing Faith Cure movement.

Simpson's major work on the subject, *The Gospel of
Healing*, was primarily an anthology of tracts that had
circulated widely before being collected in 1885. His treatment
differs little from others of the period, except perhaps in its
focus on Christ and his "fullness" as the key to both
sanctification and healing, as may be seen especially in a later
collection of his writings on the question, *The Lord for the
Body*. Part of Simpson's concern here seems to have been to
have "accentuated the positive" by avoiding such questions as
the eradication of sin. In view of what would follow, it is
important to notice the radical character of his teachings. First,
healing was provided in the Atonement:

> Redemption finds its center in the Cross of our Lord Jesus
> Christ and there we must look for the fundamental
> principle of Divine Healing, which rests on the atoning
> sacrifice. This necessarily follows from the first principle
> we have stated. If sickness be the result of the Fall, it must
> be included in the atonement of Christ which reaches as
> "far as the curse is found."[43]

Second, in his earlier book, Simpson also argued against
the use of "means" (i.e., against doctors and medicine) in favor
of divine healing:

> If that be God's way of healing, then other methods must
> be man's ways, and there must be some risk in deliber-
> ately repudiating the former for the latter. . . . for the
> trusting and obedient child of God there is the more
> excellent way which his Word has clearly prescribed.[44]

A close colleague of Simpson who shared the same ethos
was Adoniram Judson Gordon. As pastor of the Clarendon
Street Baptist Church in Boston, A. J. Gordon worked out his
teachings on healing somewhat more in dialogue with the
emerging Christian Science of Mary Baker Eddy, but he clearly
shared most features of the Holiness tradition. In the early
1870s Gordon became associated as a trustee with the "faith
work" of Charles Cullis. Later in that decade, during D. L.

Moody's campaign in Boston in 1877, Gordon observed several instantaneous healings and overcame his initial reservations about the teaching.

Gordon's very popular *The Ministry of Healing* breathes very much the spirit and sources of Cullis's thought. The chapter on the testimony of the Scripture begins with the statement that "in the atonement of Christ there seems to be foundation laid for faith in bodily healing."[45] Gordon carefully avoided the Holiness doctrines of eradication and second blessing, but he clearly paralleled sanctification and healing as the two-fold work of the Spirit whose benefits may be at least partially received in this life. Gordon saw "two streams of blessings started from the personal ministry of our Lord, a stream of healing and a stream of regeneration; the one for the recovery of the body and the other for the recovery of the soul."[46] He insisted that both were valid for the whole dispensation of the Spirit.

Perhaps a better barometer of the development of the healing doctrines was Captain R. Kelso Carter, an associate of A. B. Simpson in the early years of the Christian and Missionary Alliance. Variously a Presbyterian and a Methodist, Carter was a mathematician, novelist, sheep rancher, and physician, as well as one of the most prominent defenders of faith healing. Carter claimed to have been healed of a "stubborn heart disease" under the ministry of Charles Cullis in 1879 and was associated with many facets of his ministries. In 1882 Carter and a man named George McCalla together issued the call for the first convention on the subject. Carter's book *The Atonement for Sin and Sickness; or, A Full Salvation for Soul and Body* (1884) was an early popular defense. Something of Carter's role, and also the extent to which these questions agitated a wider audience in the culture, is illustrated in the fact that he was chosen to represent the affirmative side in an 1887 debate on the question of faith healing in *Century* magazine.

Carter's book, perhaps more than any other, clearly reveals the Holiness roots of the healing doctrine. The first two chapters argue in turn the Atonement basis for "pardon for all past sins" and the "cleansing from all inbred sin" before developing a biblical basis for "bodily healing, as provided for in the Atonement." Carter cites various Wesleyan writers to affirm that "only in the Wesleyan view of the matter is the Atonement believed to be *instantaneous* in its application to unrighteousness, or inward depravity."[47] This became the model for healing because "the Atonement has provided for the body all that it has provided for the soul."[48] Thus "he who finds in Jesus the perfect cleansing of the soul and the keeping power against all sin, can be equally consistent in placing his body beneath the same wonderful salvation."[49]

This pattern was true of Carter's own experience: "I began to believe that my Divine Master not only took upon himself my sins, but also bore my bodily sicknesses, and that I might, through simple faith, be free from the latter, just as well as from the former."[50] Nor was Carter reluctant to universalize his own experience:

> It is a remarkable fact, that no one has been known to seek the healing power for the body, without receiving a distinct spiritual baptism; and further, that everyone known to the writer (a very large number), who has been *entirely healed* in body, is or has become a believer in and professor of entire sanctification of soul.[51]

SECOND THOUGHTS

By the end of the century, however, Carter had second thoughts about the positions taken in the book. In 1897 he published with a Holiness publisher, the Christian Witness Company, some retractions under the title *"Faith Healing" Reviewed After Twenty Years*. This book maintained the doctrines of faith healing in general, but backed away from two positions of the earlier book: (1) that healing was definitely and mechanically included in the Atonement so that any continuing disease was a sign of continuing sin or lack of faith, and (2) that the use of "means" (medical help and medicine) was to be avoided as a sign of lack of faith.

The reasons for this change were quite practical. On 1 March 1887, the day the *Century* essay was published, Carter was struck with an "attack of brain prostration." For three years he struggled with his health until finally convinced by a doctor to try a little medicine that proved to be the correct remedy and enabled him to return to his work. The following year saw a new "record of meetings held and souls converted and saints consecrated to a deeper life" and convinced him of the rightness of his change.

This experience sent Carter back to his Bible and led to a "delightful sense of freedom" since he "no longer felt called upon to ransack the universe for a reason for any ache or pain that came along. It did not follow that he was a transgressor because he was a sufferer." Passages like Job became more important, and ordinary hygiene and "laws of health" more sensible. Most importantly, the lack of healing was now consigned to God's inscrutable will, though Carter continued the practice of anointing the sick with oil.[52] Theologically he now wished to postpone some of the effects of the Atonement he had earlier wished to claim immediate:

> That the Atonement of Christ covers sickness and disease as well as sin, is but to say that the effects are necessarily embraced in the root cause. There was and could be no error there. But to claim that ALL the results of the Atonement are NOW open to the present living Christian is a grave mistake. . . . we may err, and have erred, in endeavoring to appropriate at the present time some of the final fruits of that sacrifice.[53]

In place of the more radical earlier doctrine of healing in the Atonement, Carter now taught healing as a "special favor," sometimes bestowed, sometimes withheld, according to "the supreme will of our Lord."

Carter also provided an interesting summary of the state of the healing doctrines at the turn of the century with regard to these questions, distinguishing between the "extreme" position of his earlier book ("healing in the Atonement") and the more moderate "special providence" view of the latter book. He reported that Cullis had never been as extreme as many of the followers; he had always given medicine and continued to suffer from a severe heart problem, though his preaching often sounded more like the extreme view. A. B. Simpson was considered to have "practically" occupied a similar position, something of a crisis having been forced on him and the Christian Alliance by the "failure of the holiest

missionaries to withstand the African fever purely by faith."
Carrie Judd Montgomery "does not like any one to attempt
much modification of the theory," but her husband had ill
health and she continued to wear glasses.

These figures constituted the mainstream and most
noticed leadership of the Healing movement. The more strictly
defined Holiness movement, though its teaching had in many
ways given birth to the healing teachings through a radicalization of its doctrine of entire sanctification, remained somewhat
ambivalently related to these currents. This is reflected particularly in the stance of the leadership of the National Holiness
Association. John Inskip, the first president of the National
Camp Meeting Association, had experienced healing when
working with William McDonald at a meeting in a Boston
Methodist Church in 1871 and was willing to publish through
Cullis a report of this experienced in 1879.[54] Though the letter
does not reveal any direct commitment to healing in the
Atonement, Inskip reported that he was

> glad of this opportunity to take rank with the fanatics who
> believe in God's method of curing people, and who think
> that the Scriptures mean just what they say in declaring
> that the "prayer of faith shall save the sick, and the Lord
> shall raise him up."[55]

In 1892 William McDonald, also to some extent associated
with Cullis, published a book, Modern Faith Healing, taking
essentially the position of Carter's second book, that "the
special answer to prayer is the proper ground, and not the
general provision in the Atonement for all believers."[56] A
similar position was taken by Daniel Steele, also associated
with Cullis and his work. Steele rejected the doctrine of
healing in the Atonement and advocated the Wesleyan distinction between the "grace of faith and the gift of faith." He was
inclined to

> regard the modern eager desire for the gifts of the Spirit
> instead of the graces of the Spirit comprised in that charity
> (I Cor. xiii), which has been aptly styled, "the greatest
> thing in the world," as a sign not of real spiritual progress,
> but rather of decline in the divine life.[57]

DISAGREEMENTS IN THE HOLINESS ASSOCIATION

The more classically and Methodistically oriented of the national leadership attempted to maintain this position throughout the rest of the century, forbidding this topic (and premillennialism!) to be discussed at meetings under the auspices of the National Holiness Association. Thus Asbury Lowrey opposed premillennialism and the extreme healing doctrines in *Divine Life* concerned "lest we divert attention from holiness to novelties and elevate the cure of the body above the healing of the soul."[58] At the turn of the century the *Christian Witness* was still fighting for the "original and correct position of the modern holiness movement upon the doctrine of faith healing," the position represented by Carter in *"Faith Healing" Reviewed.*[59]

But this position was not easily maintained. As the Holiness movement spread throughout the country during the rest of the century and spawned numerous local associations, the control of the national leadership weakened and with that the resistance to the tendency of the Holiness teachings to overflow into variations on the healing doctrines. Thus, for example, in the Southwest:

> With the coming of the doctrine of entire sanctification came also the doctrine of divine healing. A veritable tidal wave of bodily healing swept through the land. . . . There would be healing services at almost every campmeeting, where the sick would come to the altar for prayer and anointing.[60]

This report condemns, however, extremes like the denial of means, the tendency to substitute healing for the pursuit of holiness, and interestingly, especially the work of B. H. Irwin, who was mocked for his unsuccessful efforts to cure an obviously crippled young woman.

But even with these qualifications, it is clear that the Holiness movement as such carried the healing emphasis in most of its variations. This could be illustrated at length, but a few examples will suffice. As early as 1862 B. T. Roberts, founder of the Free Methodist Church, editorialized in his journal, the *Earnest Christian and Golden Rule*, on the theme

"The Lord our Healer," citing most of the passages that would come into prominence later, to argue a "connection between sin and sickness."[61] Among several references to the theme in this journal over the years was a major essay by Asa Mahan, who became interested in the issue after the healing of his wife. Mahan appeals to the usual text in Matthew 8:16–17 to defend something that sounds very close to the doctrine of healing in the Atonement.

> If the fact that Jesus bore our sins in His own body on the tree, is a valid reason why we should trust Him now to pardon our sins, the fact that "He bare our sicknesses" is an equally valid reason why we should now trust Him to heal our diseases. We have the same revealed basis for trust in the one case as in the other.[62]

Mahan's essay follows the normal pattern of argument, both exegetically and historically, that one finds in most of the late nineteenth-century defenses of divine healing.

By the end of the century some emphasis on divine healing was a common feature of the Holiness movement, especially in more radical circles where the impulse was the strongest. In 1895 W. B. Godbey, a Kentucky evangelist and author of a widely circulated multivolume commentary on the New Testament, noted that

> since the rise of the holiness movement divine healing has become so common as to be no longer a matter of controversy. With candid Bible readers I have witnessed it ever and anon the last twenty-five years. It is rapidly coming to the recognition and appreciation of the church.[63]

Godbey would also suggest that "as the church becomes enlightened and moves up on to the highlands of entire sanctification, the recognition of the Omnipotent healer will become as common as in New Testament times."[64]

In 1897 Seth Cook Rees elaborated his vision of *The Ideal Pentecostal Church*, which would include as a basic theme "The Power of the Lord is Present to Heal the Sick" (the title of chapter 15). Here he argued that concern about fanaticism should not cause people to neglect healing:

Now, that some have gone to unwarrantable extremes, and even into fanaticism, on divine healing, there can be no doubt. But may this not be said, as well, of experiences vastly more important? There is probably not a man in all our prisons who was placed there for counterfeiting the copper cent. So the devil counterfeits only the good, God-sent and God-ordained things, and the more valuable the genuine the more elaborate and labored his imitation. Let us not reject the gold because there is some brass in circulation.

When Pentecost was come "the power of the Lord was present to heal." Let us then help each other's faith. It is much more Christ-like than to break off the heads of the tender shoots of trust in God and his power and willingness to heal.[65]

By the turn of the century, divine healing was a theme to be incorporated in official and semi-official statements of faith. In 1901, for example, the General Holiness Assembly in Chicago adopted a doctrinal statement that contained among only six items the following:

5. We wish to declare it as our belief that the sick may be healed through the prayer of faith, and that if God's people generally would measure up to the New Testament requirement in the matter of holy living, including particularly the matter of consecrating their bodies to the Lord, marvelous instances of divine healing would be far more numerous than they now are, God would be better glorified and the general testimony of the church would be much more effective on the outside world.[66]

Among the more radical wings of the Holiness movement the advocacy of divine healing would be a special matter of pride and emphasis. By 1901 the *Guide to Holiness* carried announcements like the following:

The Harvest Home Camp Meeting of the Pentecostal Band, will be held in Indianapolis, Ind., July 20 to August 5, inclusive. It will be a radical holiness rallying point. A treat for believers in Divine healing and the second coming of Christ. A veritable canvass city. Over one hundred preachers and mission workers will be present.[67]

All of this means that by the turn of the century most of the currents that had adopted the doctrine of Pentecostal baptism in the Spirit had also begun to teach a variation on the theme of divine healing.[68] The third theme of the four-square gospel was largely in place. Before turning to the fourth, however, we need to notice one other development.

Our argument so far has been that the rise of the healing doctrines was largely a radicalization of the perfectionist push of the Holiness teachings. We have tried to demonstrate this not only by tracing this historical evolution, but also by showing that the connection is present in every major manifestation of the Healing movement in the late nineteenth century. Historians of Pentecostalism and of the Healing movement in general have usually suggested that John Alexander Dowie of Zion City, Illinois, was the major source of Pentecostal doctrines of healing.

Our response to this is that this position largely ignores the fact that the healing doctrines were widespread before Dowie. It also ignores the extent to which Dowie himself reveals that his own teachings were rooted in the same radicalization of Holiness teachings, though he also reveals a tendency to extract the healing doctrines from their Holiness context and give them a slightly different theological grounding. This move is clearly evident in the report of the founding meeting of the International Divine Healing Association in 1890, dominated by Dowie. The debates at the meeting produced the following interchanges:

> Mr. Hugh Craig, of the Oakland Branch, asked: "Would it not be wise that the object of the association shall be the promotion not only of the Scriptural teaching of healing, but of the Scriptural teaching of Salvation and Divine Healing?"

> Mr. Dowie replied: "No. I am just as earnest in wanting to see Salvation as any one can be. . . . but this Association is not formed to promote that work, all-important thought it is, for it would at once come into collision with the churches. . . . Of course, a local president would understand that he cannot, and it would be improper to attempt to prevent a member's saying that he believes the Lord is coming or that he wants to be wholly *sanctified* but the

object of the Association is to promote the doctrine of
HEALING THROUGH FAITH IN JESUS. . . . therein is the
point wherein we differ with the Christian Alliance,
which has for its motto, 'Christ our Saviour, Christ our
Sanctifier, Christ our Healer and Christ our Coming
King.' "

And later, the discussions would reveal the extent to which
Holiness theology lay behind the teachings:

> Mr. Morgan: ". . . I don't think that the churches have a
> patent right on salvation; I don't think that the National
> Holiness Association has a patent right on Divine Holi-
> ness. Every man that has been born again has a right to
> preach Christ; every man that has been sanctified wholly
> is commissioned to proclaim the great salvation in its
> fullness, and I bless God that I am able to do it every
> day. . . . but I am in favor of everything that shall guard
> the work from scandal."

> Mr. Dowie: "Amen. . . . we have always taught that you
> can't get healing without salvation, and you can't get
> entire sanctification without salvation and healing. No-
> body wants to limit testimony to a ridiculous extent, but I
> cannot undertake to promote a new church organization. I
> can help you to form a Divine Healing Association, and no
> more."[69]

These debates reveal how even the Divine Healing Association
of Dowie was speaking out of the broader Holiness ethos—and
in dialogue with the Christian Alliance of A. B. Simpson and
the National Holiness Association. But the debates of the
convention also reveal how in Dowie the themes of healing
were being extracted from their soteriological rooting in
redemption and being restated in a more distinctly Pentecostal
vein. Healing becomes more a manifestation of Pentecostal
"power" and an evidence of "God also bearing witness with
them, both by signs and wonders, and by manifold powers
(miracles) and by gifts of the Holy Spirit."[70]

NOTES

1. Morton T. Kelsey, *Healing and Christianity in Ancient Thought and
Modern Times* (New York: Harper and Row, 1976).

2. Evelyn Frost, *Christian Healing* (London: A. R. Mowbray, 1940).

3. In a letter to the Elector of Brandenburg, dated 4 December 1539, quoted by Benjamin B. Warfield, *Counterfeit Miracles* (New York: Charles Scribner's Sons, 1918; reprint, London: Banner of Truth, 1972), p. 306. See also Luther's comments on extreme unction in "The Babylonian Captivity of the Church," *Luther's Works*, ed. Abdel Ross Wentz (Philadelphia: Muhlenberg, 1959), 36:120ff.

4. See Morton Kelsey, *Healing and Christianity*, p. 233, and Bengt R. Hoffman, *Luther and the Mystics* (Minneapolis: Augsburg, 1976), who is convinced that Luther did affirm a sort of Charismatic healing, dealing with the issue on pages 195–201.

5. John Calvin, *Institutes of the Christian Religion*, Library of Christian Classics edition, ed. John T. McNeill (Philadelphia: Westminster Press, 1960), bk. 4, ch. 19, sect. 19, p. 1467.

6. See Owen's "Discourse on Spiritual Gifts," in *The Works of John Owen*, William Gould, ed. (Edinburgh: T. and T. Clark, 1862), vol. 4, ch. 4, pp. 462–63.

7. In *Counterfeit Miracles*.

8. See Henry J. Cadbury, ed., *George Fox's "Book of Miracles"* (Cambridge: University Press, 1948). "Miracles of healing" are also described in his *Journal*.

9. W. B. Godbey, *Spiritual Gifts and Graces* (Cincinnati: God's Revivalist Office, 1895), p. 27.

10. Dudley Wright, ed., *The Epworth Phenomena* (London: William Rider and Son, 1917). Compare J. Gordon Melton, "John Wesley and the Supernatural," *Spiritual Frontiers* 6/7 (Autumn-Winter 1974): 115–33, and the similar ch. 9 in Paul Lambourne Higgins, *John Wesley: Spiritual Witness* (Minneapolis: T. S. Denison, 1960), also representing the perspective of the Spiritual Frontiers Fellowship.

11. See the modern edition of John Wesley, *Primitive Physic*, with an introduction by A. Wesley Hill (London: Epworth, 1960), and the editor's fuller treatment of *John Wesley Among the Physicians: A Study of Eighteenth-Century Medicine* (London: Epworth, 1958).

12. Kelsey, *Healing and Christianity*, p. 235, especially the list of citations in footnote 44.

13. *The Journal of the Rev. John Wesley, A.M.*, ed. Nehemiah Curnock (London: Epworth, 1912), 3:55–56.

14. Letter of 16 November 1762 to Dr. Warburton, Bishop of Gloucester, in the Telford edition of Wesley's *Letters*, 4:344.

15. See Endre Zsindely, *Krankheit und Heilung im älteren Pietismus* (Zurich: Zwingli Verlag, 1962), especially sect. 3C on "*Gebetsheilung im Pietismus.*"

16. John Albert Bengel, *Gnomon of the New Testament*, rev. and ed. Andrew Faussett (Edinburgh: T. and T. Clark, 1857), 1:575–76.

17. See the comments on James 5:14 by Bengel, *Gnomon*, 5:39–40.

18. These developments are sketched by William G. Bodamer, Jr., "The Life and Work of Johann Christoph Blumhardt" (Ph.D. diss., Princeton Theological Seminary, 1966), pp. 161–71.

19. Ibid., pp. 34–44.

20. Blumhardt's report of this event was widely distributed—against his will. See *Blumhardt's Battle: A Conflict with Satan*, trans. Frank S. Boshold (New York: Thomas E. Lowe, 1970).

21. Bodamer, "The Life and Work of Johann Christoph Blumhardt," pp. 44–55.

22. See *Answers to Prayer; or, Dorothea Trudel* (Boston: Henry Hoyt, n.d.).

23. See Arthur T. Pierson, *Forward Movements of the Last Half Century* (New York and London: Funk and Wagnalls, 1905), especially ch. 9, "The Growth of Faith-Work."

24. The literature on Müller is extensive and begins in 1837 with Müller's own publication of the first section of *A Narrative of Some of the Lord's Dealings with George Müller, written by himself*, later collected by G. Fred Bergin into the *Autobiography of George Müller*, whose centenary edition of 1905 contained a preface and final chapter by Arthur T. Pierson (London: J. Nisbet, 2nd ed., 1906). In 1861 the retired president of Brown University, Francis Wayland, wrote a commending introduction to an American edition of the early sections as *The Life of Trust*, ed. H. Lincoln Wayland (Boston: Gould and Lincoln, 1861). The most sophisticated biography to date appears to be that of Roger Steer, *George Müller: Delighted in God* (Wheaton, Ill.: Harold Shaw, 1975).

25. See lectures 4 on "Prevailing Prayer" and 5 on "The Prayer of Faith" in Charles G. Finney, *Lectures on Revivals of Religion* (New York: Leavitt, Lord, 1835), critical edition ed. William G. McLoughlin (Cambridge, Mass.: Harvard University Press, Belknap Press, 1960), pp. 52–88.

26. R. Kelso Carter, *"Faith Healing" Reviewed* (Boston and Chicago: Christian Witness, 1897), p. 109. More generally on Cullis, see W. H. Daniels, *Dr. Cullis and His Work* (Boston: Willard Tract Repository, 1885); W. E. Boardman, *Faith-Work; or, the Labours of Dr. Cullis in Boston* (London: W. Isbister, 1874); and Raymond J. Cunningham, "From Holiness to Healing: The Faith Cure in America, 1872–1892," *Church History* 43 (December 1974): 499–513, largely extracted from his "Ministry of Healing: The Origins of the Psychotherapeutic Role of the American Churches" (Ph.D. diss., Johns Hopkins University, 1965).

27. Boardman, *Faith-Work*, pp. 22–23.

28. Charles Cullis, *Faith Cures; or, Answers to Prayer in the Healing of the Sick* (Boston: Willard Tract Repository, 1879), p. 13.

29. *Dorothea Trudel; or, The Prayer of Faith*, with an introduction by Charles Cullis, 3d ed. (Boston: Willard Tract Repository, 1872).

30. Daniels, *Dr. Cullis and His Work*, p. 339.

31. W. E. Boardman, *"The Lord That Healeth Thee"* (London: Morgan and Scott, 1881), pp. 10–11. This book was also published in the United States as *The Great Physician* (Boston: Willard Tract Repository, 1881).

32. Ibid., p. 11.

33. Ibid., p. 47.

34. Mary M. Boardman, *Life and Labors of the Rev. W. E. Boardman* (New York: D. Appleton, 1887), p. 232.

35. Mrs. M. Baxter, Divine Healing (Brighton: Christian Herald, n.d.), consisting of articles reprinted from the Christian Herald and the Prophetic News.

36. Carrie F. Judd, "Faith Reckonings," Triumphs of Faith 1 (January 1881): 2–3. This editorial was also published as a tract from the Oakland home under the author's married name, Montgomery.

37. R. L. Stanton, Gospel Parallelisms: Illustrated in the Healing of Body and Soul (Buffalo: Office of Triumphs of Faith, 1884), p. 13.

38. Ibid., pp. 15–17.

39. Ibid., p. 152.

40. Ibid., p. 174.

41. Narrated in A. E. Thompson, The Life of A. B. Simpson (New York: Christian Alliance Publishing, 1920), ch. 8.

42. Ibid., p. 64.

43. A. B. Simpson, The Gospel of Healing, rev. ed. (New York: Christian Alliance Publishing, 1915), p. 34; see The Lord for the Body (New York: Christian Alliance Publishing, 1925), p. 29. The latter book expanded The Discovery of Divine Healing, published in 1903.

44. Simpson, The Gospel of Healing, p. 70.

45. A. J. Gordon, The Ministry of Healing: Miracles of Cure in All Ages (Boston: H. Gannett, 1882), p. 16. On Gordon's teaching, see ch. 2 of Ernest B. Gordon, Adoniram Judson Gordon: A Biography (New York: Fleming H. Revell, 1896).

46. Gordon, The Ministry of Healing, p. 43.

47. Robert Kelso Carter, The Atonement for Sin and Sickness; or, a Full Salvation for Soul and Body (Boston: Willard Tract Repository, 1884), pp. 12–13.

48. Ibid., p. 17.

49. Ibid., p. 38.

50. Ibid., p. 1.

51. Ibid., p. 38.

52. A description of this development is included as an appendix to R. Kelso Carter, "Faith Healing" Reviewed, pp. 153–61.

53. Ibid., p. 167.

54. This letter appears in Boardman, "The Lord That Healeth Thee," pp. 135–38.

55. Ibid., p. 138.

56. William McDonald, Modern Faith Healing (Boston: McDonald and Gill, 1892). The summary is from Carter, "Faith Healing" Reviewed, p. 13.

57. Daniel Steele, Half Hours with St. Paul (Boston: McDonald and Gill, 1894), especially ch. 35, "Faith Healing," p. 250.

58. Asbury Lowrey, "Spirit Leading and Other Truths Carried to Excess," Divine Life and Bible Expositor 20 (May 1893): 133.

59. N. Hammond Follin, in the introduction to J. N. Short, Divine Healing (Chicago: Christian Witness, n.d.), p. 1.

60. C. B. Jernigan, Pioneer Days of the Holiness Movement in the Southwest (Kansas City, Mo.: Pentecostal Nazarene Publishing House, [1919]), p. 165.

61. B. T. Roberts, "The Lord Our Healer," *Earnest Christian and Golden Rule* 4 (July 1862): 1–7.

62. Asa Mahan, "Faith-Healing," *Earnest Christian* 48 (September 1884): 76.

63. Godbey, *Spiritual Gifts and Graces*, p. 25.

64. Ibid., p. 27.

65. Rees, *The Ideal Pentecostal Church*, p. 81.

66. S. B. Shaw, ed., *Echoes of the General Holiness Assembly Held in Chicago May 3–13, 1901* (Chicago: S. B. Shaw, n.d.), p. 31.

67. *Guide to Holiness* 75 (July 1901): 23.

68. I have not been able to pin down exactly where the Moody/Torrey tradition of revivalism stood on this issue. The standard biographies are completely silent on the issues, and a survey of Moody's major writings reveals little. Moody clearly avoided the issues and apparently would not, from hints in his comments on prayer, have been susceptible to any mechanical doctrine of the "prayer of faith." On Torrey, see T. J. Shanks, ed., *College Students at Northfield* (New York: Fleming H. Revell, 1888), pp. 201–3. As with Spirit baptism, Torrey seems to be more involved, but his book—a defense of miraculous healing and a moderate doctrine of healing in the Atonement while critical of such extremes as the denial of "means"—was written in 1924, almost a quarter-century after the emergence of Pentecostalism, a movement that Torrey loathed. As happened in many places, Torrey may well have modified his teachings in the meantime to avoid any confusion with Pentecostal teachings. His book was *Divine Healing* (New York: Fleming H. Revell, 1924; reprint, Grand Rapids: Baker, 1974). See also the discussion of Torrey in J. Sidlow Baxter, *Divine Healing of the Body* (Grand Rapids: Zondervan, 1979), pp. 96–97. We do know that Torrey at one point asked John Alexander Dowie to pray for his daughter. Dowie exploited this incident in his *Leaves of Healing* 5 (8 April 1899): 457–64. There is a brief discussion of this incident in Edith Lydia Waldvogel, "The 'Overcoming Life': A Study of the Reformed Evangelical Origins of Pentecostalism" (Ph.D. diss., Harvard University, 1977), pp. 123–24.

69. See the appendix containing a "Full Report of the First General Convention of the Divine Healing Association" to John Alexander Dowie and Mrs. Dowie, *Our Second Year's Harvest* (Chicago: International Divine Healing Association, 1891), pp. 172, 174–75.

70. Ibid., p. 168.

35 Our Lord's Return to Earth Again.

J. M. K. Acts 1: 9,10, 11. J. M, KIRK.

1. I am watch-ing for the com-ing of the glad mil - len - nial day,
2. Je-sus' com-ing back will be the an-swer to earth's sorrowing cry,
3. Yes, the ran-somed of the Lord shall come to Zi - on then with joy,
4. Then the sin and sor-row, pain and death of this dark world shall cease,

When our blessed Lord shall come and catch his wait-ing Bride a - way; Oh! my
For the knowledge of the Lord shall fill the earth and sea and sky; God shall
And in all his ho - ly mountain nothing hurts or shall de-stroy; Per - fect
In a glorious reign with Je - sus of a thousand years of peace; All the

heart is fill'd with rapt-ure as I la-bor, watch and pray, For the Lord is coming
take a-way all sickness and the suff'rer's tears will dry, When our Saviour shall come
peace shall reign in ev - 'ry heart, and love with-out al - loy, Aft - er Jesus shall come
earth is groaning, cry-ing for that day of sweet re - lease, For our Je - sus to come

D. S.-*will be bound a thousand years, we'll have no tempter then, Aft-er Jesus shall come*

FINE. CHORUS.

back to earth a-gain. Oh! our Lord is com-ing back to earth a - gain,
is com-ing back to earth a-gain,

back to earth a-gain.

D. S.

Yes, our Lord is com-ing back to earth a - gain; Sa - tan
is com-ing back to earth a-gain,

CHAPTER VI

THE RISE
OF PREMILLENNIALISM

When in 1914 a group of Pentecostals met to form what would become the Assemblies of God, the largest of the white Pentecostal denominations in the United States, they rejoiced not only in the international impact of their movement, but also in "the prophecy which has become predominant in all this great outpouring, which is 'Jesus is coming soon' to this old world in the same manner as he left it to set up his millennial kingdom."[1] Some, such as Robert Mapes Anderson and David William Faupel, have argued that this theme is in fact the integrating core of the Pentecostal message.[2]

This eschatological motif certainly permeated the earliest literature of the movement, has resurfaced in key periods like the Latter Rain revival of the 1940s, appears even in the Catholic Charismatic movement where the themes of classical Pentecostalism have been most transformed by a new theological context, and characterizes the more distant cousins of Pentecostalism like the African independent churches. It at least deserves, as we have argued in the first chapter, a place among the four defining themes of the Pentecostal *gestalt* of characteristic theological claims. At the same time it presents a challenge to the general thesis that has emerged from this study—that the historical lineage of Pentecostalism is to be traced primarily through the nineteenth-century Holiness traditions and more indirectly back to themes of Methodism and perhaps even to Pietism and Puritanism.

We are led by history to expect a linking of eschatology and pneumatology in movements like Pentecostalism. Those movements most intensely experiencing the personal infusion of the Spirit seem to long most ardently for a return of Christ and a corresponding cosmic transformation of this world order. To a certain extent this conjunction is present in the biblical texts most used by Pentecostals. In the account of Pentecost (Acts 2), for example, Peter quotes the prophet Joel to argue that what has just taken place is the prophesied effusion of the Holy Spirit in the Last Days. N. Q. Hamilton finds the Holy Spirit and eschatology also clearly connected in the writings of Paul, where "it is the Spirit which bridges the gap between the present and the future."[3]

Whether by a common influence of such biblical texts or by some similar experiential dynamic, we find that the more Spirit-oriented movements in the history of the church have had a particular fascination with prophetic and apocalyptic themes. Thus Montanism closely linked pneumatology and eschatology.[4] Similarly, though with a very different content, Joachim of Fiore looked forward to a new age that would be characterized by its association with the Third Person of the Trinity.[5] These themes are clearly conjoined in the nineteenth-century Irvingite movement.[6] Or, from the other side, it is worth noting that the sequence of American "prophecy conferences" in the late nineteenth century was broken by a conference on the Holy Spirit, the only topic allowed to break into the usual pattern of eschatological fascination.[7]

Reflecting on such phenomena, Emil Brunner has commented that

> we can trace in the history of Christendom something like a law, that the more vitally hope is present in the Ekklesia, that is, the more powerfully life in the Spirit of God is present in it, the more urgent is its expectation of the Coming of Jesus Christ; so that the fulness of the possession of the Spirit and the urgency of expectation are always found together, as they were in the primitive community.[8]

Stressing such facts, we might most easily argue that the turn to a doctrine of the Holy Spirit in the late nineteenth century involved almost of necessity a turn to eschatology. We would then turn immediately to notice the rising impact of the premillennial movement of the nineteenth century from its origins among the British Plymouth Brethren, especially the followers of John Nelson Darby, through its greater impact in America in the series of prophecy conferences beginning in 1878, and finally in the rise of the "Bible institutes" at the turn of the century that became the model of Pentecostal educational institutions.[9] Our Pentecostal *gestalt* of themes would then be the product of the "elective affinities" between a certain late nineteenth-century pneumatology and this pervasive new eschatology. Indeed, insofar as an explanation of this development has been attempted, it has been largely along these lines, seeing dispensational premillennialism as one of several nineteenth-century sources of modern Pentecostal thought.[10]

We do not wish to deny entirely the general thrust of this argument, but several factors must be allowed to qualify it. In the first place, it is not clear that Pentecostal eschatology, with its emphases on the inauguration of the "new order of the latter rain" and the "restoration of spiritual gifts" as a prelude to the return of Christ, fits as easily into dispensationalist categories as it is sometimes assumed. It was generally premillennial in expecting a millennial kingdom to be inaugurated by an imminent return of Christ, but contradicted dispensational distinctives by adopting different (generally tripartite) periodizations of human history, by applying many Old Testament promises to the church, by appropriating more directly texts (the Lord's Prayer, the Sermon on the Mount, and so forth) that dispensationalists relegate to the millennial kingdom, and so on.[11] Such evidence suggests that the Pentecostal eschatological motif has its own integrity, but that this theme could coalesce with or, perhaps better, express itself through a variety of distinct eschatological schemes from dispensationalism through British Israelism that circulated in the fluid, popular Evangelical culture of the late nineteenth century.

There is also the danger of a cultural and historiographical distortion in dealing with these materials. The most accessible written sources and often the more elaborately articulated theological reflection on Pentecostal eschatology occur in precisely those wings of the movement most cultural- ly and theologically akin to dispensational fundamentalism. These traditions, such as those clustered in the Assemblies of God, have drawn their membership most fully from fundamen- talist circles and have over the years most fully assimilated themselves into that theological culture.

Though further research needs to be done, there is some evidence that the further one moves away from these cur- rents—into the more Holiness branches of Pentecostalism or into black or other ethnic Pentecostal groups—the less the eschatology is expressed in the characteristic forms of dispen- sational thought. This fact also suggests that we should not too quickly assume that Pentecostal eschatology is merely the assimilation of the themes of emerging dispensationalism.[12]

But perhaps as important, to accept immediately at face value the thesis that Pentecostal eschatology is a borrowing of dispensational eschatology would qualify the results of our pursuit so far of the roots of our first two themes, the baptism of the Holy Spirit and divine healing. It may well be that our thesis thus far should be qualified by a greater recognition of more pluralistic sources than we have suggested. But before adopting this more obvious solution, we need to examine more closely the traditions to which we have been led by our investigations in earlier chapters to see if the emergence of Pentecostal eschatology may be a product of dynamics internal to these movements.

This search, at first glance, seems doomed to failure because the Methodist and Holiness traditions have histori- cally had little interest in eschatology or have inclined toward a postmillennial eschatology often viewed as the opposite of the premillennial, not only by virtue of its expectation of a millennium preceding the return of Christ (thus making the return less imminent), but also because it provided a more "this-worldly" eschatological hope that could support social transformation and other broader cultural commitments. But closer examination of the eschatological patterns of the currents that have come to our attention in the search for the roots for other Pentecostal distinctives reveals dynamics and issues internal to these movements that not only help to explain the rise of Pentecostal eschatology, but also shed light on wider developments. As this argument unfolds, we shall be more inclined to see the emergence of Pentecostal eschatology as a parallel development (or occasionally an antecedent) to the rise of dispensationalism, though, of course, we shall see common dynamics and a great deal of intermingling.

To enter the tangled maze of the history of eschatological and millennial views is to despair of reconciling contrary views and discerning patterns of development. Little of the scholarly work that has been done, moreover, has pursued the questions as we would pose them; or when our questions have been asked, the work has been uncritical or apologetic.[13] In spite of these difficulties, a broad outline of development can be drawn which, however oversimplified it may be, illumines the emergence of Pentecostal eschatology. This outline will require, as in earlier chapters, glancing at Puritanism and Pietism, dwelling on early Methodism, giving attention to the coalescing of this tradition with American revivalism, discerning the transformations that took place within perfectionistic revivalism, and finally uncovering the new shape of the eschatology dominating the late nineteenth-century currents.

PURITAN AND PIETIST INFLUENCES

Pentecostal eschatology, as it emerged in the late nineteenth century, was a departure from the schemes that had dominated for a couple of centuries the religious currents to which it was most closely related. Puritanism and Pietism, for example, both contained a commitment to "reform" whose logic required an optimism about the future and the possibility of change. Though Puritan eschatology was more varied, in general it looked forward to a "latter-day glory" of the church, or (to use the title of a volume of 1678 sermons by John Howe) *The Prosperous State of the Christian Interest Before the End of Time.*[14]

Interestingly from the perspective of Pentecostalism, the latter-day glory was usually understood to be associated with a special outpouring of the Holy Spirit. But the Puritan vision expected a collapse of the papacy, the conversion of the Jews, and an era of the success of missions that would be "millennial" in character. Increasingly this view tended toward what we would call today postmillennialism, identifying this era with a millennium discerned in Revelation 20. This view looked forward to the return of Christ, but not imminently because of the expected period of latter-day glory that needed to occur before that event. As we shall see later in America, periods of "revival" would accentuate the hope that this era might be dawning.[15]

Also hinting at a broader than sometimes noticed consensus in this era was Pietism's hope for "better times" ahead for the church. Pietism, as we have had occasion to notice elsewhere, tended to break from the classic Lutheran dialectic of good and evil, with its emphasis on justification, by shifting the emphasis to the individual in regeneration and sanctification; and by emphasizing, on the historical plane, the individual and elevated "hope" and an era of better times ahead.[16] Philipp Jakob Spener announced this teaching in his *Pia Desideria* and expanded on the theme in his *Behauptung der Hoffnung künfftiger Besserer Zeiten* ("Assertion of Hope for Future Better Times") in 1693. Spener, too, looked forward to the fall of Rome and the conversion of the Jews, but was less inclined than the Puritans to be explicitly "millennial" (or "postmillennial") in his description of the era of better times to precede the return of Christ.[17]

It was, however, John Albert Bengel, Pietism's great biblical scholar, who would in his fascination with the Apocalypse attempt to date these events more fully. His work in prophecy and chronology converged to produce a chronological system that coordinated these "most favorable times" with the rise of Pietism, the founding of the Bible societies, and the spread of missions—and dated this era as roughly 1617–1836. This latter date would mark the climax of a period of tribulation and the overthrow of the "Beast" upon the return of Christ, which would then usher in the technical millennium.

Bengel is therefore somewhat ambiguous by later standards, expecting better times both to precede and to follow the return of Christ. This scheme was deeply influential through Bengel's *Gnomon*.[18]

WESLEY AND FLETCHER: PULLING
IN DIFFERENT DIRECTIONS

Though Wesley was heir to all these currents, on eschatology, as on many other points, he is exceedingly difficult to interpret. Both postmillennialists and premillennialists would later claim his for their lineage.[19] Much depends on one's hermeneutic of Wesley and especially on which texts are made normative—those in which he is passing on received tradition, or those in which his own distinctive theological impulses are given the most freedom. Wesley's own *Explanatory Notes upon the New Testament,* for example, as we have already indicated, are often only an abridgment of Bengel's *Gnomon,* and his comments on the Apocalypse incorporate as well much of the *Ekklärte Offenbarung* of Bengel. Wesley himself did not have strong opinions about the issues involved, but does pass on Bengel's scheme with some diffidence and warning that "every part of this I do not undertake to defend."[20]

Actually such issues were really of very little interest to Wesley, whose focus was, as we have already suggested, much more exclusively soteriological. When once he generated some controversy by reporting Bengel's predictions, he responded in a 1788 letter:

> I said nothing, less or more, in Bradford church, concerning the end of the world, neither concerning my own opinion, but what follows:—that Bengelius had given it as his opinion, not that the world would then end, but that the millennial reign of Christ would begin in the year 1836. I have no opinion at all upon the head: I can determine nothing at all about it. These calculations are far above me, out of my sight. I have only one thing to do,—to save my soul, and those that hear me.[21]

And as we have already argued, Wesley's soteriology was a form of "realized eschatology" that emphasized the continuity between the salvation experienced in this life and the glory yet to come. Though Wesley could refer to and affirm events of a "last time" (the Second Coming, judgment, and so forth), he tended to relegate these to a vague and distant future that did not impinge much on this life. His real interest was in questions of how much the salvation that other theological traditions relegated to heaven could be experienced in this life. His discussions of the possibility of entire sanctification seem to assume a pattern that does not give much weight to an imminence of the return of Christ.[22] They certainly reflect a distaste for eschatological and apocalyptic speculation.

Not all of Wesley's followers, however, were so inclined. George Bell, soon after converting to Methodism, announced the end of the world on 23 February 1763, only to be soundly repudiated by Wesley.

Much more significant for our purposes, however, is the thought of John Fletcher. We have already suggested the importance of Fletcher's doctrine of dispensations, which he used to interpret the progress of both individual spiritual experience and the history of the race. Both move through dispensations of the Father, the Son, and the Holy Spirit. In human history the points of demarcation are marked by John the Baptist and Pentecost. In personal spiritual development the key points are conversion and the special reception of the Spirit associated with entire sanctification. We have already sketched the tensions between Wesley and Fletcher over elements of this scheme and the importance of Fletcher's way of casting the issues for the rise of the doctrine of a baptism of the Spirit and associated Pentecostal terminology.

What is noteworthy at this point is the significance of this difference for eschatology. Fletcher was much more inclined toward speculation on such matters, and this tendency is revealed in his doctrine of dispensations. In his posthumously published *Portrait of St. Paul*, Fletcher would argue that each dispensation has its correlate promise. Thus, "under the dispensation of the Father, the grand promise was that which respected the external manifestation of the Son." Under the dispensation of the Son, another "promise was given for the exercise of faith and hope . . . respecting the full manifestation of the Holy Ghost." This was, of course, fulfilled at Pentecost. And finally, under the present dispensation of the Holy Ghost, we have "the promise of Christ's second coming to 'gather his wheat into the garner, and to burn up the chaff with unquenchable fire.' " But since the dispensations also reflect stages in spiritual growth, this coming of Christ, which is disregarded by many . . . is so fully expected by those who live under the dispensation of the Spirit, that they are constantly "looking for, and hastening to the coming of the day of God."[23]

Such passages in Fletcher have a decidedly non-Wesleyan tone to them. And whatever the reason, Fletcher seems to have looked forward to an imminent return of Christ, to occur in the next generation if not in his own. At one point he predicted the return of Christ between 1750 and 1770 and urged Wesley to give more attention to such themes and not to judge harshly those who wished to pursue such matters.[24] In 1775 he wrote again to Wesley advocating the eschatological schemes of an unnamed "great divine abroad" with whom he had been in discussion.[25]

But even more important than Fletcher's own mind-set or the actual use to which he put his doctrine of dispensations is the fact that it had tendencies of its own or a distinct logic that, given more freedom in another time and place, could be elaborated in an increasingly Pentecostal direction. As we have suggested, it makes Pentecost an event in the *Heilsgeschichte* comparable to the coming of Christ, at least in marking out the dispensations, and the defining event of the present disposition of the church age. And, combined with an emphasis on the correlated promises, as in Fletcher, this structure of thought can explicitly accentuate eschatology. But it in other, more subtle ways also pushes in the same direction.

The Pentecostal accounts in Acts (and perhaps the Lukan theology as a whole) tend to link eschatology and pneumatology, as we have already seen. When these texts are elevated to the hermeneutical key by which the whole of Scripture is read, these tendencies may gain force. It may be as well that emphasizing Pentecost in this way accentuates the discontinuity between the testaments.

Wesley and other Methodists less inclined to Pentecostal rhetoric could more easily appropriate Old Testament models of piety, especially such figures as Noah and Abraham, who are described as having lived "perfectly before the Lord." When Christian piety becomes, however, more a matter of being filled with the Spirit descended at Pentecost, Old

Testament applications become a little more difficult, and there is a corresponding tendency to read the Old Testament primarily as anticipation of the event of Pentecost, thus reinforcing a basically prophecy/fulfillment pattern of reading the Scriptures. And hopefully without pushing too far, it may also be possible to discern more emphasis on divine sovereignty than in the more synergistic patterns of Wesleyan cooperation with divine initiative.

The key texts in the Pentecost accounts suggest that the basic stance of the Christian is to "tarry and wait" for the enduement from above. In both the personal and eschatological vision the key idea is "descent" and a "breaking in" from beyond, more characteristic of the apocalyptic mind-set and somewhat at odds with the more gradual, growth-oriented patterns of postmillennialism or development toward perfection. All these shifts are in the direction of fundamentally Pentecostal motifs.

Such concerns, of course, anticipate our story to some extent. But on the point of eschatology, as well as with regard to the rise of the doctrine of a Pentecostal baptism of the Holy Spirit, we must notice the significance of Fletcher's points of divergence from Wesley's thought. Again, the patterns of Wesley would dominate Methodism and the movements under its influence for a century. But when Fletcher's Pentecostal framework became more prominent in the late nineteenth century, his doctrine of dispensations also came to the fore.

Whatever Fletcher's intention in this doctrine, it is clear that the terminology itself became a bridge to dispensationalism just before the turn of the century. Fletcher becomes enshrined in the lists of antecedents of dispensationalism, even where he is so otherwise little known as to be rather anonymously described as "a Mr. Fletcher," who taught "a doctrine of dispensations."[26]

But it was Wesley's thought that set the tone for a full century—on eschatology as well as the vocabulary for entire sanctification—and pulled in a different direction. Wesley's own emphasis on Christian perfection was key in this regard. His individual soteriology, with its thrust toward a "realized" or "anticipated" eschatology, affirmed a certain level of vanquishment over evil in this life. This perfectionist soteriology tended as well to an optimistic social vision. The result was an ambiguous position that could easily move in the direction of postmillennialism, as is revealed in the following citation:

> And it is meet for all those who love his appearing to pray that He could hasten the time that his Kingdom of grace may come quickly, and swallow up all the kingdoms of earth; that all mankind, receiving Him for their King, truly believing in His name, may be filled with righteousness, and peace, and joy, with holiness and happiness—till they are removed hence into His heavenly kingdom, there to reign with Him forever and ever. . . . We pray for the coming of His everlasting kingdom, this kingdom of glory which is the continuation and perfection of the kingdom of grace on earth.[27]

Wesley was so oriented to soteriology that his followers could combine a basically Wesleyan scheme of salvation with a variety of eschatologies without an obvious sense of betrayal. But the basic thrust of Wesley's thought was probably better captured by the less apocalyptic and more postmillennial schemes of thought. Thus, while Wesley himself did not self-consciously adopt a millennial scheme, he helped to unleash forces that could and would move in that direction. This development took place especially in America, where Methodism was to find a special home and a context that would allow its Arminian and perfectionist tendencies fuller freedom of development.

MILLENNIALIST CURRENTS IN REVIVALISM

The American revivalist currents had already developed a millennial tradition. Periods of revival often appear to the participants to be ushering in a new era of God's special blessing. In the Great Awakenings of the eighteenth century, Jonathan Edwards had begun to wonder if the revivals under his ministry might not be the beginning of the millennium that God would call forth in the new world—the latter-day glory of the church for which the Puritans had longed:

Indeed, I have often said, as I say now, that I looked upon
the late wonderful revivals of religion as forerunners of
those glorious times so often prophesied of in the Scriptures, and that this was the first dawning of that light, and
beginning of that work which, in the progress and issue of
it, would at last bring on the church's latter-day glory . . .
and Christ's kingdom shall be everywhere established and
settled in peace, which will be the lengthening of the
millennium.[28]

C. C. Goen has suggested in a noted article that Edwards
drew on the exegesis of Daniel Whitby and Moses Lowman in
England to develop a postmillennial vision that marked a
"new departure" in American eschatology.[29] This vision was
far from what would develop later in Pentecostalism. In many
ways Edwards sounds more like his contemporary Wesley. For
one thing, Edwards was not attracted to the extraordinary gifts:

I don't expect a restoration of these miraculous gifts in the
approaching glorious times of the church, nor do I desire
it: it appears to me that it would add nothing to the glory
of those times, but rather diminish from it. For my part, I
had rather enjoy the sweet influences of the Spirit,
shewing Christ's spiritual divine beauty, and infinite
grace, and dying love, drawing forth the holy exercises of
faith and divine love, and sweet complacence, and
humble joy in God, one quarter of an hour, than to have
prophetical visions and revelations for a whole year.[30]

For another, Edwards's view was postmillennial, expecting a
more gradual yet imminent dawning of the millennial era
before the return of Christ.

The significance of Edwards for our story seems to be that
he contributed to the expectation of a literal millennium and
helped generate a tradition of millennial thinking that would
grow in force over the next century. Those who stood in the
tradition of Edwards cultivated and refined this doctrine.
Joseph Bellamy issued a noted sermon on the topic that would
be appended to the writings of Edwards, and Samuel Hopkins
published *A Treatise on the Millennium* in 1793.[31]

Thus, when Methodism arrived in America and began to
intermingle with the indigenous revival movements early in
the nineteenth century, it found a formal doctrine of the

millennium. Methodism's perfectionistic tendencies were given free rein in the new and optimistic nation, and they in turn accelerated and heightened the postmillennial expectations. This development took place particularly in Oberlin perfectionism, which, as we have seen, represented in so many ways the synthesis of Methodism and American revivalism. This new synthesis radically "Arminianized" the New England traditions, making the inauguration of the millennium contingent on human effort, and, riding the crest of the Second Great Awakening, would link the themes of perfection, reform, and millennial expectation.

Charles G. Finney did not fully articulate his millennial expectations, but his views are implicit in many statements like the following on social reform:

> Now the great business of the church is to reform the world—to put away every kind of sin. The church was originally organized to be a body of reformers. The very profession of Christianity implies the profession and virtually an oath to do all that can be done for the reformation of the world. The Christian church was designed to make aggressive movements in every direction—to lift up her voice and put forth her energies in high and low places—to reform individuals, communities and governments, and never rest until the Kingdom and the greatness of the Kingdom under the whole heaven shall be given to the saints of the Most High God—until every form of iniquity shall be driven from the earth.[32]

Finney was prone to say that if the "church would do its duty," the millennium would come in "six months" or "three years" or some such timing that made the event imminent. But Finney was radically Wesleyan in that his *Systematic Theology* is so soteriologically oriented that he never gets around to developing formally the doctrine of the millennium. He apparently left that task to other colleagues at Oberlin.

The *Oberlin Evangelist* was the major organ by which the Oberlin vision was communicated. Among its regularly announced goals was "to call the attention of Christians to the fact that the millennium is to consist in the entire sanctification of the church."[33] The spread of Holiness seemed to announce the arrival of the millennium, just as a century before, the revivals under Edwards had created a similar expectation. In 1841 the *Evangelist* carried a series of twenty-three essays on the millennium authored by editor Henry Cowles.

Reflecting the reform and ferment of the age, Cowles noticed "a heaving in the elements of the moral and social world portentous of no common change" that seemed to suggest that "the present is, or at least is becoming, an age of the study of prophecy."[34] Cowles argued that an imminent millennium was the obvious answer to their longings and devoted five essays to delineating the social and religious state during the millennium: Christ's kingdom will replace the empire of the world; war, oppressive rule, and slavery will be vanquished; a system of civil government may remain; the right knowledge of God will be prevalent; God will be present with his people as never before; the Holy Spirit will be given "in glorious and immense effusions"; piety and holiness will be widespread; the "great mass of the people will be Christians"—including conversion of the Jews and "numerous throngs of Gentiles"; hypocrisy and dissension will no longer trouble the churches, and so on.[35]

Cowles then dealt with the time of the commencement of the millennium. After rejecting various schemes designed to predict the exact date, he opted instead for attempting to discern the hand of Providence in the events of history. Among the signs of "some deep pervading action in the vast elements of the social and moral atmosphere," he pointed to such facts as this, that

> knowledge is gone and going abroad; knowledge on almost every subject pertaining to the improvement of society, and the multiplication of human comforts. The arts and sciences—pioneers of the millennium—are making all things ready for the children of God to possess the earth. The recent improvements in the printing art are such as would have been deemed miraculous. What need be more manifest than that God is preparing this instrument for his own use in converting the world, and sustaining the millennium. . . . Geographical knowledge has laid the world open before the Christian's eye. . . . God has given Christian nations remarkable access to the

heathen. To say nothing of the facility of reaching them
which commerce affords, the political relations of Europe
and of our own nation have laid open immense portions of
the heathen world to the gospel. . . . God has exalted the
influence of the Christian nations—and crushed that of
the heathen. . . . God has secured the general peace of the
civilized world.[36]

These and parallel religious developments convinced Cowles
that "we are amply justified in laying out our plans upon this
basis: THE MILLENNIUM IS AT HAND."[37] The essays go on to
treat other themes: the restoration of the Jews, the fate of the
wicked, whether the thousand years is literal or figurative
(Cowles opted for a figurative sense), and so forth. For our
purposes, only one further theme calls for notice.

Cowles understood that the church had a role in ushering
in the millennium. He polemicized against those who "think
God will bring in the millennium by a sort of miracle and
chiefly without human agency." He found this a "dreadful
mistake. Were it believed and acted on by the whole church,
we should never have a millennium to the end of time." These
Arminian-sounding themes are confirmed by an attack on
those (Calvinist) theological views that discouraged "the zeal
and efficient labor of the church":

. . . that salvation is possible to none but the elect—that
man can do nothing but wait God's time to convert him—
that salvation is a thing of fate and not of free choice—
that God does his own work alone and asks no Christian's
interference—that God wants none to be saved but those
whom he actually does save.[38]

The result is to place an ominous responsibility on the church:
"Just as long as the church shall withhold the agency, so long
will she retard the Millennium."[39] The last essay of Cowles is
then a ringing call to action with the advice to "expect great
things," to "expect great changes," and to expect opposition
against both changes in sentiment and reform in action." One
must "live as if such a Millennium were at the door, and
waiting only for our cooperation to be ushered in with all its
light and love."[40]

This, then, is something of the millennial vision that dominated the traditions to which our earlier investigations in search of the theological roots of Pentecostalism have led us. The problem for our thesis is that this position is very different from the eschatology that we find in Pentecostalism—it is, in fact, what has generally been considered to be the opposite of the premillennial theology that dominates early Pentecostalism.

Have we been misled by the clues that on the other themes directed our attention to Oberlin perfectionism as perhaps the key middle term between Methodism and Pentecostalism? Not necessarily. There is a way of construing the relationship between postmillennialism and premillennialism that makes the radically optimistic view of Oberlin a key step on the way from the former to the latter.

PROPHETIC VERSUS APOCALYPTIC

This construct involves the apparently paradoxical claim that it was precisely the most radical wing of postmillennialism that eventually became most tempted by the premillennial position. Postmillennialism, particularly in the radical version of Oberlin, promised more than it could deliver. It raised hopes and taught the expectation of an imminent millennium which failed to materialize. Optimism faded into despair. The only way to sustain the hope of the millennium was to radically rearrange the chronology along the lines of premillennialism.

We can better understand this suggestion by examining the biblical parallel of how the prophetic vision in the Old Testament was transformed into the apocalyptic world view that often followed. One of the most useful recent efforts to explain this development may be found in the work of Paul Hanson. He has defined "prophetic eschatology" as

> a religious perspective which focuses on the prophetic announcement to the nation of the divine plans for Israel and the world which the prophet has witnessed unfolding in the divine council and which he translates into the terms of plain history, real politics and human instrumentality; that is, the prophet interprets for the king and the

people how the plans of the divine council will be effected within the context of their nation's history and the history of the world.[41]

On the other hand, "apocalyptic eschatology"

focuses on the disclosure (usually esoteric in nature) to the elect of the cosmic vision of Yahweh's sovereignty—especially as it relates to his acting to deliver his faithful—which disclosure the visionaries have largely ceased to translate into the terms of plain history, real politics, and human instrumentality due to a pessimistic view of reality growing out of the bleak post-exilic conditions.[42]

Hanson discerned in the pre-exilic prophets through Second Isaiah a subtle prophetic balance between "vision of the cosmic realm and translation into historical terms"—the "vital tension between vision and realism which is the heart of genuine ethical religion."[43] Eschatology is the point of continuity when prophecy begins to evolve into apocalyptic as the tension between vision and reality falls apart, when the experience of the world can no longer be related to the religious vision. Despite differences in the "form of prophetic and apocalyptic eschatology, it must be emphasized that the essential vision of restoration persists in both, the vision of Yahweh's people restored as a holy community in a glorified Zion."[44]

For Hanson, then, apocalyptic is an effort to maintain intact that vision in the face of a new historical reality requiring a more pessimistic analysis of the course of human history and of the potential of human instrumentality. The answer is largely to shift the responsibility of effecting the restoration to the supra-historical divine sovereignty.

The shift from postmillennial to premillennial eschatology in nineteenth-century America is greatly illumined by this analysis—indeed, it was in many ways a shift from ethical prophetism to ahistorical apocalypticism. Certainly it involved a shift of focus from the prophetic to the apocalyptic texts of Scripture. Arminian and perfectionist tendencies heightened the postmillennial expectations just as the events of history began to pull the rug out from under them. The tension between vision and reality began to disintegrate under internal conflicts created by heightened unrealistic expectations and under external attack a history took new turns that consistently and cumulatively accentuated the gap between the millennial hope and actual historical experiences. The only way to maintain the millennial hope *and* its imminence was to put the pieces of the eschatological vision into a new configuration. The millennial hope was preserved by placing the return of Christ before the millennium to become the cataclysmic event that would bridge the growing gap between hope and historical reality.

A CHANGING VISION

Almost as soon as it was articulated, the Oberlin postmillennial vision began to show cracks and flaws. As the 1840s and 1850s came and went, internal tension grew as, for example, Oberlin's commitment to abolitionism came into conflict with its commitment to nonviolence. Soon, and especially in the Civil War, adherents had to choose between peace and anti-slavery. Such choices seemed to postpone the millennium; life became more complex, and evil seemed more intransigent than was first thought.

After the Civil War, revivalist postmillennialism was dealt lethal blow after lethal blow. Great waves of immigration from the late 1840s forced a new pluralism involving large contingents of Catholics (for many revivalists the increase of "Romanism" could only expand the base of "antichrist"), new forms of Protestantism (such as German Lutherans who did not easily fit into the revivalist and temperance ethos), and eventually large numbers of Jews and other non-Christians. Concurrently there was the rise of biblical criticism and the new sciences (geology, Darwinism, and so forth) that shook traditional views of the Scriptures and of human origins—and gave impetus to a more liberal interpretation of Christianity or even its abandonment. All this was taking place in the context of harsh urbanization and industrialization, the burdens of which often fell heavily on rural Protestants migrating to the cities out of middle and southern America in the wake of the revivalist impact.

The postmillennial vision became unthinkable to many in this context. Instead of a world growing better and better, many saw only progressive decline and a world growing worse and worse. Indeed, the literary battles between the postmillennialists and the premillennialists often turned on an empirical issue: Was progress or decline the better description of the direction of the culture? Postmillennialists and their near cousins, the more liberal advocates of progress, appealed (as Cowles did in the quotation cited earlier) to growing literacy, the advance of missions, the growth of science and commerce, and so on.

Premillennialists were those who began to have doubts about these dreams. They observed the same passing scene and gave it a different reading. In 1878 there began in New York a series of prophecy conferences advocating premillennialism which continue into the present. In 1914 at the Chicago Prophetic Bible Conference, there was a panel discussion of figures who reflected on the sorts of dynamics that lay behind their conversion to premillennialism—significantly almost always from postmillennialism. Typical of these was the testimony of the Rev. Howard W. Pope, superintendent of men at Moody Bible Institute:

> This truth of the premillennial coming of our Lord came to me in two installments, probably because I was unable to receive it all at once. When I graduated at Yale University and Theological Seminary, our instructor in theology dismissed the whole subject with about two sentences, saying that this truth was a harmless delusion held by certain people called Adventists. . . .

> But about twenty years ago, when I was a [Congregationalist] pastor in New England, I was studying the general subject of missions, and reached the conclusion that this world would never be converted by the agencies now in operation. I recalled that New England had had some chance, having had the gospel for two hundred and fifty years; and yet there was not a city, town, or hamlet in all New England where all the people had ever been converted. The thing began to look rather discouraging to me. . . . I discovered that in the the last one hundred years of missions about three millions of heathens had been

> converted; while during that same time three billions of
> people have been born, lived and died, and never heard
> that there is a Christ. At that rate, I thought, when are we
> ever likely to overtake the procession? I reached the
> conclusion, that it was simply a hopeless case; that this
> world would never be converted. . . . I reached that
> conclusion without any reference to premillennial teach-
> ing.[45]

Such growing convictions predisposed Pope to adopt premillennialism sometime later.

This radical shift that took place in the mainstream of
Evangelical revivalism between Charles G. Finney and Dwight
L. Moody is one of the most remarkable developments on the
religious scene in the nineteenth century. Compare Finney's
explosive optimism, cited earlier, with this self-confident
pronouncement of Moody a half-century later:

> The pre-millennial advent means Christ coming before the
> millennium. There will be no millennium till he comes.
> That is plain Scripture. Many people have got an idea that
> we are going to get the millennium by means of tele-
> phones, steam-engines, swift Atlantic steamers, and all
> the appliances of modern civilization. These things, they
> imagine, are to bring the millennium and then at the end
> of the millennium Christ will come. But it is Scripture that
> Christ will come first. He must come before his reign of a
> thousand years. He is to usher in the millennium by his
> coming. If the post-millennial view is correct, when is the
> millennium to commence? Certainly it hasn't come yet,
> nor does it seem to be coming. Look at London with its
> millions in degradation and sin. Look at our own country
> with its great cities like Chicago, with Anarchists and
> Communists propagating their doctrine. If the world is to
> become better first, we are very far from the millennium
> yet. But death is here, sin is here.[46]

Similar sentiments would be expressed at the 1886
(second) prophetic conference by A. T. Pierson, prominent
missionary leader and advocate of premillennialism:

> What is the real character of our civilization? We may as
> well face the facts. It is gigantic in invention, discovery
> and enterprise, achievement, but it is gigantically worldly;

sometimes and somewheres monstrously God-denying
and God-defying. . . . Philosophy now blooms into a
refined and poetic pantheism or a gross, blank materialism
or a subtle rationalism or an absurd agnosticism. Science
constructs its systems of evolution and leaves out a
personal God; . . . Such men as Strauss and Renan, Hegel
and Comte, Goethe and Kant, Mill and Spencer, Darwin
and Huxley, Matthew Arnold and Theodore Parker are
specimens of men who owe their education, refinement,
accomplishment, to the very Christianity they attack. . . .
We have the ripest form of worldly civilization, but the
RIPENESS BORDERS ON ROTTENNESS . . . and that
awful anarchy which is the last result of atheism even
now threatens to dissolve society itself. . . . Our golden
age is far from unfolding even the promise of millennium.[47]

This analysis was elaborated and developed into a standard
litany of the "evils of the age" and the "signs of the times."
The approaching end was signaled, not by progress, but by
decline.[48]

This shift would require the subtle adaptation of earlier
visions. Whereas the postmillennial vision had looked forward
to the conversion of the world, hopes were now scaled down
to worldwide evangelism with much more pessimism about
the percentage of response. Evangelism became less a tool for
transforming the culture and more and more a process of
calling out a "select few," the elect, who should be about the
task of witness while preparing as a bride to meet the
Bridegroom.

But, however we explain the phenomenon, it is clear that
this new eschatological vision swept the world of conservative
revivalism late in the nineteenth century and with few
exceptions came to be the dominant position in nearly all
those constellations where the Pentecostal baptism and the
doctrines of faith healing were advocated. This was clearest in
the revivalistic mainstream. Where there had been reticence
about the doctrines of divine healing (as in the Moody/Torrey
circles), no such hesitation appears. Moody led the way and
set the tone on this question.[49] Others were quick to follow.
A. B. Simpson and A. J. Gordon, for example, were strong
advocates of the doctrine.

PREMILLENNIALISM IN THE HOLINESS MOVEMENT

On this issue, however, the Methodist wing of the Holiness currents showed no more resistance. Premillennialism was, with healing, one of the issues most resisted by the leadership of the National Holiness Association. Such figures as G. W. Wilson[50] and Daniel Steele consistently polemicized against the new doctrines in various books.

Steele was particularly active in these polemics. He noticed that those in the Reformed traditions were more attracted to premillennialism—as evidenced by statistics about conveners and attenders at the prophecy conferences. He felt that the new doctrines were a fundamental affront to characteristic themes of Methodism:

> We can see how an old-fashioned Calvinist, who believes in irresistible grace, can accept this doctrine; but how an Arminian, trained to magnify human freedom and the suasive power of gospel motives for the renovation of the will, through the Holy Spirit applying truth assented to by the intellect, and taught to reject salvation by mere sovereignty, can accept the Millenarian idea of the universal triumph of Christ, surpasses our poor understanding.[51]

This correlation was noticed by others as well[52] and helps to explain why the Methodist side of the Holiness movement withstood the pressure longer—so much so that even in the twentieth century, when A. M. Hills penned the first full systematic theology of the movement, he faced a dilemma on the issue. He himself, originally a Congregationalist nurtured at Yale and Oberlin, was staunchly postmillennial, but his denomination, the newly formed Church of the Nazarene, was predominantly premillennial. He solved the problem by producing a systematic theology with two eschatologies, a postmillennial one penned by himself and a premillennial one penned by a leader of that perspective.[53]

But even Steele showed signs of the shift that would take place in Holiness thought late in the nineteenth century. Fletcher's doctrine of dispensations was regularly analyzed in Steele's works, and these expositions were widely reprinted in various Holiness periodicals. We have already noted Steele's call for an adoption of the vocabulary of Pentecost.

Where these seeds are sown, the movement to premillennialism is more natural. Just as postmillennialism may be seen as the social correlate of the doctrine of entire sanctification—both emphasizing the role of human agency and the process of gradual transformation culminating in a level of the vanquishment of sin and evil within history—so may premillennialism be seen as the social correlate of the doctrine of the baptism in the Holy Spirit—both emphasizing an instantaneous event of transformation, the divine agency, and a human response of "tarry and wait" for the "blessing" or the "blessed hope."

Thus, by the mid-1890s major leaders of the more radical wings of the Methodistic Holiness movement had become advocates of the new doctrine. This shift could be illustrated extensively, but a few examples will suffice. W. B. Godbey reveals the struggle that some Methodists endured over the doctrine:

> A great holiness evangelist said to Bro. Pickett, "I am a postmillennialist." In reply to Bro. Pickett's request for his reason, he responded, "I have to be a postmillennialist in order to be a Methodist." When Bro. Pickett told me, it grieved me, because I had congratulated myself that that brother like myself was saved from Methodism. I was born a Methodist—my father was a Methodist preacher, but when the Lord baptized me with the Holy Ghost and fire in 1868, He cremated the Methodist along with the Free Mason, the Odd Fellow, the College President and the candidate for the episcopacy.[54]

George D. Watson, a southern evangelist and prolific author (often on themes of eschatology and the necessity of the Holiness "bride" to prepare to meet her "bridegroom"), changed his views about 1896:

> For twenty-five or thirty years of my life I accepted the old Roman Catholic notion, which is accepted by most Protestants, that the second coming of Christ would be after the millennium, and at the time of the general judgment. Then, for a few years, I was unsettled in my views on that subject for I saw so many portions of Scripture that could not have any reasonable interpretation in harmony with that old theory.

Early in 1896 I began to pray very earnestly for the Holy
Spirit to open up the Scriptures to me clearly on that
subject. In two or three weeks afterward the Spirit began
unfolding to my mind, in a remarkable way, the Book of
Revelation, and the parables of Jesus and other Scriptures
on the pre-millennial coming of Christ, and the light on
that subject has been increasing ever since.[55]

By the 1890s W. B. Godbey claimed that the Holiness
movement was largely premillennial in conviction:

Some were shouting, "Behold, He cometh! Behold, He
cometh!" I have been shouting it for twenty years. What a
wonderful flood of light on this subject is inundating the
world! Only two years ago Brother Carradine got light on
it, and preached it, and Dr. Watson preached his first
sermon on it, and there has been a regular revelation on
the subject in the last few years. You do not find one
sanctified man in a thousand who is not looking for the
speedy coming of the Lord.[56]

In 1897 Martin Wells Knapp, editor of *God's Revivalist*,
announced a new policy indicating that "the Aim of the
Revivalist"

is to present a Pentecostal experience as the basis of
genuine revival life in the individual and the Church, and
to ignore no Bible doctrine which is an incentive to or
result of this life. We are fully persuaded that one of these
doctrines is that of the second coming of our Lord, as
taught in the New Testament, and that every fully-devel-
oped Pentecostal experience includes this Pentecostal
expecting of the coming of the King. While in no sense of
the word do we substitute this for the main issue of the
sanctifying work of our Savior, yet we design to give its
notice its proper place in our columns, and may for a time
give it more attention, to make amends for a past neglect,
than we otherwise would.[57]

And so, by the turn of the century at least the most radical
wings of the Holiness movement had worked this theme into
their theology. Sanctification was no longer, as it had been at
Oberlin half a century earlier, a part of God's transformation of
the world and his means of inaugurating the millennium. As

C. W. Ruth would preach in a turn-of-the-century camp meeting, "What is the holiness movement but a call to God's people to put on the wedding garment?"[58]

With this development the stage has been set for the emergence of Pentecostalism. Nearly every wing of late nineteenth-century revivalism was teaching in one form or another all the basic themes of Pentecostalism except for the experience of glossolalia, or "speaking in tongues."

NOTES

1. Assemblies of God, *Combined Minutes, First General Council* (1914), p. 2, as quoted in Robert Mapes Anderson, *Vision of the Disinherited: The Making of American Pentecostalism* (New York: Oxford University Press, 1979), p. 79.

2. See Anderson, *Vision of the Disinherited*, ch. 5, "The Pentecostal Message." David William Faupel of Asbury Theological Seminary, Wilmore, Kentucky, argues this case in a dissertation for the University of Birmingham, England.

3. Neill Q. Hamilton, *The Holy Spirit and Eschatology in Paul*, Scottish Journal of Theology Occasional Papers, no. 6 (Edinburgh: Oliver and Boyd, 1957), p. 33. See also Marie E. Isaacs, *The Concept of the Spirit*, Heythrop Monographs, no. 1 (London: N. p., 1976), and Eduard Schweizer et al., *Spirit of God* (London: Adam and Charles Black, 1960).

4. On Montanism, see especially Maurice Barnett, *The Living Flame: Being a Study of the Gift of the Spirit in the New Testament With Special Reference to Prophecy, Glossolalia, Montanism and Perfection* (London: Epworth, 1953).

5. For Joachim's use of apocalyptic texts and imagery, see the works of Marjorie Reeves, especially *Joachim of Fiore and the Prophetic Future* (London: SPCK, 1976).

6. The five volumes of the *Collected Writings of Edward Irving*, ed. G. Carlyle (London: Alexander Strahan, 1864), are supplemented by two volumes of *The Prophetical Works of Edward Irving* (London: Alexander Strahan, 1867). See also C. Gordon Strachan, *The Pentecostal Theology of Edward Irving* (London: Darton, Longman and Todd, 1973).

7. A. C. Dixon, ed., *The Person and Ministry of the Holy Spirit* (Baltimore: Wharton, Barron, [1891]).

8. *The Christian Doctrine of the Church, Faith and the Consummation*, Dogmatics (London: Lutterworth, 1962; original German publ., 1960), 3:400. This passage was drawn to my attention by J. Rodman Williams, "The Holy Spirit and Eschatology," a paper presented at the 1980 annual meeting of the Society for Pentecostal Studies and published in *Pneuma* 3 (Fall 1981): 54–58. Williams, a leader of the Presbyterian wing of the Charismatic movement, suggests that he personally had "no joy in the expectation of the return of the

Lord" before he "knew the Holy Spirit." Since then he reports that "we can hardly wait for this full manifestation." These comments and the Brunner quote, however, do not appear in the published version.

9. This story is most recently chronicled by Timothy P. Weber, *Living in the Shadow of the Second Coming: American Premillennialism, 1875–1925* (New York: Oxford University Press, 1979; rev. ed, Grand Rapids: Zondervan, 1983), and earlier by Ernest R. Sandeen, *The Roots of Fundamentalism: British and American Millenarianism, 1800–1930* (Chicago: University of Chicago Press, 1970).

10. See especially the essays by Melvin E. Dieter and William Menzies in Vinson Synan, ed., *Aspects of Pentecostal-Charismatic Origins* (Plainfield, N.J.: Logos International, 1975), and Edith Lydia Waldvogel, "The 'Overcoming Life': A Study of the Reformed Evangelical Origins of Pentecostalism" (Ph.D. diss., Harvard University, 1977), pp. 123–24.

11. On dispensationalism, see Daniel P. Fuller, *Gospel and Law: Contrast or Continuum? The Hermeneutics of Dispensationalism* (Grand Rapids: Wm. B. Eerdmans, 1980); Clarence B. Bass, *Backgrounds to Dispensationalism* (Grand Rapids: Wm. B. Eerdmans, 1960); and C. Norman Kraus, *Dispensationalism in America* (Richmond: John Knox, 1958).

12. Some of the ideas in these two paragraphs I owe to conversations with Prof. Gerald T. Sheppard of Emmanuel College, Toronto, and his paper, "Pentecostals and Dispensationalism: The Anatomy of an Uneasy Relationship," presented at the 1983 annual meeting of the Society for Pentecostal Studies and published as "Pentecostalism and the Hermeneutics of Dispensationalism: Anatomy of an Uneasy Relationship" in *Pneuma* 6 (Fall 1984): 5–33.

13. In addition to the literature cited in other footnotes, I have found especially useful a study by Robert K. Whalen, "Millenarianism and Millennialism in America, 1790–1880" (Ph.D. diss., State University of New York at Stony Brook, 1971).

14. The sermons, however, were not published until 1715. They are included in only some editions of the works of Howe, but are excerpted in Iain H. Murray, *The Puritan Hope: A Study in Revival and the Interpretation of Prophecy* (London: Banner of Truth, 1971), pp. 241–55.

15. In this disputed area of Puritan eschatology, I am following the views of Iain H. Murray, *The Puritan Hope*, and the contributors to Peter Toon, ed., *Puritans, the Millennium and the Future of Israel: Puritan Eschatology 1600 to 1660* (London: James Clarke, 1970).

16. Thus Jürgen Moltmann will argue that his "theology of hope" may be seen as an elaboration of the dynamic of Pietism (from notes taken in lectures on "*Glauben und Wissen*," Tübingen, summer semester, 1980).

17. These issues are well treated by K. James Stein, "Philipp Jakob Spener's Hope for Better Times for the Church—Contributions in Controversy," *Covenant Quarterly* 37 (August 1979): 3–20.

18. The *Gnomon* exists in several forms, the later English versions having been modified to conform with later eschatological views when the chronology failed to take place in the nineteenth century as anticipated. Bengel's chronology is reproduced in some detail by J. C. F. Burk, *A Memoir of*

the *Life and Writings of John Albert Bengel* (London: William Ball, 1837), pp. 291–93. See also Gottfried Mälzer, *Johann Albrecht Bengel: Leben und Werk* (Stuttgart: Calwer Verlag, 1970), pp. 220ff.

19. See, for example, Harris Franklin Rall, *Was Wesley a Premillennialist?* (New York: Methodist Book House, 1921), originally published in Rall, *Modern Premillennialism and the Christian Hope* (New York: Abingdon, 1920), arguing that he was not. For the opposite case, see Nathaniel West, *John Wesley and Pre-millennialism* (Cincinnati: God's Revivalist, 1894).

20. Quoted from the preface to his "Notes of the Revelation of Jesus Christ," in the *Explanatory Notes* (various editions).

21. Letter to "Mr. Christopher Hopper" with no date but the year 1788, reprinted in the 1872 Jackson edition of Wesley's *Works*, 12:319.

22. The most helpful treatment of these themes is by Clarence L. Bence, "Processive Eschatology: A Wesleyan Alternative," *Wesleyan Theological Journal* 14 (Spring 1979): 45–59. See also his related dissertation, "John Wesley's Teleological Hermeneutic" (Ph.D. diss., Emory University, 1981).

23. *The Portrait of St. Paul* (New York: Phillips and Hunt, n.d.), pp. 168–69. This and the other citations are found in a section entitled "the true minister believes and preaches the three grand promises of God, together with the three great dispensations of grace," to be found in the second part of the book as reprinted in the different versions of Fletcher's *Works*.

24. John Fletcher, "Letter to Wesley, " *Arminian Magazine* 16 (1793): 370–76, 409–416.

25. John Fletcher, "A Letter on the Prophecies" (presumed to be to Wesley on the basis of internal evidence), in *The Works of the Rev. John Fletcher* (London: John Kershaw, 1826), 4:529–50.

26. See, for example, Arnold Ehlert, *A Bibliographic History of Dispensationalism* (Grand Rapids: Baker, 1965), pp. 41–42. This booklet reprints articles from *Bibliotheca Sacra*, vols. 101–2.

27. These words are from Wesley's exposition of the petition "thy kingdom come" in the Lord's Prayer as given in his sixth sermon on "The Sermon on the Mount," usually numbered 26 in editions of his sermons.

28. Letter of 5 March 1743/4 to William McCulloch, reprinted in Jonathan Edwards, *The Great Awakening*, Works of Jonathan Edwards, ed. C. C. Goen (New Haven: Yale University Press, 1972), 4:560.

29. C. C. Goen, "Jonathan Edwards: A New Departure in Eschatology," *Church History* 28 (March 1959): 25–40.

30. Edwards, "The Distinguishing Marks," in *The Great Awakening*, 4:281.

31. I have not seen the Bellamy sermon, but it is apparently appended to the 1794 edition of Edwards's *Humble Attempt*. Samuel Hopkins, *A Treatise on the Millennium* (Boston: Isaiah Thomas and Ebenezer Andrews, 1793; reprint, New York: Arno Press, 1972).

32. "The Pernicious Attitude of the Church on the Reforms of the Age," in a series of "letters" published by Finney in *Oberlin Evangelist*, this letter being originally published 21 January 1846, but excised from later editions of the letters in book form until restored in Charles G. Finney, *Reflections on Revival*, comp. Donald W. Dayton (Minneapolis: Bethany Fellowship, 1979).

33. This appears in a list of purposes regularly carried in early issues of the *Oberlin Evangelist.*

34. Henry Cowles, "The Millennium—No. 1," *Oberlin Evangelist* 3 (17 February 1841): 28.

35. Henry Cowles, "The Millennium—No. 9," *Oberlin Evangelist* 3 (9 June 1841): 94.

36. Henry Cowles, "The Millennium—No. 10," *Oberlin Evangelist* 3 (23 June 1841): 101.

37. Ibid.

38. Henry Cowles, "The Millennium—No. 11," *Oberlin Evangelist* 3 (7 July 1841): 110.

39. Henry Cowles, "The Millennium—No. 12," *Oberlin Evangelist* 3 (21 July 1841): 119.

40. Henry Cowles, "The Millennium—No. 23," *Oberlin Evangelist* 3 (22 December 1841): 204.

41. Paul D. Hanson, *The Dawn of Apocalyptic* (Philadelphia: Fortress, 1975), p. 11.

42. Ibid., pp. 11–12.

43. Ibid., pp. 17, 31.

44. Ibid., p. 12.

45. *The Coming and Kingdom of Christ* (Chicago: Bible Institute College Colportage Association, [1914]), pp. 75–76.

46. *D. L. Moody at Home* (London: Morgan and Scott, [1910]), p. 163.

47. A. T. Pierson, "World Wide Evangelism," in *Prophetic Studies of the International Prophecy Conference, Chicago, 1886* (Chicago: Fleming H. Revell, 1886), p. 31.

48. See, for example, the influential defense of premillennialism by W. E. Blackstone, *Jesus Is Coming* (New York: Fleming H. Revell, 1898), translated into some forty languages, or such later studies as Henry Clay Morrison, *Is the World Growing Better, or Is the World Growing Worse?* (Louisville: Pentecostal Publishing, 1932).

49. The most recent study of Moody's theology is Stanley N. Gundry, *Love Them In: The Proclamation Theology of D. L. Moody* (Chicago: Moody, 1976). On Torrey, see Roger Martin, *R. A. Torrey: Apostle of Certainty* (Murfreesboro, Tenn.: Sword of the Lord, [1976]).

50. G. W. Wilson, *The Signs of Thy Coming* (Boston: Christian Witness, 1899).

51. Daniel Steele, *Steele's Answers: A Substitute for Holiness, or Antinomianism Revived* (reprint, Salem, Ohio: Schmul Publishers, n.d.), pp. 91–92.

52. See, for example, Whalen, "Millenarianism and Millennialism in America, 1790–1880."

53. A. M. Hills, *Fundamental Christian Theology* (Kansas City, Mo.: Nazarene Publishing House, 1931).

54. W. B. Godbey, *An Appeal to Postmillennialists* (Nashville: Pentecostal Mission Publishing, n.d.), pp. 5–6.

55. George D. Watson, *Steps to the Throne* (Cincinnati: God's Revivalist, [1898]), p. 5.

56. W. B. Godbey and Seth Cook Rees, *The Return of Jesus* (Cincinnati: God's Revivalist Office, n.d.), p. 16.

57. As reported in A. M. Hills, *A Hero of Faith and Prayer; or, Life of Rev. Martin Wells Knapp* (Cincinnati: Mrs. M. W. Knapp, 1902), p. 154.

58. *Electric Shocks From Pentecostal Batteries; or, Food and Fire from Salvation Park Camp-Meeting* (Cincinnati: M. W. Knapp, 1899), p. 122.

PENTECOSTAL POWER

CHARLOTTE G. HOMER   CHAS. H. GABRIEL

1. Lord, as of old at Pen-te-cost Thou didst Thy pow'r dis-play,
2. For might-y works for Thee, pre-pare And strengthen ev-'ry heart;
3. All self con-sume, all sin de-stroy! With earn-est zeal en-due
4. Speak, Lord, be-fore Thy throne we wait, Thy prom-ise we be-lieve,

With cleans-ing, pu-ri-fy-ing flame De-scend on us to-day.
Come, take pos-ses-sion of Thine own, And nev-er-more de-part.
Each wait-ing heart to work for Thee; O Lord, our faith re-new!
And will not let Thee go un-til The bless-ing we re-ceive.

CHORUS

Lord, send the old-time pow'r, The Pen-te-cos-tal pow'r! Thy floodgates of

blessing on us throw o-pen wide! Lord, send the old-time pow'r, the

Pen-te-cos-tal pow'r, That sinners be converted and Thy name glo-ri-fied!

THE EMERGENCE
OF PENTECOSTALISM

Our search for the theological roots of Pentecostalism has brought us full circle. In the first chapter of this book we argued that only by "bracketing" for the moment the phenomenon of speaking in tongues could we understand theologically the nature of Pentecostalism and be able to place it in its theological and ecclesiastical context. Our analysis there led to the identification of four Christological themes defining the basic *gestalt* of Pentecostal thought and ethos: Christ as Savior, as Baptizer with the Holy Spirit, as Healer, and as Coming King. This description was confirmed by an explication of the logic with which these themes are intertwined in Pentecostal rhetoric.

This four-fold analysis has now also been confirmed by the extent to which it has permitted a description of the historical and theological process in which these themes emerged and coalesced to form the Pentecostal tradition. The first theme locates Pentecostalism within the conversionist-oriented revivalist tradition. The second theme is the key one, and chapters 2, 3, and 4 have been devoted to tracing the evolution of the Wesleyan doctrine of entire sanctification into the Pentecostal doctrine of baptism in the Spirit. By the end of the nineteenth century, popular American revivalism, the Holiness movement proper, and the broader "deeper Christian life" spiritualities of the time were suffused with Pentecostal rhetoric and variations on the doctrine of a Pentecostal baptism of the Holy Spirit.

With this basic outline made clear, the rest of the story falls into place. It becomes apparent in chapter 5 that the rise of faith healing, while it had broader roots, may be seen largely as a radicalization of the Holiness doctrine of instantaneous sanctification in which the consequences of sin (i.e., disease) as well as sin itself are overcome in the Atonement and vanquished during this life. Likewise, in chapter 6 we have seen how the internal logic and transformations of Holiness thought in the nineteenth century tended in the direction of premillennialism so that by 1900 this theme had coalesced with the others to produce the "full" or "four-fold gospel" that lies at the heart of Pentecostalism.

Once these themes have been identified, it is striking the extent to which they seem to permeate late nineteenth-century popular Evangelicalism and Fundamentalism. Indeed, one might argue that the whole network of popular "higher Christian life" institutions and movements constituted at the turn of the century a sort of pre-Pentecostal tinderbox awaiting the spark that would set it off. This fact could be illustrated at length; a few examples will have to suffice here.

By the end of the century, the Holiness movement proper was preoccupied not only with the Pentecostal reformation of Wesleyan doctrine, but also more specifically—despite the efforts of the national leadership to oppose "sidetracks" from the central focus—with the themes of the four-fold gospel. A poignant illustration may be found in the reports of the Salvation Park Camp Meeting in Cincinnati, one of several meetings in a series of volumes entitled *Electric Shocks From Pentecostal Batteries*. The Four themes we have developed in our study formed virtually the organizing principle of the reports. In the preface to the 1900 edition, Martin Wells Knapp quoted the words of Seth Cook Rees:

> We have been in the ministry of Christ's gospel for twenty-seven years, and this camp was the nearest "back-to-Pentecost" of anything we have ever witnessed; not because there were about five hundred souls saved or sanctified in the ten days, for we have a few times witnessed a larger number than that in the same length of

time; but never have we seen anything more thorough and satisfactory than the work here. The conversions and sanctifications were more distinct, definite, demonstrative. Not less than one hundred were anointed for healing according to the fifth chapter of James; and a very large proportion of them received the distinct instantaneous witness in their bodies to healing. Perhaps as large a proportion of those seeking received the witness to healing as did those seeking salvation. In this camp the Holy Ghost has again set at naught the folly of those who claim that to allow healing a place in the teachings of the Holiness Movement is detrimental to "holiness." We know something of camp meeting work; and we have never attended a camp where these things were warned off as "side-tracks" that had anything like the power that was manifest here. When we preached on the "Return of our Lord," the altar was packed and overrun with seekers for salvation.[1]

Martin Wells Knapp urged "those who desire to spread the tidings of a full gospel, to do so by the circulation of this booklet" of "electric sparks" from a "Pentecostal battery."[2] Two years later at the same meeting, testimonies abounded along the lines of "I know in whom I have believed. The Lord is my Savior, Sanctifier, Healer, and coming King."[3]

Indeed, when Pentecostalism emerged in the next few years, leaders of the Holiness movement recognized that it was only the gift of tongues that set it apart from their own teachings. For example, the Rev. B. W. Huckabee, the editor of the *Pentecostal Advocate* (a journal close to the roots of the present Church of the Nazarene), reported after meeting some of the "tongues people" a letter from a friend indicating that

they preached the full gospel, emphasizing the ministry of holiness and also the universality of the gospel invitation. They taught with great conviction the immediate return of our Lord, and the necessity of being filled with the Holy Spirit as a preparation for the rapture. They taught divine healing; in fact, the full gospel as we understand it, with this addition, the gift of tongues.[4]

At the end of chapter 4 we noted that by 1890 A. B. Simpson, the major figure behind the Christian and Missionary

Alliance that stood midway between the strictly Holiness currents and the broader premillennial revivalists of the late nineteenth century, had articulated his teachings in the form of a four-fold gospel expressed in the slogan "Christ our Savior, Christ our Sanctifier, Christ our Healer, and Christ our Coming Lord." This is obviously very close to the Pentecostal formulation, requiring only the transmutation of the second theme into "Christ the Baptizer with the Holy Ghost." By the middle of the last decade of the nineteenth century Simpson was moving, especially in his Bible studies, toward more explicitly Pentecostal language. It is, therefore, not unexpected that when Pentecostalism did emerge, some observers thought it a split within the Christian and Missionary Alliance.

But these same four themes are also to be found, though perhaps somewhat muted, in the more Reformed revivalism of popular Evangelicalism at the turn of the century. We have already referred to various books by Adoniram Judson Gordon, leading figure behind contemporary New England Evangelicalism. To see his commitment to the themes of the four-fold gospel, we need only to note his major books: *The Ministry of Healing; or, Miracles of Cure in All Ages* (1882); *The Two Fold Life; or, Christ's Work for Us and Christ's Work in Us* (1883); *Ecce Venit* (1889); and *The Ministry of the Spirit* (1894). We have also noted that a similar pattern is discernible in the writings of R. A. Torrey, who served at the turn of the century as the head of the Moody Bible Institute and is remembered today in part for his violent polemics against Pentecostalism. Popular Evangelicalism was indeed at the time but a hairsbreadth from Pentecostalism.

That hairsbreadth of difference was the experience of speaking in tongues as the evidence of having received the baptism with the Holy Spirit. This phenomenon was not a natural part of the currents that we have surveyed in this study and, indeed, is a significant *novum* for the most part that truly does set Pentecostalism apart from the other "higher Christian life" movements. But the question of "evidence" was not new or entirely foreign to these circles.

From the time of Puritanism and classical Methodism, the question of assurance had been at the fore. Wesley's own concern for the presence of the moral fruit of the Spirit as a

confirming witness was a moderating influence in his teachings, but his willingness to speak of a "direct witness of the
Holy Spirit" was a major basis for accusations of "enthusi-
asm."[5] This concern cropped up in various forms in the
nineteenth century and was often radicalized along with the
other developments that we have traced.

In Phoebe Palmer and the early Holiness movement these
themes were muted, though controversy did arise about the
role of "testimony" as an evidence of having received the
"blessing."[6] In the late nineteenth century, however, issues of
"evidence" came more distinctly to the fore. Though no doubt
the case is extreme, Hannah Whitall Smith left in her papers
that were published posthumously a report of a "Dr. R." who
argued that the "Baptism of the Holy Spirit was a physical
thing, felt by delightful thrills going through you from head to
toe, and that no one could really know what the Baptism of the
Spirit was who did not experience these thrills."[7]

Whatever the reason, by the end of the century the more
moderate Holiness leadership was warning against excessive
concern for physical and emotional signs. Thus in 1891
Methodist Asbury Lowrey, writing in the pages of Divine Life,
pitted the classical Wesleyan doctrines of assurance against
"expecting any outward signs" in an essay entitled "Evidences
of Full Salvation."[8] The issue was clearly surfacing, and we
should not be surprised to see the question put explicitly by
the end of the century. Once the question was put, the account
of Pentecost in Acts, especially as read through certain Pauline
texts in Corinthians 12–14, provided a ready-made answer:
the "evidence of speaking in unknown tongues."

This phenomenon of speaking in tongues was not unknown at the time. Assiduous searches for antecedents to
contemporary Pentecostal practice have compiled lists of
reports of such outbreaks that occurred at an increasing rate of
frequency from 1870.[9] Illustrative of these incidents, but not
included among the lists, so far as I know, is this event taking
place in 1881 in a midwestern Holiness camp meeting:

> One day in the midst of a great sermon, a woman from
> Carrol County, a holiness professor, sprawled out at full
> length in the aisle. This, in itself, was not much to be

thought of, for to tumble over now and then was to be
expected. But the unexpected happened in this case. It
kept some of the sisters busy to keep her with a measur-
ably decent appearance. Directly she began to compose a
jargon of words in rhyme and sing them with a weird
tune. She persisted till the service was spoiled and the
camp was thrown into a hubbub. Strange to say, the camp
was divided thereby. Some said it was a repetition of
speaking in unknown tongues as at Pentecost. But every
preacher on the ground without exception declared it to
be of the devil. But the camp was so divided in opinion
that it had to be handled with the greatest of care.[10]

This incident illustrates the fact of speaking in tongues and
foreshadows the variety of interpretations that would be
attached to the practice a couple of decades later.

It is worth noting that these incidents were widespread
and apparently unrelated. There seems to have been a tendency for the practice to arise spontaneously in many contexts.
As far away as Sweden, for example, Lewi Pethrus, later to
emerge as the major leader of Pentecostalism in that country,
reported a similar experience in 1902. Though a Baptist,
Pethrus had heard in his youth of the doctrine of the baptism
of the Holy Spirit from Salvation Army officers. This raised for
him the question of whether such an experience was for today.
Then in 1902, he was returning aboard a ferry from a prayer
meeting held in the home of Norwegian advocates of the
"Holiness experience," at which themes of the deeper Christian life and divine healing had been explored. As he paced on
board ship and prayed, he had an experience in which "under
the influence of a mighty power which filled [his] entire being
[he] began to speak words that [he] could not understand."[11] It
was not until five years later, after reports from the Azusa
Street Revival in America reached him, that Pethrus received
the categories that he would use to interpret his experience as
having spoken in tongues as an outward sign of having
received the baptism of the Holy Spirit.

Thus we may now understand much better the context in
which, as reported in chapter 1, an independent Holiness
evangelist by the name of Charles Fox Parham described an
incident at Bethel Bible College of Topeka, Kansas:

In December of 1900 we had our examination upon the subject of repentance, conversion, consecration, sanctification, healing, and the soon coming of the Lord. We had reached in our studies a problem. What about the second chapter of Acts? . . . I set the students at work studying out diligently what was Bible evidence of the baptism of the Holy Ghost.[12]

It was this assignment, at least according to later reports, that a few days later led Agnes N. Ozman to "receive the Holy Spirit" and purportedly to speak in the Chinese language. This event is usually regarded as the beginning of Pentecostalism.

This book leaves unanswered many questions. It would be tempting to follow out the denouement of many themes identified in this volume, such as the rise of the "finished work" doctrine of sanctification that split Pentecostalism into Holiness and non-Holiness segments. But this and related issues are a part of the history rather than the prehistory of Pentecostalism. They belong to a study of the theological history of the movement, not to a search for the theological roots of Pentecostalism.

NOTES

1. *Electric Shocks—No. II, from Pentecostal Batteries; or, Pentecostal Glories from Salvation Park Camp-Meeting—1900* (Cincinnati: M. W. Knapp, 1900), pp. 3–4.

2. Ibid., p. 4.

3. *Electric Shocks—No. IV, from Pentecostal Batteries; or, Salvation Park Camp-Meetings, 1902* (Cincinnati: Mrs. M. W. Knapp, 1902), p. 115.

4. B. W. Huckabee, *Pentecostal Advocate* (14 March 1907): 8.

5. On Wesley's doctrine of assurance and its antecedents, see Forest T. Benner, "The Immediate Antecedents of the Wesleyan Doctrine of the Witness of the Spirit" (Ph.D. diss., Temple University, 1966); Arthur S. Yates, *The Doctrine of Assurance* (London: Epworth, 1952); and Mark Noll, "John Wesley and the Doctrine of Assurance," *Bibliotheca Sacra* 132 (April-June 1975): 161–77.

6. On the "testimony" controversy, see Melvin E. Dieter, *The Holiness Revival of the Nineteenth Century*, Studies in Evangelicalism, no. 1 (Metuchen, N.J.: Scarecrow Press, 1980), pp. 35–37.

7. Ray Strachey, *Group Movements of the Past and Experiments in Guidance* (London: Faber and Faber, 1934), p. 167.

8. *Divine Life* 16 (April 1891): 85–87. A similar article under the same name by the same author appeared earlier in *Divine Life* 10 (March 1887): 235–37.

9. Illustrative of this would be the list compiled by William W. Menzies, *Anointed to Serve* (Springfield, Mo.: Gospel Publishing House, 1971), pp. 29–33.

10. A. M. Kiergan, *Historical Sketches of the Revival of True Holiness and Local Church Polity* (Fort Scott, Kans.: Church Advocate and Good Way, 1971), p. 31.

11. Lewi Pethrus, *A Spiritual Memoir* (Plainfield, N.J.: Logos International, [1973]), p. 20.

12. Parham, *The Life of Charles F. Parham*, pp. 51–52.

BIBLIOGRAPHICAL ESSAY

This book has been based largely on a personal collection of more than 4,000 volumes gathered over a decade. Complete bibliographical description and analysis of this material would produce a bibliography larger than the volume itself. More extended bibliographical and discussion notes have been provided in the body of the text, and full bibliographical information has been given there for both actual citations and for materials relevant to aspects of the issues treated. Here is offered a more analytical overview of the source material used and the discussions in the secondary literature about its interpretation.

Much of the material used in this work, particularly pieces relating to times subsequent to classical Methodism, has not been collected by the major libraries and has not been incorporated into the major national and subject bibliographies. Only within the last decade or so has bibliographical control of this material been at all possible. The first efforts at this task were a series of "Occasional Bibliographic Papers of the B. L. Fisher Library" published at Asbury Theological Seminary, Wilmore, Kentucky. These include Donald W. Dayton, *The American Holiness Movement: A Bibliographic Introduction* (Wilmore, Ky.: B. L. Fisher Library, 1971), originally published in the 1971 *Proceedings* of the American Theological Library Association; David W. Faupel, *The American Pentecostal Movement: A Bibliographical Essay* (Wilmore, Ky.: B. L. Fisher Library, 1972), originally published in the 1972 *Proceedings* of the American Theological Library Association; and David D. Bundy, *Keswick: A Bibliographic Introduction to the Higher Life Movements* (Wilmore, Ky.: B. L. Fisher Library, 1975).

More recently the massive and careful work of Charles Edwin Jones has provided the standard bibliographies in this area. Most useful for this study has been his *Guide to the Study of the Holiness Movement*, American Theological Library Association Bibliography Series, no. 1 (Metuchen, N.J.: Scarecrow Press and American Theological Library Association, 1974), with 7,338 entries. Also relevant is his two-volume sequel, *A Guide to the Study of Pentecostalism* (Metuchen, N.J.: Scarecrow Press and American Theological Library Association, 1983). These bibliographies are, of course, not complete and, unfortunately, do not indicate the location of materials described, but they have become the standard tools for study of these subjects.

My personal collection of materials, currently housed in the Seminary Library, the jointly maintained library of Bethany Theological Seminary and Northern Baptist Theological Seminary, contains most of the materials cited in this volume. This collection has been supplemented by materials in a number of other libraries, especially the B. L. Fisher Library of Asbury Theological Seminary, which in addition to other materials in this area has such special collections as the archival materials of the Christian Holiness Association, and the "Holy Spirit" collection in the library of Oral Roberts University, which is the most complete collection of early Pentecostal materials. Beyond these libraries one has to go to the numerous collections of the various schools spawned by the Pentecostal and Holiness movements. Here and there one finds the volumes missing in the larger collections. Garland Publishing (New York) has published under my editorship a forty-eight volume facsimile reprint series under the title "The Higher Christian Life: Sources for the Study of the Holiness, Pentecostal and Keswick Movements." Many key materials used in this study have been reprinted in this series.

CHAPTER I
TOWARD A THEOLOGICAL ANALYSIS
OF PENTECOSTALISM

This chapter is based largely, as is indicated, on a comparative analysis of early statements of faith and efforts to articulate the message of Pentecostalism. These are derived from a large range of sources, but the best collection of such material is to be found in Walter J. Hollenweger, *Handbuch der Pfingstbewegung* (Geneva: Privately published, 1965–67). This ten-volume Zürich dissertation has been deposited by the author in major libraries around the world and has been copied in microfilm by the Board of Microtext of the American Theological Library Association. Extracts have been published in several languages (French, German, Spanish, and English) with somewhat differing contents. The English edition is published as *The Pentecostals* (London: SCM Press; and Minneapolis, Minn.: Augsburg, 1972), but contains only a few samples in the appendixes of the materials used in this chapter.

The analysis of this chapter has built on the efforts of several scholars to produce a typology of the strands of Pentecostalism. The best discussion of these issues may be found in David W. Faupel, *The American Pentecostal Movement* (Wilmore, Ky.: B. L. Fisher Library, 1972), where Faupel builds on the work of Everett L. Moore, "Handbook of Pentecostal Denominations in the United States" (M.A. thesis, Pasadena College, 1954).

Because Pentecostalism has been interpreted largely in nontheological terms, the literature of theological analysis is small. In many ways the most useful book is still Frederick Dale Bruner, *A Theology of the Holy Spirit: The Pentecostal Experience and the New Testament Witness* (Grand Rapids: Wm. B. Eerdmans, 1960). This study, originally a Hamburg dissertation, is finally very critical of Pentecostalism, but it does take the time to penetrate into the inner logic of Pentecostal belief and practice and supplies in an appendix an extensive collection of source texts. Also very helpful is a chapter entitled "The Message of Pentecostalism" in Robert Mapes Anderson, *The Vision of the Disinherited: The Making of American Pentecostalism* (New York: Oxford University Press, 1979). This fact is all the more remarkable because in general this work is marred by an antitheological bias that underplays the theological aspect of Pentecostalism.

My analysis of the four-fold character of Pentecostal thought is original, but relies heavily on the writings of Aimee Semple McPherson, the founder of the International Church of the Foursquare Gospel, for the clues to this analysis. Her writings around this theme have been conveniently collected by Raymond L. Cox, *The Four-Square Gospel* (Los Angeles: Foursquare Publications, 1969). Sarah E. Parham, *The Life of Charles F. Parham, Founder the Apostolic Faith Movement* (Joplin, Mo.: Tri-State Printing, 1930; reprint, Joplin, Mo.: Hunter Printing, 1969), conveniently reprints early documents and sermons that have been important in establishing my analysis. Also key for the understanding of the logic of early Pentecostalism is D. Wesley Myland, *The Latter Rain Covenant and Pentecostal Power with Testimonies of Healing and Baptism* (Chicago: Evangel Publishing House, 1910; reprint, Springfield, Mo.: Temple Press, 1973).

CHAPTER II
METHODIST ROOTS OF PENTECOSTALISM

Classical Methodism is, of course, better studied theologically and bibliographically than the eddies it has produced that are the focus of this book. Until more volumes of the Oxford Edition (recently shifted to Abingdon Press) appear, the nineteenth edition of Wesley by Thomas Jackson, ed., *The Works of the Rev. John Wesley, A.M.* (London: John Mason, 1829) remains indispensable for the Wesley corpus. Also crucial are the twentieth-century critical editions of the letters and sermons: John Telford, ed., *The Letters of the Rev. John Wesley, A.M.* (London: Epworth, 1931), and Edward H. Sugden, ed., *Wesley's Standard Sermons* (London: Epworth, 1921). Unfortunately neither is complete. For the crucial questions for this study, the poetry and hymns of the Wesleys must not be neglected. For these we must still turn to G. Osborn, ed., *The Poetical Works of John and Charles Wesley* (London: Wesleyan Methodist Conference Office, 1869).

The key issue in this chapter is how to relate Wesley's thought to that of his associate John Fletcher. Unfortunately I have not been able to locate the vital documents from the controversies at Trevecca College that led to Fletcher's resignation. They are apparently not available in the Methodist Archives now located in the library of the University of Manchester, England. Fortunately some correspondence from the period has been preserved in Luke Tyerman, *Wesley's Designated Successor* (London: Hodder and Stoughton, 1882). The essential writings of Fletcher are his *Checks to Antinomianism* and *The Portrait of St. Paul*, both available in various editions of Fletcher's *Works* (I have used a recent reprint; Salem, Ohio: Schmul Publishers, 1974). There is little secondary literature on Fletcher, but there is a significant dissertation that speaks to the issues of this study by John Allan Knight, "John William Fletcher and the Early Methodist Tradition" (Ph.D. diss., Vanderbilt University, 1966).

The last decade has seen a controversy about how to interpret the relationship between Wesley and Fletcher on these issues. This book had its origins in an effort to answer questions raised by Herbert McGonigle, "Pneumatological Nomenclature in Early Methodism," *Wesleyan Theological Journal* 8 (Spring 1973): 61–72. My earliest attempts to work with these issues, "Asa Mahan and the Development of American Holiness Theology," *Wesleyan Theological Journal* 9 (Spring 1974): 60–69, and "From 'Christian Perfection' to 'The Baptism of the Holy Ghost,'" in H. Vinson Synan, *Aspects of Pentecostal-Charismatic Origins* (Plainfield, N.J.: Logos International, 1975), pp. 39–54, located the issues largely in the nineteenth century. The significance, however, of subtle differences between Wesley and Fletcher had become clear by the time of "The Doctrine of the Baptism of the Holy Spirit: Its Emergence and Significance," *Wesleyan Theological Journal* 13 (Spring 1978): 114–26.

The essay by McGonigle and my own efforts have helped to prompt several independent efforts to evaluate the evidence on these questions. An early response to McGonigle was William Arnett, "The Role of the Holy Spirit in Entire Sanctification in the Writings of John Wesley," *Asbury Seminarian* 29 (April 1974): 5–23. Since then the position that I have taken in this book has been severely criticized by Timothy L. Smith in such essays as "The Doctrine of the Sanctifying Spirit in John Wesley and John Fletcher," *Preacher's Magazine* 55 (September-November 1979): 16–17, 54–58, a preliminary study for "How John Fletcher Became the Theologian of Wesleyan Perfectionism, 1770–1776," *Wesleyan Theological Journal* 15 (Spring 1980): 68–87, and "The Holy Spirit in the Hymns of the Wesleys," *Wesleyan Theological Journal* 16 (Fall 1981): 32–37.

Smith's reading of the literature has prompted its own reaction, including such essays as J. Kenneth Grider, "Evaluation of Timothy Smith's Interpretation of Wesley," *Wesleyan Theological Journal* 15 (Fall 1980): 64–69, and Ken Bible, "The Wesleys' Hymns on Full Redemption and Pentecost: A Brief Comparison," *Wesleyan Theological Journal* 17 (Fall 1982): 79–87. The literature of the early stages of these debates has been surveyed by Rob L. Staples, "The Current Wesleyan Debate on the Baptism with the Holy Spirit" (privately circulated paper available from the author, no date but c. 1979).

CHAPTER III
THE AMERICAN REVIVAL OF CHRISTIAN PERFECTION

The rise of the Holiness currents, including the emergence of the more moderate Keswick spirituality, is now most conveniently narrated in Melvin E. Dieter, *The Holiness Revival of the Nineteenth Century*, Studies in Evangelicalism, no. 1 (Metuchen, N.J.: Scarecrow Press, 1980). Much work needs to be done in sorting out the theological developments in antebellum Methodism and their relationship to the varieties of the emerging Holiness currents of importance to this book. Allan Coppedge has disputed the reading that I have given to this material in his essay, "Entire Sanctification in Early American Methodism: 1812–1835," *Wesleyan Theological Journal* 13 (Spring 1978): 34–50. More supportive of my reading would be John A. Knight, "John Fletcher's Influence on the Development of Wesleyan Theology in America," *Wesleyan Theological Journal* 13 (Spring 1978): 13–33.

Again Timothy L. Smith has been attempting to dispute the position taken in this book by arguing for more congruence between classical Methodism and later developments. His major essays on this period include "Christian Perfection and American Idealism, 1820–1900," *Asbury Seminarian* 31 (October 1976): 7–34; "The Doctrine of the Sanctifying Spirit: Charles G. Finney's Synthesis of Wesleyan and Covenant Theology," *Wesleyan Theological Journal* 13 (Spring 1978): 92–113; "Righteousness and Hope: Christian Holiness and the Millennial Vision in America," *American Quarterly* 31 (Spring 1979): 21–45; and his introduction, "How Finney Helped Americans Discover the New Covenant: Righteousness Through Grace," to Charles G. Finney, *The Promise of the Spirit* (Minneapolis: Bethany Fellowship, [1980]).

The key issue in this period is the interpretation to be given to the development and significance of Oberlin perfectionism, the Wesleyan-like theology and spirituality that developed in the midst of Finneyite revivalism. The literature on this question begins with James H. Fairchild, "The Doctrine of Sanctification at Oberlin," *Congregational Quarterly* 18 (1876): 237–59; includes the fiercely polemical writings of Benjamin B. Warfield that originally appeared in the *Princeton Theological Review* (1921), but were later collected into the two volumes of *Perfectionism* (New York: Oxford University Press, 1931) and reprinted in a one-volume edition by the Presbyterian and Reformed Publishing Co., 1958; and more recently finds expression in such works as Barbara Brown Zikmund, "Asa Mahan and Oberlin Perfectionism" (Ph.D. diss., Duke University, 1969), though the last of these is not particularly oriented to the questions at the heart of this work.

CHAPTER IV
THE TRIUMPH OF THE DOCTRINE
OF PENTECOSTAL SPIRIT BAPTISM

In spite of the essays cited under chapter 3, especially those by Timothy Smith, I am inclined to date the rise of the doctrine of the baptism with the Holy Spirit to the period from 1855 to 1870, arguing that only then does it become a developed and articulated *doctrine* that goes beyond the use of Pentecostal images and metaphors. It is at least clear that the major impact of the teaching may be seen after 1870. The key texts in the emergence of the doctrine include William Arthur, *The Tongue of Fire; or, the True Power of Christianity* (New York: Harper and Brothers, 1856); the writings of Phoebe Palmer, especially *The Promise of the Father* (Boston: H. V. Degen, 1859); and particularly the first president of Oberlin, Asa Mahan, *The Baptism of the Holy Ghost* (New York: Palmer and Hughes, 1870).

The growing impact of this doctrine within the Holiness movement proper may be traced through such books as Adam Wallace, ed., *A Modern Pentecost* (Philadelphia: Methodist Home Journal Publishing House, 1873; reprint, Salem, Ohio: Convention Book Store, H. E. Schmul, 1970), and Charles J. Fowler, *Back to Pentecost* (Philadelphia: Christian Standard, 1900), representing the more restrained mainstream of the Holiness movement; and in the more radical wing by such books as Seth Cook Rees, *The Ideal Pentecostal Church* (Cincinnati: M. W. Knapp, Revivalist Office, 1897), and Martin Wells Knapp, *Lightning Bolts From Pentecostal Skies* (Cincinnati: Revivalist Office, 1889). The theological tensions these developments produced for the Holiness movement are best seen in A. M. Hills, *Holiness and Power for the Church and the Ministry* (Cincinnati: Revivalist Office, 1897). This last volume also serves as a good catalogue of various views on the question in the late nineteenth century.

The emergence of the "third-blessing heresy" within the Holiness context is a crucial development on the way to Pentecostalism. Attention was first drawn to the significance of B. H. Irwin by H. Vinson Synan, *The Holiness-Pentecostal Movement in the United States* (Grand Rapids: Wm. B. Eerdmans, 1971). Since then further work has been done by Craig Charles Fankhauser, "The Heritage of Faith: An Historical Evaluation of the Holiness Movement in America" (M.A. thesis, Pittsburg [Kansas] State University, 1983). Irwin left little articulation of his teaching. The most important sources are two leaflets, *The Baptism of Fire* and *Pyrophobia*, both originally published as articles in the *Way of Faith*, the first on 13 November 1895, p. 2, and the second on 28 October 1896, p. 2.

One of the contributions of this book is to focus attention on a Canadian counterpart to Irwin, R. C. Horner, a figure studied infrequently and hardly at all in terms of Pentecostalism. Horner was much more prolific than Irwin, had read Wesley and understood the novelty of the new doctrines, and reveals more clearly the dynamics at work in this interesting development within the Holiness teachings. Horner's life and teachings are illustrated in his autobiographical *Ralph C. Horner, Evangelist: Reminiscences from His own Pen, also Reports of Five Typical Sermons* (Brockville, Ont.: Published for Mrs. A. E. Horner by Standard Church Book Room, n.d.). His teachings are more fully developed in two volumes of *Bible Doctrines* (Ottawa: Holiness Movement Publishing House, 1909). His understanding of Wesley's distance from his own teaching and that of the late nineteenth-century Holiness movement may be seen in his *Pentecost* (Toronto: William Briggs, 1891).

The impact of this teaching on evangelist D. L. Moody and the more widely known proto-Fundamentalist revivalist tradition can be traced more easily. Sarah Cooke, *The Handmaiden of the Lord; or, Wayside Sketches* (Chicago: S. B. Shaw, 1900), provides a contemporary account of Moody's own experience, while the most developed secondary treatment is to be found in J. C. Pollock, *Moody: A Biographical Portrait of the Pacesetter in Modern Mass Evangelism* (New York: Macmillan, 1963). Moody's teaching can best be seen in such books as *Secret Power* (Chicago: Fleming H. Revell, 1881) and is analyzed by Stanley N. Gundry, *Love Them In: The Proclamation Theology of D. L. Moody* (Chicago: Moody, 1976). For Moody's successors, see R. A. Torrey, *The Baptism with the Holy Spirit* (New York: Fleming H. Revell, [c. 1895 and 1897]) and *How to Obtain Fullness of Power* (New York: Fleming H. Revell, 1897), as well as J. Wilbur Chapman, *Received Ye the Holy Ghost?* (New York: Fleming H. Revell, 1894).

On the Keswick tradition more directly, see the already cited bibliography by David D. Bundy, *Keswick: A Bibliographic Introduction to the Higher Life Movements,* Occasional Bibliographical Papers of the B. L. Fisher Library, no. 3 (Wilmore, Ky.: B. L. Fisher Library, 1975). For the teaching of American Keswick figures see such writings as A. B. Simpson, *The Fulness of Jesus; or, Christian Life in the New Testament* (New York: Christian Alliance Publishing, 1890); or A. J. Gordon, *The Ministry of the Spirit* (New York: Fleming H. Revell, 1894) and *The Two-Fold Life; or, Christ's Work for Us and Christ's Work in Us* (New York: Fleming H. Revell, 1895). This position is surveyed in Edith Lydia Waldvogel, "The 'Overcoming Life': A Study in the Reformed Evangelical Origins of Pentecostalism" (Ph.D. diss., Harvard University, 1971).

CHAPTER V
THE RISE OF THE DIVINE HEALING MOVEMENT

The history of the Healing movement is somewhat better studied. The most wide-ranging book is that by Morton T. Kelsey, *Healing and Christianity in Ancient Thought and Modern Times* (New York: Harper and Row, 1976). David E. Harrell in *All Things Are Possible* (Bloomington: Indiana University Press, 1975) attempts a history of the modern Healing movement as it has influenced the recent Charismatic movement, but surprisingly picks up the story in the middle. Much more useful is the work of Raymond Cunningham, who sketches the nineteenth-century antecedents to the twentieth-century movements. My work developed independently of his, but found striking confirmation in his essay, "From Holiness to Healing: The Faith Cure in America, 1872–92," *Church History* 43 (December 1974): 499–513.

The Healing movement in America really begins with Charles Cullis of Boston, whose work is described in contemporary accounts by W. H. Daniels, *Dr. Cullis and His Work* (Boston: Willard Tract Repository, 1885), and W. E. Boardman, *Faith-Work; or, the Labours of Dr. Cullis in Boston* (London: W. Isbister, 1874). Cullis's own statement may be found in *Faith Cures; or, Answers to Prayer in the Healing of the Sick* (Boston: Willard Tract Repository, 1879).

Other major late nineteenth-century books on healing include W. E. Boardman, *"The Lord That Healeth Thee"* (London: Morgan and Scott, 1881), published in the United States as *The Great Physician* (Boston: Willard Tract Repository, 1881); R. L. Stanton, *Gospel Parallelisms: Illustrated in the Healing of Body and Soul* (Buffalo: Office of Triumphs of Faith, 1884); Carrie Judd Montgomery, *The Prayer of Faith* (Buffalo: H. H. Otis, 1880); A. B. Simpson, *The Gospel of Healing*, rev. ed. (New York: Christian Alliance Publishing, 1915), and related writings; A. J. Gordon, *The Ministry of Healing: Miracles of Cure in All Ages* (Boston: H. Gannett, 1882); and especially R. Kelso Carter, *The Atonement for Sin and Sickness; or, A Full Salvation for Soul and Body* (Boston: Willard Tract Repository, 1884), and *"Faith Healing" Reviewed* (Boston and Chicago: Christian Witness, 1897); William McDonald, *Modern Faith Healing* (Boston: McDonald and Gill, 1892).

CHAPTER VI
THE RISE OF PREMILLENNIALISM

Millennialism has been more studied than any other theme in this study, yet it remains difficult to understand. On the seventeenth century I have found most useful such works as Iain H. Murray, *The Puritan Hope: A Study in Revival and the Interpretation of Prophecy* (London: Banner of Truth, 1971); Peter Toon, ed., *Puritans, the Millennium and the Future of Israel: Puritan Eschatology 1600 to 1660* (London: James Clarke, 1970); and K. James Stein, "Philip Jakob Spener's Hope for Better Times for the Church—Contributions in Controversy," *Covenant Quarterly* 37 (August 1979): 3–20. For understanding the issue in John Wesley I have followed Clarence L. Bence, "John Wesley's Teleological Hermeneutic" (Ph.D. diss., Emory University, 1981). On Edwards I have followed the well-known essay by C. C. Goen, "Jonathan Edwards: A New Departure in Eschatology," *Church History* 28 (March 1959): 25–40.

The most important surveys of the rise of premillennialism within the nineteenth century remain Clarence Bass, *Backgrounds to Dispensationalism* (Grand Rapids: Wm. B. Eerdmans, 1960); C. Norman Kraus, *Dispensationalism in America* (Richmond: John Knox, 1958); Ernest R. Sandeen, *The Roots of Fundamentalism: British and American Millenarianism, 1800-1930* (Chicago: University of Chicago Press, 1970); and Timothy P. Weber, *Living in the Shadow of the Second Coming: American Premillennialism, 1875– 1925* (Grand Rapids: Zondervan, 1983). None of these, however, really correlates the theme with the traditions at the center of this study. Most helpful have been the chapter on the theme in Edith Lydia Waldvogel, "The 'Overcoming Life': A Study of the Reformed Evangelical Origins of Pentecostalism" (Ph.D. diss., Harvard University, 1977), and Robert K. Whalen, "Millenarianism and Millennialism in America, 1790–1880" (Ph.D. diss., State University of New York at Stony Brook, 1971).

For the understanding of the dynamic behind the rise of premillennialism and its coordinate turn to apocalyptic categories in the nineteenth century, I have found most helpful the analysis of the shift from prophetic to apocalyptic categories within the biblical sources by Paul D. Hanson, *The Dawn of Apocalyptic* (Philadelphia: Fortress, 1975).

The rise of premillennialism in the late nineteenth-century Holiness movement is not well studied yet. Illustrative of the negative reception given the movement by those more completely rooted in classical Methodism would be Daniel Steele, *A Substitute for Holiness; or Antinomianism Revived; or, The Theology of the So-Called Plymouth Brethren Examined and Refuted*, 2d ed. (Boston and Chicago: Christian Witness, 1899), and George W. Wilson, *The Signs of Thy Coming; or, Premillennialism, Unscriptural and Unreasonable* (Boston: Christian Witness, 1899). For the more radical nineteenth-century illustrations of Holiness premillennialism, see such writings as W. B. Godbey, *An Appeal to Postmillennialists* (Nashville: Pentecostal Mission Publishing, n.d.); George D. Watson, *Steps to the Throne* (Cincinnati: God's Revivalist, [1898]); W. B. Godbey and Seth Cook Rees, *The Return of Jesus* (Cincinnati: God's Revivalist Office, n.d.).

Index of Persons

Adams, Benjamin M., 90
Anderson, Robert Mapes, 143
Arthur, William, 74, 87
Barth, Karl, 120
Baxter, Mrs. Michael, 125
Baxter, Richard, 37
Beecher, Edward, 66
Bell, George, 150
Bellamy, Joseph, 154
Bengel, John Albert, 119–20, 148–49
Benson, Joseph, 49, 71
Blumhardt, Johann Christoph, 120–21
Boardman, W. E., 67, 104, 123–27
Boland, Jeremiah, 98
Boole, William H., 90
Booth, William, 95
Bosanquet, Mary, 50
Bresee, Phineas, 93
Brown, Charles, 78
Brumbeck, Carl, 15
Brunner, Emil, 144
Burwash, Nehemiah, 99–100
Bushnell, Horace, 67
Byrum, Russell R., 94
Calvin, John, 116–17
Carter, R. Kelso, 129–31, 133
Carwardine, Richard, 64
Chapman, J. Wilbur, 101, 104
Chiles, Robert, 68
Clarke, Adam, 68–69
Clibborn, Arthur S., 95
Conzelmann, Hans, 53
Countess of Huntingdon, 49
Cowles, Henry, 72, 156–57, 161
Cullis, Charles, 67–68, 104, 122–25, 127–29, 131, 132
Darby, John Nelson, 145
Davies, Edward, 92
de Fleury, Claude, 41, 42

Degen, Henry V., 67, 76
Dittus, Gottliebin, 121
Dowie, John Alexander, 136
Dunning, H. Ray, 69
Durnbaugh, Donald, 40
Earle, A. B., 67, 96, 123
Eddy, Mary Baker, 128
Edwards, Jonathan, 70, 153–54, 156
Ellyson, E. P., 94
Faupel, David W., 18, 143
Finney, Charles Grandison: influence of, 64, 66, 94, 104, 106; millennial views, 155, 162; on prayer, 122; on sanctification, 69–70, 71–72, 100–102
Fish, Henry C., 73
Fison, J. E., 53
Fletcher, John: doctrine of dispensations, 51–53, 92–93, 95, 149–53, 164; influence of, 74–75, 80; and Wesley, 49–54, 67, 71
Fowler, Charles J., 92
Francke, August Hermann, 121
Frost, Evelyn, 115
Godbey, W. B., 134, 165–66
Goen, C. C., 154
Goodwin, Thomas, 37
Gordon, Adoniram Judson: on the Holy Spirit, 106–7; influence of, 105, 176; on healing, 127–29; millennial views, 163
Gossner, Johannes Evangelista, 121
Hamilton, N. Q., 144
Hanson, Paul, 158–59
Hills, A. M., 71, 94, 103, 164
Hollenweger, W. J., 23
Hopkins, Samuel, 154
Horner, R. C., 98–100
Horton, Stanley, 21
Huckabee, B. W., 175

Subject Index

perfectionism, 64, 66–72, 75–
76, 79, 105, 155, 158; on sanctification, 68–69, 71
"Oneness," 18
Oxford Movement, 56n27
Pacifism, 76
Patterns of themes, 18, 19–21, 26, 28,
31n22, 32n23, 32n29, 35. See
also Motifs
Pentecost: event, 9, 10, 24, 26, 27, 36,
49, 50, 51, 52, 72, 73, 74, 88, 92,
98, 99, 100, 101, 104, 106, 107,
135, 144, 150, 151, 152, 164,
174, 177; Wesley on, 84n69;
"new," 74
Pentecostal Fellowship of North
America, 17, 19
Pentecostalism: and church growth,
10; and culture, 10, 17, 74–75,
160; and Catholicism, 10, 15, 37;
definition of, 15–16; and divine
healing, 115–37; and eschatology, 147; hermeneutics, 22–26;
history, 9–10, 20; "idea," 91;
inner logic of, 21, 22, 27, 28;
language and imagery, 71–74,
79, 87, 88, 164, 173, 176; Methodist roots, 35–54; and Premillennialism, 143–67; and Spirit
baptism, 87–108; themes, 91–
92, 93, 99, 108, 143, 173, 179;
theological analysis of, 15–28;
typology of groups, 18. See *also*
Gestalt
Pentecostal movement. See Pentecostalism
Perfection: doctrine of, 43–44, 46,
47, 49, 50, 52, 63, 72, 76, 79, 87,
93, 152; "sinless," 47; teleological character, 68–69, 70
Perfectionism, 11, 63–80, 105, 115,
117, 147, 152, 153, 155, 159. See
also Oberlin theology: on p.
"Perfect love," 57, 95, 99
Pietism: influence of, 37–38, 119–
21, 143, 147; theology of, 23,
148; and Wesley, 41–42, 117–
18
Pilgrim Holiness Church, 91
Plymouth Brethren, 121, 145
Pluralism, 75
Pneumatology, 43, 144, 145, 151. See
also Christocentrism

Postmillennialism, 146–65
Power, 25, 50, 53, 74, 77, 88, 89, 90,
93, 94, 95, 96, 97, 99, 100, 103,
104, 106, 115, 127, 137, 178. See
also Enduement
Prayer: and faith, 119, 121, 122, 124,
132, 135, 141n68; role of, 31n22,
64, 96, 116, 119, 121, 122, 124,
178
Premillennialism, 20, 21, 55n13, 133,
140–67, 174; dispensational,
145; and Holiness movement,
164–67; rise of, 143–67; and
Wesley, 38, 55n13
Presbyterian Church, the, 126
Primitive church, 72, 73, 144. See
also Early church
Primitivism: motif, 40–42; of Wesley,
41–42, 45
Princeton theology, 25
Process sanctification. See Sanctific-
ation
Prophecy, gift of, 93
Protestantism, 10, 38, 40
Psychic phenomena, 118
Psychological research, 15–16
Puritans. See Puritanism
Puritanism, 37–38, 117, 143, 147,
153, 176
Quakerism, 42, 117
Quietism, 81n19
Radicalism: and Wesley, 43, 76, 78
Radicalization of doctrines, 100, 124,
128, 132, 136, 174, 177
"Receiving" the Holy Spirit, 49–50
Reductionism; reduction theory, 11,
16, 19
Reformation, the, 19; English, 39
Reformed tradition, 64; influence of,
89–90, 100, 176; on healing,
116–17; on millennium, 164
Regeneration, 20, 37, 92, 94, 103, 129,
148; baptismal, 38
"Release" of the Holy Spirit, 31n22
Repentance, 20, 46, 99, 129
Restoration, 46, 73, 125, 127, 145,
154
Revivalism: and baptism of the Holy
Spirit, 89–90, 100–105, 108;
influence of, 64, 66, 70, 73–74,
87, 147, 167, 173–74; millennial
currents in, 153–58, 162–63,
175–76; and Wesley, 70, 71

Scripture Index